Bloomsbury CPD Library: Secondary Curriculum and Assessment Design

By Summer Turner

BLOOMSBURY

LONDON · OXFORD · NEW YORK · NEW DELHI · SYDNEY

Bloomsbury Education
An imprint of Bloomsbury Publishing Plc

50 Bedford Square	1385 Broadway
London	New York
WC1B 3DP	NY 10018
UK	USA

www.bloomsbury.com

Bloomsbury is a registered trade mark of Bloomsbury Publishing Plc

First published 2016

British Library Cataloguing-in-Publication Data
A catalogue record for this book is available from the British Library.

ISBN:
PB: 9781472928504
ePub: 9781472928528
ePDF: 9781472928551

Library of Congress Cataloging-in-Publication Data
A catalog record for this book is available from the Library of Congress.

10 9 8 7 6 5 4 3 2 1

Typeset by Integra Software Services Pvt. Ltd.
Printed by CPI Group (UK) Ltd, Croydon, CR0 4YY

This book is produced using paper that is made from wood grown in
managed, sustainable forests. It is natural, renewable and recyclable.
The logging and manufacturing processes conform to the
environmental regulations of the country of origin.

To view more of our titles please visit www.bloomsbury.com

Contents

Acknowledgements

I owe a huge thanks to all of the team at Bloomsbury Education, but a particular mention must go to my editor Holly Gardner who has driven this book forward with determination and passion, offering me immeasurable support and guidance along the way.

This book is a team effort, it is inspired by the work of many fellow educators whose names you will find in the pages before you, but also by my colleagues, leadership team and governors at East London Science School who are a group of inspiring teachers and people. Thanks in particular to David Perks whose dream made the school a reality and who has encouraged me to pursue my interest in curriculum and assessment and to Cat Ventham for keeping me sane.

Outside of work I'm also lucky to have a strong tribe of people around me, both friends and family, who have been incredibly supportive. I owe a specific thank you to Jack Durant for being my writing companion and to Jessica, Imogen, Amanda and Anthony Turner for everything and more besides.

Lastly, I'd like to dedicate this book to all of my pupils - past, present and future.

How to use this book

The Bloomsbury CPD Library provides primary and secondary teachers with affordable, comprehensive and accessible 'do-it-yourself' continuing professional development. This book focuses on curriculum and assessment design in secondary schools.

The book is split into two halves: Part 1 **Teach yourself** and Part 2 **Train others.**

Part 1: Teach yourself

This part of the book includes everything you need to improve your curriculum and assessment design. It is split into four stages:

STAGE 1: ASSESS

Determine how much you know about curriculum and assessment design, including the history and politics which have influenced curriculum and assessment changes. Gain an understanding of the key aspects of curriculum and assessment and reflect on the areas you need to work on to develop your expertise.

STAGE 2: IMPROVE

Learn about the different thinking, theory and research which exists on the subject of curriculum and assessment design and develop your own curriculum and assessment. Explore what this looks like when put into practice in existing schools. Then take the reins yourself and begin to introduce your new curriculum and assessment systems to your school.

STAGE 3: EVALUATE

Take the time to evaluate the work that you have done so far and discover the successes, as well as the areas for improvement. Make an action plan for your continuing design journey.

STAGE 4: EXCEL

Finally you will work on embedding and developing the curriculum and assessment within your school. This is the chance to see your vision come to life.

Part 2: Train others

Having built your expertise in curriculum and assessment design, it is now your chance to share this with other teachers at your school. This section will offer advice on how to run successful CPD and the types of training which are most effective to train both leaders and teachers on curriculum and assessment design. You will be provided with detailed, resourced training plans which means you'll be ready to get started with trainings, whether they be twilight sessions, inset days or full blown events, straight away.

Online resources

For templates, questionnaires and PowerPoints from the book please visit www.bloomsbury.com/CPD-secondary-curriculum-assessment-design

Introduction

Four years ago I accepted a job that changed my world – head of English at a brand new school in East London. One part of the role stood out to me in particular: the chance to design my own curriculum and assessment for English. I had grown sick of the stock cupboard approach (teach the least dusty books in there to Key Stage 3) and the intervention sessions that GCSE classes were so often reduced to. Instead I was now being given the responsibility to make decisions about what would work best for my pupils based on my knowledge of English as a subject. I was being asked to be a subject expert again and was being trusted to be the creator of something inspirational and life-changing for the community I was to serve. I had the honour of making and laying down the stones on which the future generation will make their path.

Five years previously, teaching had chosen me to join its ranks; as I shuffled emptily around the world of media looking for some inspiration, teaching called to me, whispering through every book page I turned. The moment I returned to a classroom and witnessed the transformational power of literature when in the hands of a great teacher, I knew my soul had returned home at last. I had found my purpose in teaching children, but more importantly in teaching children MY subject; the chance to take on this intricate web of English language and literature – to untangle it and lay out the threads for my pupils: this was something special. This was something special. It turned out to be just the first step – my embracing of this curriculum opportunity and development of corresponding assessment meant I soon found myself leading on this at whole-school level.

Curriculum and assessment design

Getting to design the curriculum and assessment in your school is a phenomenal privilege – but it's also a little bit terrifying! It requires a lot of thought and deliberation as well as action. There is no silver bullet, particularly as the same approach will not necessarily work in every school. So it should be no surprise that a curriculum and its sidekick, assessment, don't spring fully-formed like Athena from the head of Zeus. You have to go through the 'struggle' which comes from exploring existing ideas, theories and research before considering how these can be implemented within your own school environment.

Holding responsibility for curriculum and assessment design in our hands can therefore seem a heavy burden. Twenty per cent of responses to the government's Workload Challenge identified 'implementing new initiatives/curriculum/ qualification change' as 'adding unnecessary burden to the general workload' and 82% of concerns 'fitted within the category of lesson planning and policies, assessment and reporting administration'. (2015)

There is also fear surrounding the process of potentially changing everything you do – this anxiety can make the status quo seem a comforting option; it is what Fromm calls the desire to 'Escape from Freedom'. This is clear in the reaction to National Curriculum levels; years of teachers arguing that they were pointless and a waste of time followed by sheer panic on the announcement of their removal and a sudden surge of people asking for them back. Many parents equally feel this fear. In Michael Tidd's blog, *My message for Lucy Powell*, he points to a Twitter exchange between the former Shadow Secretary for Education, Lucy Powell, and headteacher Tom Sherrington, in which Powell claimed that levels 'might not have been perfect [but] were well understood by everyone and now there's nothing'. The thrust of her argument was that as a parent, levels offered a shared understanding of pupil achievement and progress, that had not been replaced.

In reality, levels are simply smoke and mirrors when it comes to reporting back useful information about a child's attainment or progress but the empty gap where levels used to be makes some cling on to this false promise of information (the shared understanding Powell believes parents gain from levels). There is also a danger that this leads to schools re-creating systems of old, which (as I note in Chapter 3) is a repeated problem within education. A real movement forward will be to take on these lessons from the past and create curriculum and assessment, which build on what we have learnt.

Designing your own curriculum and assessment is hard work; but what you gain, what you learn, what impact you can have is worth every second of it. So face the fear, and do it anyway.

In Part 1 of this book I've tried to create a sense of a story about curriculum and assessment – a vision of the journey that you might take. Of course you will all be setting off at different starting points and therefore some chapters will resonate more than others. I am not claiming to have all the answers – I'm still on the journey myself – but I hope that by sharing the experiences I've had and the resources that have helped me along the way, I will be able to metaphorically take your hand and offer you support as you discover and build your own stories.

I hope that Part 1 will help to alleviate some of the burdens and fears but I also think there is reward to be found in braving the 'struggle' – it helps you to determine what you really believe in and to create a curriculum and an assessment system that is meaningful and that you are willing to stand up and fight for. My guidance would be to follow Part 1 chronologically and do the soul searching which comes with thinking through the work of others to find your own way – it will be worth it!

Part 2 explores how to run successful CPD training in curriculum and assessment design at your school. Running training, especially insets, in schools is notoriously difficult to get right and CPD often gets a bad name.

Do any of the scenarios below sound familiar?

Scenario One

First day back in January, as the cold seeps through your jumper into the very marrow of your bones, you sheepishly file into the hall – hazy memories of the end of term party still making eye contact difficult – and settle down for some new year INSET inspiration. Except that what happens is: death by PowerPoint, followed by group work with large sheets of paper and marker pens (which never see the light of day again until the next INSET session) and moaning from the usual crowd. Occasionally the dreaded flashy consultant turns up and re-hashes some out of date work on Assessment for Learning (AfL), which he clumsily links to progress measures (cue childlike rebellion through texting, Tweeting and barely repressed giggles). It works as a gentle wake up into the term, but the reality is it's a waste of day that could have been spent teaching!

Scenario Two

You have been sent on a course entitled: 'How to be an Outstanding ...[insert anything education related]'. Your school has paid £295 (it always seems to be around that number) for you to attend this prestigious training. You are given a sticker when you go in, on which to write your name – if you are a woman you then have an awkward few minutes working out where to place it so that it doesn't involve people staring at your chest – you then spend much of the rest of the day getting it caught in your hair. The day starts with introductions – you have to say your name, despite it being emblazoned on you, and an interesting fact about yourself. You spend so long trying to think of an interesting fact that you don't hear any of the other names around

---

you. As you will be working in groups for the rest of the day and having to feed back their ideas, this is particularly awkward. The day consists of a number of different activities which you complete in groups; there will be at least one card sort and if you care at all about being a good student, a moment when you have to do both the writing and the feedback for the group. You learn a couple of interesting things throughout the day but it's mostly flash over substance and nothing that you can embed in your practice. The lunch, however, is fantastic.

Scenario Three

You're in a department meeting. There are biscuits – good start! Someone comments on the quality of the biscuits, someone else declines having one with the phrase, 'ooh I better not', it takes about ten minutes to find everyone in the department and to ensure everyone has made a cup of tea. The head of department looks at the first agenda point which is about Year 11 progress towards their target grades.

45 minutes later

Each member of the team has detailed the 'progress' of their individual pupils, mostly discussing poor behaviour and rescheduling re-sits of controlled assessments (thankfully no longer). Someone has blamed SLT. Someone else has said progress measures are a load of crap. The head of department wearily ends the meeting saying, 'We'll look at KS3 next week'. This never happens.

These are examples of the worst of CPD, but they will be experiences that every teacher has had. It's no wonder CPD has had such a bad press.

Why you should still believe in CPD

The truth is, whilst I've been exposed to all of these scenarios, I have also had the experience of CPD that has been transformative – much of it through the online teaching community. When it is done well, it renews you and inspires you to be better, even when you feel like you are already giving your heart and soul. Teaching is a job like no other, some days it seems to just take and take but then suddenly it gives and in that moment, whether it be a pupil lighting up with excitement about a book they've read, a spectacular essay, a soul-moving poem, a thank you, or a truly amazing CPD session, it's all more than worth the effort.

In fact it's this that has made CPD somewhat precious to me. I feel it needs to be protected from the forces of darkness that turn it away from all the good it can do. Being inspired by other educators, building your own knowledge and taking ownership of your professionalism makes for happy, successful teachers. This in turn, makes for happy and successful pupils.

Yet the idea of teaching as something magical (which of course it is) can also mislead us into thinking it is purely an intrinsic talent, which you can hone with a few useful tricks you learn over the years, but is in need of little work. In an article in *The Guardian*, 'Overcoming the OK plateau: how to become an expert teacher', Alex Quigley refers to the 'OK plateau', a phrase originally coined by Joshua Foer in his book 'Moonwalking with Einstein', where teachers tend to stop trying to improve their practice and just get on with the job in hand. But, as Dylan Wiliam has famously said: 'Every teacher needs to improve, not because they are not good enough, but because they can be even better.' Good teachers are THE biggest lever in improving pupil attainment, so we have to do everything to support and challenge them to be 'even better'.

It's also true that in any school, both staff and pupils know what the school values by the time and resources dedicated to it. If you want your staff to get on board with something that you believe will have a positive impact on your pupils, you need to demonstrate this by spending time dedicated to this process. It can't be a one-off. A great example of this being done well is the ResearchEd movement, which started as an idea between a few people on Twitter in 2013 and quickly built into a conference of over 500 people. Three years on and the momentum hasn't stopped – there are now ResearchEd conferences all over the UK and abroad, as well as hubs within schools. WomenEd, a group dedicated to addressing the imbalance of female leadership in education, is following a similar trajectory. The success of these two movements is based on three precise factors:

1. Need – each of these movements come from a need within the education community, sometimes one we didn't even realise we had until it started to be fulfilled. This was often a specific group of teachers/educators and started by conversations between that group, usually through social networking.
2. Choice – this is a really tricky one in education; often the same people who advocate for lack of choice when it comes to types of schools, are also those who argue for more choice within a curriculum and vice versa. Yet within the world of CPD, with informed adults who have a range of interests and knowledge, it's clear that an element of choice is useful. So the fact that these movements are self-selecting is important, as is the fact that the events they run allow people to choose from a range of different workshops/lectures/seminars.
3. Sustained effort – one of the most impressive and important aspects of these movements is that they are not one-off moments but are run by people

who work hard to ensure a succession of events, blogs, projects and online discussions, which means they stay in your mind as a reminder of why they matter. This also means they pick up more and more contributors along the way; impacting on increasing numbers of teachers and educators.

Each of these factors contribute to building successful professional development in the wider education world, and it's not much of a stretch to see that they can easily be applied to school-based training.

Leading transformational CPD

The *Evaluation of CPD providers in England 2010-2011: Report for School Leaders* commissioned by the Teachers Development Agency for Schools (TDA), identified four not dissimilar principles for effective CPD:

1. CPD should be collaborative and sustained (this makes it likely to have more significant and lasting impact).
2. CPD should help improve outcomes for children and young people.
3. CPD should be based on effective needs analysis.
4. CPD should encourage participants to be reflective practitioners and use their learning to inform their professional judgement.

I suggest coming up with your own list of principles that you want to base your CPD programme on. It might be a combination of some of the above and some which relate to the context of your school. In this book the training will be based around the following principles:

- CPD should be based on needs of teachers, pupils and the school
- CPD should be targeted
- CPD should align with the school vision
- CPD should impact on pupil outcome
- CPD should inspire teachers
- CPD should be part of the culture of a school.

In Part 2 of this book, I will explore the different forms of CPD that you can run in school based on a school-led model; run by those within the school community rather than external providers. Along the way I hope to answer how these CPD sessions (which range from twilights to full-day INSETS) will match the principles of CPD outlined above and how they aim to establish a transformative approach to CPD in schools. This is particularly important in the realm of curriculum and assessment design because of the level of involvement and commitment needed from staff to make it work. It's clear that it takes hard work to achieve this kind of CPD but it can be done!

Part 1

Teach yourself

1

What's it all about?

Assessment and curriculum are inextricably bound. You only have to look at the way in which schools have begun to revitalise their Key Stage 3 curriculum in response to the end of levels to see how assessment often drives curriculum. I firmly believe that this is the wrong way around: curriculum should always drive assessment. We are beginning to see this happen – if you follow the #LearningFirst on Twitter you can see a budding network of educators looking into curriculum-led assessment. Whilst the politics of qualifications can make this difficult, this book aims to address ways in which you can design meaningful curriculum and assessment within the existing system and also explore the challenges for the profession going forward.

What is the ethos of your school?

The first step in designing your curriculum and assessment is to establish a clear vision of what you want to achieve. In order to create a system that has meaning, you will need to start with a foundation based on values and ethos. I remember as a child attending the secondary school open days to decide where I wanted to go: there were some that I just felt were right, I didn't know why but they just seemed to buzz and felt like they made sense. It was the same when choosing a university; visiting St Andrews and sitting in the office of an English professor as he waxed lyrical about Victorian poets with the sound of the sea crashing in the background – my family and I were sold on the vision. An academic institution that knows what it wants for its student body and what it will achieve is one that inspires.

In one of my favourite films, *The Way We Were*, Barbara Streisand's character Katie argues with her husband Hubbell because she wants to stand up and fight against the McCarthy witch hunts. He tells her that it's pointless and that it's not worth fighting for because 'People are more important... You and me! Not causes. Not principles' to which she passionately replies: 'Hubbell, people ARE their principles'.

I feel the same way about schools – they are the principles on which they are founded. Out of the successful schools I have visited the one thing that they have in common is a strong ethos that binds together staff and pupils. Some of this comes through a shared understanding of what the purpose of a school is – this is something I'll explore in Chapter 4.

Once you have considered the question – what is the ethos of your school? –you should have a clearer idea of the fundamentals of the curriculum, such as what subjects your pupils will study and how much time will be allocated to these. It should lead you to having a clearer sense of how you can answer a wider range of questions about your curriculum and assessment design.

> ## Reflection questions
>
> - How is this ethos present in the current school curriculum?
> - What needs to change in your curriculum and assessment so that it holds true to your ethos?
> - Is there any conflict between your ethos and the types of subjects or qualifications you offer?

What is curriculum?

According to the *New Oxford English Dictionary*, curriculum is: 'the subjects comprising a course of study in a school or college'. This dictionary definition is a good starting point; it's clear and simple, it's probably the definition we'd be most likely to give if asked. However, as you'll soon realise if you haven't already, there are rarely any simple ideas in education. Instead you have to be some kind of Sherlock Holmes character, exploring the complexities of the educational landscape.

The easiest way to understand curriculum is to know that it can actually be divided into three categories. In his SSAT pamphlet, *Principled Curriculum Design*, Dylan Wiliam explains these as:

1. the 'intended' curriculum – the curriculum as prescribed by the National Curriculum or equivalent: the specified topics, ideas, content that pupils should learn
2. the 'implemented' curriculum – the 'textbooks, schemes of work, lesson plans'
3. the 'enacted' curriculum – how this is translated into learning within the classroom, between the teacher and pupil.

1 INTENDED CURRICULUM	2 IMPLEMENTED CURRICULUM	3 ENACTED CURRICULUM

Fig. 1 Three categories of curriculum

For the purpose of this book, the focus will primarily be on the intended curriculum and how schools then move forward to an implemented curriculum. To try to advise or guide enacted curriculum would assume knowledge of an individual's classroom and pupils that I simply do not have.

The distinction between these different curricular is useful, particularly if you are leading on curriculum within your school. For instance, just because something is not included within the implemented or intended curriculum it doesn't mean that it has no place at all within a school. I think of it a bit like a book club; you can prescribe the book, the size of the group, the meeting place and time ('intended'), you can construct a list of points or questions for discussion and guide the conversation ('implemented') but it's the ('enacted') part of the group session, where people voyage on various intellectual adventures together that you can't prescribe. Much of the ideas around values, character and creativity I think happen within that enacted curriculum; within the dialogue and relationships between teachers and their classes.

Equally, the idea of curriculum for some schools may entail such things as outdoor activities, clubs and trips – the curriculum doesn't always refer to just the subjects which are being studied. The National Curriculum itself explains this: 'The school curriculum comprises all learning and other experiences that each school plans for its pupils. The National Curriculum forms one part of the school curriculum.'

What is assessment?

Assessment is equally complex in definition, although 'assessment is really just a procedure for making inferences' (Wiliam) seems a fairly good start. The amount of different types of assessment that exist within schools does make the whole thing a bit mind-boggling, though. We assess pupils constantly in school, even if it's simply through the questions we ask them. There's a much quoted statement from *Teachers: The Real Masters of Multitasking* (busyteacher.org) which says: '1,500 educational decisions made by an average teacher every school day' and what is a decision if not some kind of assessment of a situation?

So what do I mean by assessment within the context of this book? Whilst it may be painstakingly obvious to point this out, I think we first need to determine the different types of assessment.

There are two main forms of assessment: formative and summative. These assessments can be internal to a school or external (also referred to as qualifications). Within school you have in-class assessments and whole-school assessment – which usually take the form of formative (in-class) and summative (whole-school). These assessments can take all kinds of formats, although summative mostly tends to be some kind of written test whilst formative can include tests, quizzes, questioning, dialogue, verbal feedback, marking and more. An assessment system is also something slightly apart from all of these, as this brings with it ideas around data, progress measures, reporting and accountability. The wonders of the English language – so many meanings located in just one word!

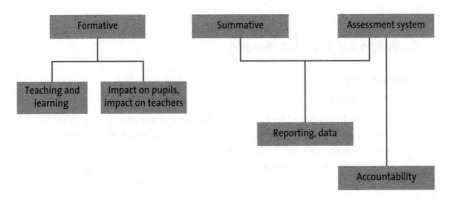

Fig. 2 Assessment flowchart

As much as it would be superb to look at the whole array of assessment, I wouldn't be able to do it all justice in this book – better for you to dig into one of the many other fabulous books in the CPD library – but I will take a close look at specific types of assessment. Assessment of all sorts must be driven by curriculum, of this I am sure. At the same time, I'm ruefully aware that this is not currently the case, particularly when it comes to external assessment. As the book will focus on designing the 'intended' curriculum and dipping into the 'implemented' curriculum, the same logic will apply to assessment. I'll explore creating whole-school assessment systems that are driven by the need to support and track the pupils in their engagement with the school curriculum. I will also look at current changes to Key Stage 3 and the freedom now given to schools to design their own assessment systems, which makes this a particularly exigent issue – Key Stage 3 has suddenly come out of the shadows to claim its moment in the spotlight and teachers have become the architects of its renovation. I'll look specifically at how this can be achieved on the ground at subject level.

I hope to balance between the ideal – of an assessment model developed solely for the purpose of formatively moving pupils towards knowledge of their subjects, and summatively being a meaningful record of their knowledge of the subjects – and the reality, where current examinations do not accurately reflect even the intended curriculum.

Chapter 1 takeaway

Teaching tip

Own the struggle

Take the time to really get to know the job that you are taking on and to consider the different strengths and areas of improvement you might have when it comes to curriculum and assessment. Consider the tensions in your thinking and in the needs of your school which might make this a difficult task and then look at where in the book you might find solutions.

Pass it on

Sharing your ideas: Blogging

It often helps to explore your ideas through the form of a blog – this also allows you to consider and engage with different viewpoints. By reflecting on what curriculum and assessment means to you and how this might relate to your/your school's ethos, you can gain an understanding of what this will mean in reality for curriculum and assessment design.

Discuss with your leadership

It can be useful to constructively challenge other members of the leadership in your school. Share your thoughts on curriculum and assessment with members of your team. Ask them how they see the values and ethos of the school matching up with curriculum and assessment. In particular it can be worth thinking about the different ranges of curriculum and assessment within the school and how linked up these are.

Share and tweet

Tweet your reflections on what curriculum and assessment mean to you by using the hashtag #BloomsCPD

CPD book club recommendation

Dylan Wiliam, *Principled Curriculum Design/Principled Assessment Design* **(SSAT Redesigning Schools Pamphlets)** (see Bibliography and further reading)

Bloggers' corner

A personal one from me on school ethos:
ragazzainglese.wordpress.com/2014/05/19/the-courage-of-conviction

TO DO LIST:

☐ Determine the school ethos/values either individually or as part of a leadership team.

☐ Write out these ethos/values so that you can use these to guide your decisions.

☐ Make notes on the different ideas around curriculum and assessment and consider what implications this has in terms of areas you might need to consider when starting the design process.

☐ Tweet your reflections on what curriculum and assessment mean to you by using the hashtag #BloomsCPD.

☐ Check out my blog post on school ethos: ragazzainglese.wordpress. com/2014/05/19/the-courage-of-conviction.

☐ Read Dylan Wiliam's pamphlets on curriculum and assessment design.

2 Self-assessment

In this chapter we will really begin to get to grips with your knowledge of curriculum and assessment design. It's important to be honest about your level of expertise so that you can take responsibility for your training and for the training of your whole staff. What do you know? What do you need to know? You will need to take into account the context and current curriculum and assessment of your school. Where do you need to begin in order to develop systems which work better for your pupils? How confident is your grasp of the different details of curriculum and assessment? What will this mean for training others? Think about your continuing professional development and what would be the most valuable training you could have at this moment in time. What is your greatest area of need?

How to complete the self-assessment questionnaire

On pages 16–31 there is a self-assessment questionnaire to encourage you to start the 'teach yourself' process by thinking very carefully about the current practices in place for curriculum and assessment design before you jump into trying to improve it.

When you are looking at your own practices and trying to form a clear view of where you are now and what the next steps will be, there are many ways of approaching it – it will depend on you as a person. For some people, it is useful to go with your gut and listen to the first thing that comes into your mind – your instinctual answer. For others, it is a better approach to spend a good amount of time really mulling over the self-evaluation questions slowly and in detail.

Quick response approach

If your preference for the self-evaluation is to go with your gut only, then simply fill in the quick response section after each question with the first thing that comes into your mind when you ask yourself the question. Do not mull over the question too long, simply read carefully and answer quickly. This approach will give you an overview of your current curriculum and assessment design understanding and practice and will take relatively little time. Just make sure you are uninterrupted, in a quiet place and able to complete the questionnaire in one sitting with no distractions so that you get focused and honest answers.

Considered response approach

If you choose to take a more reflective and detailed approach, then you can leave the quick response section blank and go straight onto reading the further guidance section under each question. This guidance provides prompt questions and ideas to get you thinking in detail about the question being answered and is designed to open up a wider scope in your answer. It will also enable you to look at your experience and pull examples into your answer to back up your statements. You may want to complete it a few questions at a time and take breaks, or you may be prepared to simply sit and work through the questions all in one sitting to ensure you remain focused. This approach does take longer, but it can lead to a more in-depth understanding of your current curriculum and assessment design practice, and you will gain much more from the process than the quick response alone.

Combined approach

A thorough approach, and one I recommend, would be to use both approaches together regardless of personal preference. There is clear value in both approaches being used together. This would involve you firstly answering the self-evaluation quick response questions by briefly noting down your instinctual answers for all questions. The next step would be to return to the start of the self-evaluation, read the further guidance and then answer the questions once more, slowly and in detail forming more of a narrative around each question and pulling in examples from your own experience. Following this you would need to read over both responses and form a comprehensive and honest summary in your mind of your

• I have done this self-assessment before. • I only want a surface level overview of my current understanding and practice. • I work better when I work at speed. • I don't have much time.	**Quick**
• I have never done this self-assessment before. • I want a deeper understanding of my current understanding and practice. • I work better when I take my time and really think things over. • I have some time to do this self-assessment.	**Considered**
• I have never done this self-assessment before. • I have done this self-assessment before. • I want a comprehensive and full understanding of my current understanding and practice and want to compare that to what I thought before taking the self-assessment. • I have a decent amount of time to dedicate to completing this self-assessment.	**Combined**

Fig. 3 How should I approach the self-evaluation questionnaire?

answers and a final view of where you feel you stand right now in your marking and feedback practice.

This is the longest of the three approaches to this questionnaire but will give you a comprehensive and full understanding of your current curriculum and assessment design practice. You will be surprised at the difference you see between the quick response and the considered response answers to the same questions. It can be very illuminating.

Rate yourself

The final part of the self-evaluation is to rate yourself. This section will ask you to rate your confidence in each area that has been covered in the questionnaire, with

Rating	Definition
1	Not confident at all.
2	Very unconfident.
3	Quite unconfident.
4	Mildly unconfident.
5	Indifferent.
6	Mildly confident.
7	A little confident.
8	Quite confident.
9	Very confident.
10	Extremely confident.

Fig. 4 Rate yourself definitions

a view to working on these areas for improvement throughout the course of the book. Read the question and on a scale of 1-10, mark how confident you feel about answering the question, either with regards to your own practice or with regards to the level of curriculum and assessment in your school. The table above shows how the scale works: the higher the number you allocate yourself, the better you feel you are performing in that area.

Top tip

Jot down your initial ideas or knowledge that come out of thinking through your answers alongside the questions. I always find these questions to be valuable – if you can't answer them yourself, then you won't be prepared to answer the same from your pupils, parents, staff and governors.

The 'you' in the self-assessment questionnaire questions is both yourself as an individual but also your school – if the answers don't overlap here, then I'd suggest you need to find a school where they do, otherwise designing any kind of system is going to be doomed from the start.

Curriculum design and assessment self-evaluation questionnaire

QUESTION 1: When you are referring to curriculum, do you mean intended, implemented or enacted, or a combination of these?

Quick response:

_____

_____

_____

_____

Questions for consideration

- Are you confident with your knowledge of these different areas?
- Can/should a leadership team determine these for the whole school?
- Is your role in curriculum design going to involve looking at all these aspects?
- Do your staff know and understand the differences?

Considered response:

_____

_____

_____

_____

_____

_____

_____

Rate yourself

QUESTION 1: When you are referring to curriculum, do you mean intended, implemented or enacted, or a combination of these?

1	2	3	4	5	6	7	8	9	10

QUESTION 2: Who should be involved in designing each type of curriculum?

Quick response:

_____

_____

_____

_____

Questions for consideration

- How much freedom do you think individual teachers and individual departments should have to design their curriculum?
- Can/should curriculum be prescribed by the state?
- If so – in what detail should this be prescribed?
- Does curriculum design require subject expertise?
- Which aspects of curriculum require prescription at whole-school level?

Considered response:

_____

_____

_____

_____

_____

_____

_____

_____

_____

_____

Rate yourself

QUESTION 2: Who should be involved in designing each type of curriculum?

| 1 | 2 | 3 | 4 | 5 | 6 | 7 | 8 | 9 | 10 |

QUESTION 3: To what extent does your intended curriculum need to match the National Curriculum?

Quick response:

_____

_____

_____

_____

Questions for consideration

- Do you work in a free school/academy/independent school?
- Do you have good knowledge of the NC?
- Does your current curriculum match the NC?
- Do you use NC levels?
- Which qualifications do your pupils study at KS4 and KS5 – how does your curriculum match this?

Considered response:

_____

_____

_____

_____

_____

_____

_____

_____

_____

_____

Rate yourself

QUESTION 3: To what extent does your intended curriculum need to match the National Curriculum?

1	2	3	4	5	6	7	8	9	10

QUESTION 4: How far does your curriculum extend beyond lessons and does this match with your school vision?

Quick response:

_____

_____

_____

_____

Questions for consideration

- What key clubs and extracurricular activities run at your school?
- What trips take place?
- Why do you run clubs, trips, competitions and so forth?
- Should more/less/the same time be dedicated to these activities going forward?

Considered response:

_____

_____

_____

_____

_____

_____

_____

_____

_____

_____

_____

Rate yourself

QUESTION 4: How far does your curriculum extend beyond lessons and does this match with your school vision?

1   2   3   4   5   6   7   8   9   10

QUESTION 5: Do you think you should teach the same curriculum to all pupils, irrespective of background?

Quick response:

_____

_____

_____

_____

Questions for consideration

- If not – how will you determine who is taught what?
- If yes – how will you enable access for all pupils to this curriculum without losing challenge?
- Is ability fixed or can it be adapted? How does this influence curriculum and assessment decisions?

Considered response:

_____

_____

_____

_____

_____

_____

_____

_____

_____

_____

_____

Rate yourself

QUESTION 5: Do you think you should teach the same curriculum to all pupils, irrespective of background?

| 1 | 2 | 3 | 4 | 5 | 6 | 7 | 8 | 9 | 10 |

QUESTION 6: What subjects should pupils study?

Quick response:

_____

_____

_____

_____

Questions for consideration

- At what point should your pupils make choices about which subjects they will study?
- Should the curriculum link up between the subjects and how?
- How do pupils build on knowledge of their subject and how do you think you should sequence your curriculum to help you achieve this?
- How do you think you can inspire pupils to love your subject? What does the curriculum need to include to allow for this?

Considered response:

_____

_____

_____

_____

_____

_____

_____

_____

_____

_____

_____

Rate yourself

QUESTION 6: What subjects should pupils study?

1   2   3   4   5   6   7   8   9   10

QUESTION 7: To what extent should your curriculum be based around knowledge and to what extent skills?

Quick response:

_____

_____

_____

_____

Questions for consideration

- Should a curriculum seek to be relevant to the pupils or should it seek to take them beyond their own experiences?
- Is it the school's responsibility to teach life skills?
- Is it the school's responsibility to teach character?
- How will you embed the teaching of functional skills?
- Is it your responsibility to teach anything else in your lessons other than your subject? How will this fit in with your curriculum?

Considered response:

_____

_____

_____

_____

_____

_____

_____

_____

Rate yourself

QUESTION 7: To what extent should your curriculum be based around knowledge and to what extent skills? Is there a compromise to be found?

| 1 | 2 | 3 | 4 | 5 | 6 | 7 | 8 | 9 | 10 |

QUESTION 8: Will your curriculum encompass academic and vocational/technical studies?

Quick response:

_____

_____

_____

_____

Questions for consideration

- What would a success story (in terms of pupil outcome) look like at the end of their school career? What would you consider to be a failure?
- What do you need to prioritise in your curriculum in order to achieve the success story?
- Can/should all pupils receive an academic education?
- Can/should all pupils receive training in vocational/technical studies?

Considered response:

_____

_____

_____

_____

_____

_____

_____

_____

_____

_____

Rate yourself

QUESTION 8: Will your curriculum encompass academic and vocational/technical studies?

1	2	3	4	5	6	7	8	9	10

QUESTION 9: Do you have an assessment system for Key Stage 3 beyond levels and is it driven by your curriculum?

Quick response:

_____

_____

_____

_____

Questions for consideration

- How does your assessment system show what pupils have learnt from their curriculum?
- Do you teach to the test?
- Would you be confident that pupils who achieve highly, according to your Key Stage 3 assessment, would be able to gain an A-level in the respective subjects?
- Does your assessment system help pupils learn how to improve?
- Does your assessment system allow you to report meaningfully to parents and pupils?

Considered response:

_____

_____

_____

_____

_____

_____

_____

_____

_____

Rate yourself

QUESTION 9: Do you have an assessment system for Key Stage 3 beyond levels and is it driven by your curriculum?

| 1 | 2 | 3 | 4 | 5 | 6 | 7 | 8 | 9 | 10 |

QUESTION 10: Are there a range of different formative and summative assessments in place and are you aware of the difference between these?

Quick response:

_____

_____

_____

_____

Questions for consideration

- Are you/your staff clear on the differences between formative and summative?
- For what purpose do you use assessment in your school?
- How often do teachers assess pupils?
- What happens to the information gleaned from assessment?

Considered response:

_____

_____

_____

_____

_____

_____

_____

_____

_____

_____

Rate yourself

QUESTION 10: Are there a range of different formative and summative assessments in place and are you aware as a staff of the difference between these?

| 1 | 2 | 3 | 4 | 5 | 6 | 7 | 8 | 9 | 10 |

QUESTION 11: Is your reporting and tracking system meaningful and does it promote excellent pupil outcomes?

Quick response:

_____

_____

_____

_____

Questions for consideration

- How do you use tracking to help pupils improve?
- How does reporting and tracking in your school monitor how much pupils know?
- By looking at reporting and tracking data can you tell how your pupils are achieving?
- Does your tracking limit pupils or maintain high expectations for all?

Considered response:

_____

_____

_____

_____

_____

_____

_____

_____

_____

_____

Rate yourself

QUESTION 11: Is your reporting and tracking system meaningful and does it promote excellent pupil outcomes?

| 1 | 2 | 3 | 4 | 5 | 6 | 7 | 8 | 9 | 10 |

QUESTION 12: How do you gauge what your pupils know?

Quick response:

_____

_____

_____

_____

Questions for consideration

- When have you found yourself feeling most aware of what your pupils know and don't know? What helped you to discover this?
- Do you think your pupils remember what you teach them? Why or why not? What could you do to help them with this, using your curriculum or assessment design?
- What do you think are the most effective ways of getting pupils to improve in your subject? How can assessment help or hinder this?

Considered response:

_____

_____

_____

_____

_____

_____

_____

_____

_____

_____

_____

_____

Rate yourself

QUESTION 12: How do you gauge what your pupils know?

1	2	3	4	5	6	7	8	9	10

QUESTION 13: How confident are your pupils and staff in their grasp of current attainment and progress?

Quick response:

_____

_____

_____

_____

Questions for consideration

- Is there any form of assessment which you have found does not help your knowledge of your pupils or how to make them progress? Why was this?
- As leadership are you aware of pupil attainment and progress across subjects?
- Do pupils know where they are succeeding and why?
- Do pupils know where they are struggling and why?

Considered response:

_____

_____

_____

_____

_____

_____

_____

_____

_____

_____

_____

Rate yourself

QUESTION 13: How confident are your pupils and staff in their grasp of current attainment and progress?

1	2	3	4	5	6	7	8	9	10

QUESTION 14: How do you use assessment data and feedback to help pupils improve?

Quick response:

_____

_____

_____

_____

Questions for consideration

- Should you teach to the test if it means pupils will achieve good exam results?
- How do you use data to impact Teaching and Learning?
- What do pupils do with the data and feedback they are given – how do they use this to improve?

Considered response:

_____

_____

_____

_____

_____

_____

_____

_____

_____

_____

_____

_____

Rate yourself

QUESTION 14: How do you use assessment data and feedback to help pupils improve?

1	2	3	4	5	6	7	8	9	10

QUESTION 15: How should you and your staff be held accountable?

Quick response:

_____

_____

_____

_____

Questions for consideration

- How important are exam results? Are these proof of a good education?
- How should you be held accountable for your pupils' progress?
- What qualifications do you want your pupils to gain?
- How should a department be held accountable?
- How should a school be held accountable?

Considered response:

_____

_____

_____

_____

_____

_____

_____

_____

_____

_____

_____

Rate yourself

QUESTION 15: How should you and your staff be held accountable?

1	2	3	4	5	6	7	8	9	10

QUESTION 16: What are the most effective forms of assessment?

Quick response:

_____

_____

_____

_____

Questions for consideration

- Do you need different types of assessment for different subjects? If so what are the range of assessments you need and why? For instance: do you need to provide an opportunity for essay writing within assessments?
- Which types of assessment give you the most knowledge about your pupils?
- Which types of assessment help pupils to improve?

Considered response:

_____

_____

_____

_____

_____

_____

_____

_____

_____

_____

_____

Rate yourself

QUESTION 16: What are the most effective forms of assessment?

1	2	3	4	5	6	7	8	9	10

The results

Well done, you have self-evaluated your practices in curriculum and assessment design and are now a step forward in the right direction to beginning the journey of curriculum and assessment design.

Take a look at how you rated your answers for each question in the questionnaire and compare your ratings with the chart below which will guide you to taking the next steps in curriculum and assessment design.

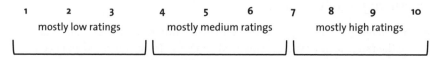

Fig. 5 How did you rate yourself?

Mostly low ratings
You need to take some time getting to know how curriculum and assessment currently works in your school. Research the basics around both and read the first couple of chapters of this book closely – making notes as you go.

Mostly medium ratings
Pick the areas you are unsure about – look to see if there are gaps within your own knowledge or in your school. Where do you/your staff need training or extra reading? This might mean exploring theories and/or case studies.

Mostly high ratings
You are very clear on how curriculum and assessment work in your school, as well as your own opinions on these topics. This puts you in a strong position to lead on designing curriculum and assessment systems for your school. This doesn't mean that you have all the answers though – be prepared to read new ideas and theories to challenge your thinking.

Now what?

The results are in. So now what? You have a full and detailed self-reflection on your curriculum and assessment design and it is important that you now make the most of it. Take the time to action plan as a result of the answers you have given and the conclusions you have drawn. Don't make this simply another bit of paperwork you have completed. Use it to really open your eyes to how far you have come, where you are now and what you want to do next. Prioritise what you want to work on and get going on it.

Chapter 2 takeaway

Teaching tip

Be honest

Be honest about what you do/do not know and the strengths and failings of your current system. In a world of school PR and social media showing off successes, it can be easy to assume that everyone else has got it right, so you need to put a face on or claim an expertise that you don't have. Actually it is those who can admit they have things to learn who are the most likely to succeed.

Pass it on

Discuss with other teachers

It is worth discussing your ideas with your network of teaching friends that you will have made since beginning teaching. The more fellow teachers you talk with, the more you will be able to build up expertise and gain different perspectives.

Pupil and parent voice

When you have some clarity on school vision, it is worth discussing these with groups of pupils and parents, to assess their needs and to see if they are on board with the school ethos.

Share and tweet

Tweet out some of your reflections or the questions you have been left with after completing the questionnaire using the hashtag #BloomsCPD

CPD book club recommendation

To get a clear picture of how to build a curriculum from strong educational principles, read *Trivium 21c* by Martin Robinson (see Bibliography and further reading)

Bloggers' corner

Check out the @staffrm blog (staffrm.io) for a range of different blogs about education, including curriculum and assessment.

TO DO LIST:

☐ Determine the specific areas of knowledge you need to build on or focus on within your school.

☐ Re-read through your answers to the questionnaire and reflect on what they reveal to you about your understanding of curriculum and assessment at this time.

☐ Use your answers to direct your reading of this book: which chapters will be most useful to you?

☐ Tweet your thoughts and questions about curriculum and assessment by using the hashtag #BloomsCPD.

☐ Check out the @staffrm blog (staffrm.io) for a range of different blogs about education, including curriculum and assessment.

☐ Read *Trivium 21c* by Martin Robinson.

3 Putting it all into context

Before beginning the practical processes of designing curriculum and assessment, it is important to ground yourself in the history and context of curriculum and assessment. We have grappled with the ideas of what we should pass on to the future generation since the very beginning of time. It is essential to understand that we are never creating something completely new, but are building on what has come before. The next few chapters aim to outline some of the thinking, policy and politics that influence curriculum and assessment today.

The missing experts

At ResearchEd 2015 (a conference focused on research in education), Sam Freedman (@Samfr – director of Teach First and former policy adviser to Michael Gove) spoke of an absence of expertise in areas such as curriculum and assessment design. The reason? Twenty five years of political meddling in state education. His belief that government should be concerned with outputs (results) rather than inputs (pedagogy) is one echoed by many in the profession.

When it comes to curriculum – and particularly assessment – there does seem to be a politician lurking around every corner. Whether it is government documents and strategies, the unwieldy tools of Ofsted (who never quite convince anyone that they are apolitical), the game-playing of national assessments or the obsession with pedagogy over curriculum – it is clear that teachers seem to feel a lack of expertise in what is the very core of a school education. According to the House of Commons National Curriculum report 2008-09, teachers claim to feel like 'deliverers' of curriculum rather than creative developers, and this detachment from the process of curriculum design has led to arguments that there has been a 'de-professionalisation' (National Association of Head Teachers) of the teaching community.

Strangely though, at the same time, a band of rebels (the poets and warriors of education) have formed throughout the UK and abroad in schools and education communities, online and in the grassroots conference movements, in an attempt to seize back ownership of what we teach in our schools. The impact of this has now been seen across the political spectrum, with politicians consistently asserting that they want to step out from the classroom.

'The Labour party's answer begins with a commitment to give all schools the freedom they need to excel.' Tristram Hunt, *The Guardian* 2015.

'We believe that the fastest and most sustainable way for schools to improve is for government to trust this country's most effective education leaders, giving them freedom and power' Nicky Morgan, 'Educational Excellence Everywhere' 2016.

'...curriculum should be set by subject experts and teaching professionals independently of government: what is taught in the classroom should not be subject to political whim.' David Laws, *The Guardian* 2015.

We have entered a new era of curriculum and assessment design, where expertise is now beginning to be developed within schools and through online networks bringing new access to research and theory.

Yet it's a confusing time, this call for a school-led system contrasts with continued involvement from politicians and causes a divide amongst educators about what we should be teaching, how we should be teaching and how consistent this should be across schools. Whilst I empathise with this confusion, I think we have to be brave enough to believe that as people who have studied our subjects and trained to teach them, we have valuable expertise.

It seems to me that to become experts within the field of curriculum and assessment design, we must simply take our knowledge and expand on this through our own research, thinking and practice.

Top tip

Twitter is a fantastic tool for online CPD for teachers and schools. It has become a platform for educational debate through discussion online and through links to relevant blogs, articles, organisations and conferences. Here are some tips for engaging with social media professionally:

1. Be ready to debate ideas but keep your cool: fight fair.
2. Be generous: share both your ideas and those of other online colleagues.
3. Use a blog to expand more widely on your Tweets.
4. Stick to your principles: don't be swayed by people simply because of their online popularity/strength of voice.
5. Remember CPD (especially that online) is something which occurs over time – don't expect it all to be perfect overnight.

Read more advice from myself and other educators here: www.theguardian.com/teacher-network/2016/feb/21/how-teachers-social-media-boost-cpd-live-chat

Who to follow:
http://www.teachertoolkit.me/2016/04/03/101educators
www.tes.com.c.tes.ent.platform.sh/news/blog/my-favourite-thinks-some-my-education-inspirations
headguruteacher.com/2015/12/27/the-people-whove-influenced-me-in-2015

Looking back to move forward

To build this expert knowledge and develop our answers to the many complex questions of the previous chapter, it is important to gain an understanding of how we got where we are today. We can do this by looking at the historical and political context within which we are working. As one audience member at ResearchEd asked: 'How do we know we lost expertise? Did we ever really have it?'

There is something to be said about taking a fresh look at the ideas of yesterday in order to create something for tomorrow. We can learn lessons from educational politics of the past: the answer does not simply lie in innovation or abandoning plans of old in the face of frustration, because this can often lead to a short-term way of thinking – understandable for politicians (Education Secretaries in particular) who may only have a short run at the job, but it's not suitable for the ongoing long-term needs of schools.

When Freedman spoke of the last 25 years of education, the implication is that schools and teachers once had the freedom to be experts. This poses the question that is core to many discussions surrounding the history of education:

Was it all better when schools were just left to get on with it?

In a discussion about curriculum in schools it's never too long before someone talks about the good old days when schools could just get on with teaching and teachers were respected as subject experts. Indeed, up until the Education Act of 1988, it's certainly true that autonomy of schools was a celebrated feature of the British education system. Politicians rarely interfered over the content of curriculum and any attempts to change this, such as the establishment of the Curriculum Study Group in 1964, were hugely unpopular and usually disbanded.

Unfortunately it wasn't all daisy chains and happy camping (or perhaps it was too much of this) as 73% of state educated pupils left school without qualifications and the rigour of the curriculum was entirely based on the school that they attended.

Assessment rules!

Yet here you have the rub: national assessment (qualifications) became the driver for curriculum. Pupils considered 'higher ability' were streamed to take O-levels whilst the rest took CSEs. Here it all gets a bit complicated – the overwhelming feeling today (and the reason the GCSE was established) is that the CSE was a very inferior qualification in comparison to the O-level and therefore left a vast range of children lacking in opportunity both in terms of their future and the quality of their academic education. At the same time, however, the CSE did offer a lot more freedom and the chance for innovation because some of the CSE was assessed within school and the exam boards were regional – made up of teachers and local representatives. This saw an increase in 'school-based curriculum development' and the introduction of what was considered more 'radical' curriculum. However the drive from exam boards (led by universities) for exams which were 'impartial, objective and related to externally assessed criteria' put a stop to this type of curriculum, and led to a contradiction between curriculum design to a certain extent still being seen as the domain of schools, but assessment controlled nationally.

Meanwhile arguments around curriculum content, when not directed by assessment, became dominated by two distinct ways of thinking: traditionalist and progressive.

The progressive versus traditionalist debate

Nothing says 'Happy New Year!' like a brawl between academics and 2016 has been no exception. Dusting off the last of the mince pies, and clearly bored with their presents there emerged the all-time favourite battle: Progressives vs Traditionalists or in its new metamorphosed form: 'There is no such thing as Progressive vs Traditionalist' versus 'There is SO a thing about Progressive vs Traditionalist'! This was a hot topic on Twitter and in numerous blog posts.

Traditional	Progressive
The curriculum is based around the existence of a traditional body of knowledge, which should be transferred to pupils.	The curriculum is based around a negotiable set of content and skills, which is determined by the needs and interests of the individual children.
Emphasis should be on *knowledge*.	Emphasis should be on *skills*.
Teaching is primarily based around direct instruction and practice.	Teaching is primarily based around activities and experiences.
Classrooms have a hierarchy, with the teacher as the authority.	Classrooms should be more egalitarian – pupil voice and choice should be taken into account.
Testing, through examinations, is an important assessment tool to measure and inform pupil progress.	There should be alternative forms of assessment such as coursework and projects, which take into account pupil feelings and skill sets.
Curriculum and Assessment are driven by subjects.	Curriculum and Assessment includes focus on cross-curricular work and discovery learning.

Fig. 6 Curriculum approaches

It is an important debate to consider when looking at the history of curriculum and assessment, as these two schools of thought have been influencing education in the UK since the beginning of the 20th century. In particular, during the late 1960s when groups of educators, inspired by figures such as Jean-Jacques Rousseau and John Dewey, argued for a more child-centred and relevant curriculum, with aspects of discovery learning[1]. One particular influence was the Plowden Report published in 1967, which argued for a child-centred curriculum based on Piaget's work on child development; arguing that we should respect children's choice and readiness for elements of the curriculum, that play is a strong tool for learning, and that subject divisions are unsuitable for children under the age of nine and perhaps even unsuitable for middle school children. This was a direct challenge to previous thinking around the content of curriculum and the pedagogy which should be used to deliver the curriculum.

Both schools of thought have often since been reduced to stereotype and have been assigned political labels: progressive as 'left-wing' and traditionalist as 'right-wing'. This can be unhelpful and can lead to blind acceptance or refusal of ideas based on ideology; there also tends to be confusion between ideas and methods. Tom Sherrington navigates this well in his blog post: *The Progressive-Traditional Pedagogy Tree*. He argues that the best approach to this is to not consider these two camps as polar opposites but as both important facets of a whole education.

Tom Sherrington on progressive vs traditional

Name: Tom Sherrington
Twitter handle: @headguruteacher
Website: headguruteacher.com
What to read: The progressive-traditional pedagogy tree

James Theobald however makes a convincing argument for viewing them as two distinct schools of thought because of the influence they have had, particularly within schools and teacher training institutes in the last 30 or so years.

James Theobald on progressive vs traditional

Name: James Theobald
Twitter handle: @JamesTheo
Website: othmarstrombone.wordpress.com
What to read: I was a teenage progressive: a defence of the debate; The reconciliation of the debate (Is it possible? Is it desirable?)

---

[1] http://www.ioe.ac.uk/services/documents/SG3_Progressive_Education_(March_2009).pdf

It is by exploring both ways of thinking that we reach a better understanding of the debates around and influences on curriculum and can be clearer about our own bias. I think we all tend to sway one way or another, either naturally or based on the company we keep, and therefore it is worth carefully considering your view point – particularly because the politicisation of these groups can make people adopt positions without thinking through the implications. It's also vital to understand the different influences on the curriculum historically and consider how this impacts on your views of curriculum today. In order to make sense of this, I will explore them as two distinct camps, even though this may be an historical distinction.

Further reading – progressive vs traditional

Ross Morrrison McGill: *8 teaching ideas to bin in 2016* (teachertoolkit.me)

Greg Ashman: *I refute it thus*; *Can a false choice be an object of research?* (gregashman. wordpress.com)

Phil Stock: *The unexamined life* (joeybagtock.wordpress.com)

Reflection questions

- How important is the transfer of knowledge in education?
- Is it more important to teach transferrable skills or to teach facts?
- Is there a body of knowledge which pupils should be taught?
- Should pupils have choice when it comes to the curriculum content?
- Should pupils be taught through direct instruction or be guided to discover learning for themselves?
- Is memorising content an important part of teaching?
- Should pupils be given opportunities to complete project work?
- Do we over test our pupils?
- Are standardised tests a good form of assessment?
- Should all pupils be assessed in the same way?

Diversity and representation

Arguments around diversity and representation in the curriculum are one of the main reasons that there were shifts in thinking about curriculum and its potential for renovation. One of the important roles that the progressive movement had was to make educators and policy makers consider the diverse body of pupils who were now being educated. This has provided us with important questions about to what extent the curriculum should reflect the experiences of those who are studying it. This was particularly important when considering ethnic backgrounds of pupils, as well as issues surrounding gender and sexuality. The needs of society and a desire for equality of experience as well as opportunity thus became a driving force behind determining the content of the curriculum. An example being The Bullock Report (1975), which directly identified the importance of children not turning their back on the language and culture of their home.

The approach by education reformers on the left in the 1980s and 1990s was to look at the problems of racism, which abounded in society. Their argument was that a mono-cultural curriculum and racist approaches to teaching were fundamental issues in schools. According to Ken Jones, in his book: *Education in Britain: 1944 to the Present*, Conservatives and right-wing media played on this by suggesting this group of teachers were deviating from the curriculum in a damaging way; using examples of extreme challenges to national ideas of education. At the same time, these educators were exploring the issue of class and how this impacted on pupils in education who came from a working class background. The tendency was to push for a range of curriculum options including a technical route for pupils not seen as academic.

Ken Jones on the history of education in Britain

Name: Ken Jones

Job title: Professor Ken Jones, Head of Department of Educational Studies, Goldsmiths University

What to read: *Education in Britain: 1944 to the Present*

These tensions over the content of the curriculum, including the debates around knowledge and skills, as well as those between academic and technical education, have been at the crux of curriculum and assessment design. It seems that the debates of the 1960s and 1970s did achieve a substantial shift forward in terms of shaping a better education for all, moving thinking from 'we are all the same' to embracing the fact that 'we are all different'. Both ends of the spectrum reached the agreement that our curriculum needs an understanding that in fact 'we are all together' (or at least should be). In the 1980s, politicians made a grab for unison by finally taking control of the curriculum (a move they seemed to have been wanting to make for a few years) and establishing a National Curriculum.

> **Further reading: history of education**
> Derek Gillard: *Education in England: a brief history*
> (www.educationengland.org.uk/history)

What has the National Curriculum ever done for us?

For teachers in my generation, the National Curriculum has always been a part of education – from our own schooling onwards – so an education system without it is almost unimaginable. It was established in the Education Act of 1988, for all pupils between the ages of five and 16. This 'broad and balanced' subject-based curriculum also included national tests as measures to keep schools accountable for the pupils in their care. The ideology behind the curriculum was said to be equality of access and opportunity. It was a winner in many respects – including particular improvements for girls: they were now required to study sciences and maths until 16 and, according to Ken Jones, there was also an improvement in the number of girls attending higher education, with the performance of most girls surpassing boys at 16+. (Jones, *Education in Britain: 1944 to the Present*)

However, it was also seen as a political grab for control, because of concerns about the local control of schools and the influences of progressive 'child-centred' approaches. This led to criticisms of the curriculum for sticking to a 'traditional' model, which many educators felt promoted a mono-cultural version of education due to the focus on standard English and British history:

> '[It] destroyed the education culture which had developed between 1944 and 1979, and began the work of creating a different one, on which old 'social actors' were marginalised and new ones rendered powerful.' (Jones, **Education in Britain: 1944 to the Present**)

At the same time, there was a concern at primary level that the content of the curriculum meant less time to focus on the essentials such as literacy and thus could possibly damage standards further rather than improve them. The political involvement in curriculum meant that any curriculum decision was seen as an ideological one. Notably these concerns continue to dominate discussion around curriculum today.

Understanding how to navigate the muddy waters of curriculum once education was no longer the preserve of the privileged few became a key debating point amongst educators. The politically sensitive nature of this led policy to focus away from curriculum (as clear in the increasingly slimmed down curriculum revisions) and more towards school effectiveness based on delivery and assessment results. Once again qualifications and assessment data ruled the roost, with curriculum following at its feet.

Arrival of the Big Bad Wolf

Then the 1990s hit, and along with 'girl power' and endless renditions of *Wonderwall* came political decisions which altered the educational landscape permanently, all within the space of three years. This began in 1991 with the establishing of SATs tests, swiftly followed by league tables (1992) and Ofsted (1993). The establishment of SATs and the publication of results in league tables created a new accountability system and subsequent competition between schools. With funding awarded to schools based on numbers of pupils, and parents given the opportunity to choose schools informed by this assessment data, schools had an incentive to ensure success at test level other than for the means of improving the learning of their pupils. Ofsted added further pressure and improper incentive, as schools knew they would be judged on their assessment data based on progress between SATs and GCSEs. Until recently this also included judgement on the way in which curriculum was delivered, including comments on pedagogy within schools.

National Curriculum change and review

These changes were not well received within the education community: in 1993-4, there was a national boycott of SATs organised by English teachers. It took another 15 years for SATs to be abolished at Key Stage 3 and a further seven years at Key Stage 2. Instead the boycott led to a revision of the curriculum including the removal of several of the more traditional elements; a slimming down of content and a less nationalised approach. The 1995 National Curriculum was thus a much different curriculum to that first introduced and put more emphasis on the use of levels throughout school to assess pupil progress. Ironically the demand for less national assessment led to a reduction of curriculum content but an increase in levelled assessment within schools. The revisions in 1995 and 1999 were attempts to reduce the problem of overloading by slimming down content and cut down the 'numbers of attainment targets and statements of attainment' (The Dearing Review (1994), The National Curriculum and its Assessment: Final Report).

The revision continued with the 2007 curriculum which was the most reduced in terms of content and focused away from proscribed content to more generic statements both in curriculum and in the assessment standards.

Game playing – the dark side of the assessment obsession

The fixation on slimming down the curriculum whilst increasing accountability around qualifications led to some schools playing the system for all it was worth. At Key Stages 2 and 3, this resulted in unreliable data and a concern that particularly in primary, teachers were being pressured to focus on teaching for the test. Likewise at the end of Key Stage 4, teachers were increasingly being held to account for their GCSE results and thus asked to focus on intervention in maths and English over other subjects. I will never forget the moment, a few years ago, when I was giving a Year 11 pupil a dressing down for having missed my English lesson and he said, 'But there's intervention on later isn't there? I'll come to that one.' The message was pretty clear about what we valued as a school and it was certainly not the subject.

This pressure, which continues today, led to teachers and school leadership attempting to play games with exam entry. In a previous role co-ordinating English at Key Stage 4, I've been in many a multi-school meeting where there was a discussion about how to enter pupils for multiple exam boards to ensure they got the required 'C' grade and at their worst where teachers were exchanging stories of rumoured cheating on Controlled Assessment tasks – from getting pupils to re-do assessments a number of times, to marks being entered despite the actual assessment being 'missing'.

School leadership teams have had a big role to play in this. At secondary level, the fear of Ofsted and league tables meant that entry into a number of different qualifications – no matter what their quality – became a usual part of school life, as did entering pupils for re-takes and playing games over which pupils to enter into which exam tier (Foundation/Higher) based on what it would do for overall school results. This had become such an accepted way of behaving that last year at an education conference I heard a headteacher stand up and openly admit that no matter what changes were coming, he and his school would attempt to game the system.

Of course this is looking at some of the worst practice around and there were (and are) still schools, leaders and teachers who were doing everything best to avoid these behaviours. They are all the more admirable for their relentless focus on what was right for the pupils in their care – but unfortunately not everyone has had this strength.

Overall the problem is not really about the fairness of school performance, it is about the quality of education being offered to pupils and the expectations that we have on them to succeed; both of which seemed to be reduced by this relentless focus on qualifications and meaningless data instead of curriculum.

All this was to change with the arrival of Michael Gove as Education Secretary. Love him or loathe him, there is no denying how much he revolutionised and stirred up debate around curriculum and assessment. Not to say we haven't still got a way to go...

The Gove reforms

In 2010, Gove commissioned a review of the National Curriculum from an expert panel who addressed some of the concerns about the quality of both curriculum and assessment. I will explore the details of this report in the following chapters but it is clear that it led to widespread reform. This has had some negative reactions from the education community (including some of those on the expert panel) due to the heavily prescribed content of the curriculum, inspired by the work of researchers such as E D Hirsch. Gove was also fairly criticised for the pace of this reform, which led teachers and school leaders into a desperate scramble to create new curriculum and assessment systems, particularly at GCSE level where teachers are now trying to assess pupils with a new numerical assessment system that they are yet to understand.

It's a lot to take in but, criticisms aside, the space created from the abolishment of National Curriculum levels; the changing of progress measures at GCSE and the rules around re-sits has given school leaders an opportunity to innovate. Whilst the content of curriculum, particularly at primary level, has increased, schools have been liberated when it comes to the ways in which they deliver and assess this curriculum. The increasing number of free schools and academies, who are completely untied from the National Curriculum, further compounds this sense of school sovereignty. It has also opened up the grounds for leaders and teachers to debate some of the core ideas around the purposes of school curriculum and assessment with the understanding that they might have be able to put these into action. The education blogosphere has been the ultimate platform for these debates.

From 1800s	• Subject-based education
1944	• Education Act (Butler Act) made religious education compulsory; the rest of the curriculum is determined by teachers/local communities
1960s	• Due to concerns about falling standards, the Ministry of Education forms the Curriculum Study Group which later becomes the Schools Council
1976	• Jim Callaghan's Ruskin Speech asking for a Great Debate in Education, includes idea of national 'core' curriculum • Abolition of Schools Council – replaced with School Curriculum & Development Committee and Secondary Examinations Council
1985	• Better Schools White Paper recommends a nationally-agreed curriculum
1986	• Establishment of National Council for Vocational Qualifications
1987	• Consultation on intended National Curriculum at the DfE under guidance of Kenneth Baker
1988	• Introduction of the National Curriculum including attainment targets and GCSEs
1989	• National Curriculum runs in primary schools
1991	• First run of Key Stage tests (SATS)
1992	• Establishment of league tables
1993	• Establishment of Ofsted • First National Curriculum review in response to teacher complaints about the curriculum and threatened boycotts of tests • National Curriculum Council and School Examinations and Assessment Council merged to form School Curriculum and Assessment Authority
1995	• Revised version of the National Curriculum including a reduction in prescribed content • Restriction of key stage tests to core subjects • Replacement of the 10 level assessment scale with 8 level descriptors
1997	• National Literacy and National Numeracy Strategies introduced • Formation of Qualifications and Curriculum Authority
1999	• Substantial revision of the National Curriculum including furthered reduction of prescribed content and overt statement of aims and purposes.
2000	• Loose National Curriculum for framework for early years • Reform of A-levels including introduction of AS-levels
2002	• National Curriculum for early years becomes statutory
2005	• QCA review of the Secondary KS3 curriculum by the DfE
2008	• QCA review becomes compulsory. • Rose Review of the Primary Curriculum • KS3 tests scrapped
2011	• Review of the National Curriculum by expert panel
2014	• Introduction of the new revised National Curriculum
2015	• Teaching of new GCSEs begins (to be assessed in 2017)

Fig. 7 Timeline

Further reading – National Curriculum

Oates, T. (2010), 'Could do better: Using international comparisons to refine the National Curriculum in England'. Cambridge Assessment

Shirley Williams (2009), The winnowing out of happiness, *The Guardian*

Chapter 3 takeaway

Teaching tip

Know your stuff

To become the missing experts, you need to do the research and reading. You have to engage with the knowledge required to become an expert. You don't have to know it all in order to make decisions or comments on curriculum and assessment design but you do owe it to your team to be basing your ideas on a concrete understanding of the history and context.

Pass it on

Be part of the debate

Attending conferences and events where teachers discuss ideas around curriculum and assessment is a good way to further your knowledge and also to contribute your own expertise. Use the Echo Chamber's 'What's On' page to find relevant events: educationechochamber.wordpress.com/whats-on/ or browse Twitter for announcements.

Share and tweet

Follow the Twitter conversation on the hashtag #LearningFirst and tweet using the hashtag to join the debate about assessment.

CPD book club recommendation

Education in Britain: 1944 to the present, Ken Jones
(see Bibliography and further reading)

Bloggers' corner

See Andrew Old's (@oldandrewuk) posts on progressive and traditional education: teachingbattleground.wordpress.com/

To do list:

- ❑ Use the questions to reflect on where your own bias lies in the traditionalist-progressive divide.
- ❑ Examine your current school curriculum and assessment systems and consider how much has been inherited from past thinking and policy.
- ❑ Write down the key mistakes from the history of curriculum and assessment that you want to avoid.
- ❑ Tweet your learning about and reflections on the history of curriculum and assessment design by using the hashtag #BloomsCPD
- ❑ Check out Old Andrew's blog posts on progressive and traditional education: teachingbattleground.wordpress.com/
- ❑ Read *Education in Britain: 1944 to the present* by Ken Jones.

4 What is the purpose of the school curriculum?

If you want a good argument, just pose the question: 'What is the purpose of a school education?' You are guaranteed a heated debate! It has even become the subject of an inquiry for the Education Select Committee (2016).

I would define the four competing schools of thought as:

- To build character
- To prepare children for the world of work
- To further social justice
- To teach academic subjects for their intrinsic value

This chapter will explore the different arguments for each of these four schools of thought and unpick the implications for curriculum and assessment design. I'll also defend the controversial position that you have to choose just one in order to create a curriculum with strong foundations.

Approaching developing a curriculum

In Ralph Tyler's book, *Basic Principles of Curriculum and Instruction*, he outlines four fundamental questions which must be answered when aiming to develop a curriculum. They can be summarised as follows:

1. What educational purposes should a school seek to attain?
2. What learning experiences can you select to achieve these purposes?
3. How can you effectively organise these experiences to best achieve your purposes?
4. How can you evaluate the effectiveness of these experiences?
   (Tyler, 1949)

These cut straight to the centre of what we need to consider when designing a curriculum: purpose, content, pedagogy, sequencing and assessment.

When looking at the history of curriculum design since the mid 1990s, it's clear we have been focused on the last of these four questions – mostly because this is the easier to set up and monitor nationally. The problem is that by cutting to the last question we lose an opportunity to create anything meaningful. The first question is somehow answered by the last without the middle two questions being considered.

Ralph Tyler on developing a curriculum

Name: Ralph Tyler

What to read: Basic principles of curriculum and instruction

Dylan Wiliam identifies 'four broad categories' of justification for education:

1. 'Personal Empowerment'
2. 'Cultural Transmission'
3. 'Preparation for citizenship'
4. 'Preparation for work'
   (Wiliam, 2013).

These more or less fit with the classifications that I suggested at the start of the chapter and which I am going to look at in more detail: building character (personal empowerment); preparing children for the world of work (preparation for work); furthering social justice (preparation for citizenship) and teaching academic subjects for their intrinsic value (cultural transmission).

Wiliam suggests that you can, and should, try to serve all of these purposes to a certain extent within a curriculum, which is a view held by many in education. Much like the progressive-traditionalist debate (see Chapter 3), there are plenty who argue it's a false dichotomy and that we must aim for a blend. It's a persuasive argument but one that is dangerously close to shutting down useful debates and, in this case, with the particular problem that it denies a key aspect of good leadership of curriculum design: prioritising.

Balancing act

I'm a fan of balance, of nuance, of navigating the grey areas of education and indeed life. I want my pupils to engage with all aspects of life; I want them to enjoy their lives, to find meaning and to achieve greatness. Like most teachers, in my classroom there is a constant balancing act to be found as I explore the best ways to teach, to inspire a love of my subject, to protect and encourage the children in my care and set them up for a life beyond school walls and rules. However, time in lessons in school and in education is short and it is precious. So as teachers we do make choices, every single moment of every single lesson we make decisions about what and how we will educate. And those decisions, those choices, are informed by a diverse collection of understandings and beliefs about the purpose of education:

- from our own beliefs, which in turn are formed from a vast array of influences and biases whether this be our own schooling, training or background
- from the beliefs of the schools in which we teach and the values and ethos it espouses
- from the beliefs of our society.

In split seconds, our minds whizz through a host of these beliefs, choices and judgements already made before determining what action to take.

Those of us who are school leaders consciously take time to think about all of these beliefs, these choices – we then help to define the ethos of our school and make decisions which determine what kind of choices we and others are able to make within our classrooms. As people who are engaged in education beyond our schools and in think tanks, companies and political bodies, we become part of an even wider community that determines the decisions our society, our school and our classroom value. Each one of us has our own narrative of how we influence and determine the decisions that our society, our schools and our classrooms value.

So our choices must reflect our ideology no matter how much we would like to escape that. I want to teach my pupils amazing, beautiful, pieces of literature and I want them to be empowered, critically-engaged citizens. But what do I think I should be judged on, what do I think I should be dedicating my time and my resources to? What do I believe my school should do? Because we do not have an infinite amount of time and money and we do have responsibilities, both self-imposed and those for which we are externally accountable whether it be to parents, government or an inspection body.

It is this prioritising that is central to understanding how you make decisions about your curriculum and assessment.

I'll now look at each of the four main schools of thought raised at the start of the chapter (p 52) and then set out my own personal conclusion. I don't think my way is THE way for everyone, but as part of understanding the process of curriculum design it helps for me to be honest about my bias.

Building character

Character is of course complicated to define. The *New Oxford English Dictionary* defines it as: 'the mental and moral qualities distinctive to an individual'. Already this provokes discussion around what we consider to be 'moral qualities' and if they are 'distinctive to an individual' then can they even be taught? However, the idea of educating for character is not a new one. Much of the discussion around teaching moral virtue comes through reading Aristotle's work, in which he argues that virtue must be practised alongside knowledge acquisition. This idea of building children who are happy and moral doesn't seem controversial. However, a recent focus (by politicians, schools and individual educators) on the explicit teaching of character through the curriculum has opened up more of a discussion about what roles school do, and should have, in 'building' character.

Both the main political parties have argued that we should look at the explicit teaching of character, with Nicky Morgan launching a multi-million pound campaign to push this in schools, including teaching character traits such as 'resilience and grit'. According to the press release, 'England to become a global leader of teaching character,' Morgan says that lessons in character are just as valuable as academic lessons because they give pupils the skills they need to succeed.

This has been welcomed by some schools, particularly new schools such as King Solomon Academy and School 21, and is inspired by the KIPP chain of schools in America that teach and grade pupils based on character. This includes giving pupils a 'character report card' where they are marked for showing examples of any of the 24 different character traits (which come from the book, *Character Strengths and Virtues: A Handbook and Classification* by C Peterson and M Seligman).

1. Zest	7. Hope	13. Wisdom	19. Leadership
2. Grit	8. Humour	14. Bravery	20. Forgiveness
3. Self-control	9. Creativity	15. Integrity	21. Modesty
4. Social intelligence	10. Curiosity	16. Kindness	22. Prudence/Discretion
5. Gratitude	11. Open-mindedness	17. Citizenship	23. Appreciation of beauty
6. Love	12. Love of learning	18. Fairness	24. Spirituality

Fig. 8 Character traits

James O'Shaughnessy, founder of Floreat Education and previous Head of Policy for David Cameron, is a strong advocate of this approach to teaching character. He discusses this in the article, 'Why character is key to a perfect education' in *The Telegraph*. In that article O'Shaughnessy quotes Martin Luther King Junior, taking from King's piece on *The Purpose of Education* where King says:

> 'Intelligence plus character – that is the goal of true education.'
> Martin Luther King Junior

This blended approach where character shares an equal purpose alongside academic study is quite common, but it is the call for specific character lessons, rather than it being just part of the wider experience of a curriculum, which is important to consider when it comes to curriculum and assessment design. Andreas Schleicher, the Director for Education and Skills for the Organisation for Economic Cooperation and Development (OECD) has argued that in fact character should be modelled rather than taught and it is this approach which holds British school children back in comparison to children in Singapore, China and Japan. Whilst he thinks character is important, he argues: 'I don't think it's an issue of an additional school subject. It's a lot more about how we teach.' ('UK 'may lose out' to Asian countries in developing 'soft skills' for life in new rankings', *The Telegraph*).

James O'Shaughnessy on teaching character

Name: Lord James O'Shaughnessy
Job title: Founder of Floreat Education
What to read: Why character is key to a perfect education (*The Telegraph*)

Potential implications for curriculum and assessment design

- Lessons within the curriculum to teach character skills.
- An assessment system which incorporates assessing for character.
- Subject curriculum to be developed with room for teaching character strengths.
- School-agreed vision on what a 'good character' is and how this links to morality and ethics.
- Decisions to be made about where character fits with PSHE, or if it will be incorporated into this.

Reflection questions

- What does teaching character mean to you and your school?
- Do you think character can be taught or is it modelled?
- Is it the school's responsibility to build character?
- Can/should you assess character?

Preparing for the world of work

The idea that school life is simply a stepping stone to the 'real' world of work is one that gains traction in the world of media and politics. The idea being that 'academia' is something very different from the functional skills and knowledge needed to be useful in the workplace. Some people, including famous entrepreneurs such as Sir Richard Branson, have gone further and criticised the education system as it stands: 'In this country, we still hold an outdated view of education and expect everyone to take the traditional path at school. Students are individuals, yet school curriculums encourage conformity.' (edtechnology.co.uk: 'Richard Branson rejects "one size fits all" education')

For some, this means taking a more progressive and creative approach to education, such as project and cross-curricular work or creating work with real life contexts such as learning about maths through looking at a school or local council budget issue. Others such as Michael Mercies, CEO of Young Enterprise argue that we should be teaching children from primary upwards the skills they will need for their future careers, and should encourage pupils to make subject choices based on their future careers rather than out of a love for education in itself, which he argues is a preserve of 'the minority'. Instead 'it is equally, if not more important, for people to get the soft skills employers value.' ('What's wrong with education for education's sake?' *The Telegraph*)

This idea of making room for soft skills, such as teamwork, critical thinking, empathy and communication, within the curriculum has a significant impact on curriculum and assessment design. One way this can be achieved is through the extended curriculum and involvement with organisations like the Duke of Edinburgh's Award or Young Enterprise. However, a number of organisations and employers have suggested taking this further by considering adjusting lessons to allow for elements such as teamwork and critical thinking to take precedence. McDonalds have even gone so far as to create a campaign to promote the teaching of soft skills: backingsoftskills.co.uk. Some schools, such as the Expeditionary Learning schools in America, have adapted their curriculum to embrace a 'learning by doing' philosophy. The XP Free School in Doncaster is the first UK school to adopt this model and focuses on teaching through discovery and craftmanship.

Essentially this means considering whether you want to dedicate lesson time to these skills and if so whether this involves sacrificing other elements of the curriculum. Dividing the curriculum into vocational/technical and academic is another option to consider if driven by the purpose of preparing pupils for the world of work.

This is something which has been taken seriously in Finland, where they have decided to scrap subject teaching and replace it with topic-based study including vocational topics such as 'cafeteria services' and academic study based on cross-subject topics such as the European Union.

Potential implications for curriculum and assessment design

- Opportunities for learning in a real-life context.
- Built in teaching of soft skills.
- Opportunities for pupils to pursue a technical or vocational path.
- Early decisions on subject choice to enable pupils to pursue a career path.
- Built in work experience.
- Reducing/removing subject-based teaching

Reflection questions

- Is it your responsibility to prepare pupils for the world of work?
- If so, how do you think you can best achieve this?
- Are you in favour of subject-based teaching or topic-based teaching?
- Should learning soft skills be a part of your curriculum and if so should this be in the everyday curriculum or in the extended curriculum?
- Are soft skills able to be taught and assessed or are they learnt through modelling and practice?
- Are real-life contexts important for learning?
- Should your assessment system include opportunities to be assessed on project work and qualifications such as the Duke of Edinburgh Award?

Education for social justice

State education has always been linked with ideas around social justice, even if only by association: the entitlement of all children to an education. However, there are also many educators who see education as having a particular purpose, which is to make society better (more equal). This idea of education as a way to improve society and to prepare pupils to take part in citizenship stretches across the political and educational divide. There are different strands such as: empowerment, teaching of social values, aiming to create an 'ideal' society within a school and teaching with the goals of citizenship in mind.

Initially this progressive political outlook became inextricably linked to the progressive education movement, in which the new thinkers in education challenged the curriculum and pushed for content and qualifications that had the lives of the learners at its heart. This has been the kind of teaching which has been 'Hollywood-ised' ever since: from *To Sir, with Love* to *Dangerous Minds* and even in the UK reality TV market from Phil Beadle to the Channel 4 Educating series and Jamie Oliver's *Dream School*. Education has been viewed as a vehicle for social change and teachers romanticised as social justice warriors (SJWs). Such is the power of the social justice movement that members of both progressive and traditional camps have become advocates.

The progressive approach is based on ideas around pupil voice and choice, including a relevant curriculum. This includes offering a range of courses for pupils to choose from, and being critical of canonical bodies of knowledge. This can also include non-traditional subjects such as citizenship and PSHE. In terms of

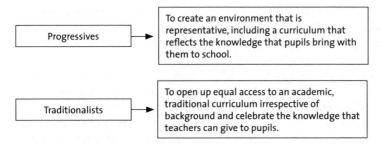

Fig. 9 Progressive and traditionalist views on social justice in education

assessment, the progressive approach tends to be sceptical of standardised tests and instead tends to embrace a range of assessment methods such as coursework and spoken work.

Many traditionalists consider the progressive approach as something which, whilst well meaning, in fact limits the opportunity for equality because it limits the expectations of children based on their backgrounds. Traditionalist approaches to a socially just curriculum suggest that by giving all children the opportunity to study an academic curriculum, you are creating equality of opportunity. This includes a knowledge-led approach to curriculum, which has become more popular in state schools since the recent re-thinking of the content of the National Curriculum and the increase of academies and free schools. This also means using standardised tests so that all pupils are being measured in the same way. This is currently seen as the education of the Conservative party or of those on the right, although it has been a feature of Labour education policy in the past – Harold Wilson was an advocate of a grammar school approach for all – and has begun to find consensus across the spectrum.

Diversity

One of the most interesting and complex parts of the argument for education having a social purpose, is when considering the diversity (or lack of diversity) of the curriculum. A traditional curriculum is often accused of being 'white, male and stale' – this is particularly true when discussing the canon of English literature and also in arguments about the studying of British history.

Jeffrey Boakye, a head of English in East London, explores many of these ideas in his blog: unseenflirtspoetry.wordpress.com. In one post, 'And then, "Killamanshank": stumbling my way towards curriculum diversity', he describes his teaching of a unit of work which was focused on modern London and multiculturalism and in which his classes compared texts by Zadie Smith, Dizzee Rascal, Doc Brown, Sway, Plan B, William Blake and Charles Dickens alongside non-fiction articles about

London. His conclusion: 'This was the first time that my students had seriously discussed writers and artists of colour regarding issues that affect people of colour. [...] an alarming reminder of the lack of diversity in the usual curriculum.'

Considering social justice, also means considering opportunity of access, which has led to much discussion around the types of assessment that best levels the playing field. Again this is something which is fought over; with some claiming standardised testing as the fairest option – read Daisy Christodoulou on this ('Tests are inhuman – and that is what is so good about them'). Whilst others argue that portfolio or coursework assessment is more equalising – see the ATL work on this ('Common ground on assessment and accountability in primary schools'.)

Potential implications for curriculum and assessment design

- Determine whether to take a traditional subject-based approach to promotion of social justice or a progressive topic-based approach.
- Explore how to develop diversity within the curriculum.
- Make text and content choices which are representative of the school body.
- Include classes on politics and citizenship.
- Look for forms of assessment which offer the most equal opportunities for pupils from all backgrounds.

Reflection questions

- Should your curriculum be centred around improving social justice?
- Does everything you teach need to be assessed?
- Do you believe in equality of opportunity or equality of outcome?
- How should this affect your curriculum and assessment?
- To what extent is your current curriculum motivated by thoughts around social justice?
- Do vocational and academic qualifications hold the same merit?
- What types of qualifications can pupils expect to achieve at your school and are these the right qualifications?

Teaching academic subjects for their intrinsic value

'[Education is] the valuation of cultural accomplishments through which society renews and acquires the intellectual and moral resources necessary to understand itself and face the future.'
('Wasted: Why Education Isn't Educating' Furedi, 2009)

For Furedi, a vocal advocate for the intrinsic value of academic education, we must think about curriculum as academics and value the importance of ideas and culture for themselves but also as the makings of our society. This is a challenge to the assumption that an academic education is narrow but also to the assertion that it doesn't prepare children for the 21st century world. We incorrectly assume that the world is changing more than it ever has and therefore the study of traditional subjects is irrelevant, but it is this which remains as our cultural foundations.

Another argument Furedi makes, is that by politicising the curriculum through a focus on social justice, we also risk dumbing down the subjects taught and focusing instead on imposing a set of 'fashionable values'. He argues that this then diminishes the intellectual culture of a school including the academic authority of the teacher, leading to the loss of expertise – teachers are subject experts, but by devaluing academic education, we diminish this expertise.

In his blog, Michael Fordham also argues the case for the study of academic disciplines in a series of posts that examine what should make up a school curriculum. He argues that:

> 'academic disciplines are [...] sophisticated forms of knowledge that have evolved over time which stand currently as our best means of making sense of the world beyond our immediate experience.'
> (Michael Fordham, 'The merits of the academic disciplines')

In his follow-up posts, he explains the implications of this on curriculum design – in particular the decision not to include vocational subjects as part of the curriculum. His ideas focus around this concept of prioritising – that by trying 'to blend academic disciplines, creative arts, life skills and vocational subjects' you end up making a mess of them all.

This argument is also emphasised in Martin Robinson's book *Trivium 21c: preparing young people for the future with lessons from the past* and on his connected blog. He looks at the purpose of education from a teaching perspective, but also as a parent thinking about what he would like his daughter to experience in her education, and argues for an education which uses knowledge of the past to build wonder and appreciation of humanity. By approaching the purpose of education for its own sake, we 'have a chance of building up the principles that should endure in the future: the freedom to know, to think, play, love, work, create or even the freedom to not do these things.' (2015)

For those who are driven by this school of thought, the day-to-day curriculum should be primarily focused around the transmission of and engagement with academic subjects, although there are arguments about which subjects this should include. It is through this that the other purposes can be achieved, if that is so desired – so tackling a difficult subject might also build resilience, debating a philosophical concept might lead to consideration of moral virtue and strengthen communication. Assessment therefore must be driven by the curriculum and used to help pupils and teachers see to what extent they have remembered what has been taught.

Potential implications for curriculum and assessment design

- Knowledge-driven curriculum
- Academic disciplines
- Focus on liberal arts, including Latin and philosophy
- Assessment driven by the curriculum.

Reflection questions

- Does your current curriculum inspire pupils to love learning for its own sake?
- Can a purely academic curriculum serve the needs of all your pupils?
- Should the curriculum be politicised or based on traditional subjects?
- Can you blend academic and vocational study effectively?
- Are your teachers considered academic authorities?
- Can/should other purposes be achieved implicitly through academic study?

Navigating the grey

I hope that by outlining the four schools of thought above, and posing questions for you to reflect on, that I have helped you towards consolidating your own thoughts on which of the four schools you favour individually or in combination. I personally have found myself genuinely torn over this question of purpose. It's something which has caused many a restless night as I've wrestled with the different arguments. I think it is key to begin by looking at the range of perspectives and arguments and to question your own bias. Certainly when I began teaching, I think like most teachers I had an idealistic view of what education should achieve and wanted to encompass all the different purposes. As a designer of curriculum, however, it has become clear to me how important it is to determine or at least prioritise a primary purpose. This is also important when considering how to build an assessment system – we know that we tend to value what we measure, so it is important to consider what you can and should assess.

Determining purpose has also influenced the choices I've made, both consciously and sub-consciously, about which research I've read and the school curriculums that have helped inspire my own design. Therefore it's important that I am clear now about the purpose that has motivated me as a curriculum and assessment designer.

Over the years I have found myself firmly moving towards the belief that teaching has to be grounded in academic knowledge – to be taught for its own intrinsic value. This has been a challenge to my natural bias, which was leaning towards a more progressive social justice style of curriculum. I haven't changed my aspirations for the pupils I teach, in fact I think they have been elevated, but like Robinson, I now believe that an engagement with knowledge of the past is the path to freedom; if we are to challenge the status quo we can't do this without a base of knowledge otherwise we become the mob of Shakespeare's *Julius Caesar* simply swayed by the rhetoric. We should place the importance on people who have done the thinking so that these become our academic authorities.

Furedi's argument that we no longer look to teachers as intellectual authorities also rings true to me and seems particularly dangerous. This is especially relevant for those teachers aiming to design curriculum and assessment because it comes back to the idea of a loss of expertise; how can teachers feel confident in designing a curriculum when they are no longer seen as having expertise in the knowledge of their subjects? Instead the child-centred approach places more authority with the child – awarding the knowledge they bring to the classroom the same distinction as that brought by the teacher.

This goes beyond schools. We seem, as a society, to have a problem with the idea of teachers or schools as academic. Yet some of my best examples of interacting with pupils have come through engaging with them academically.

Case study 1

It makes me think of one of my pupils a few years ago; a troubled young boy in my Year 8 class. He was renowned throughout the school for being disruptive, for fighting and general trouble making. As with many troubled and troubling children, he was full of emotion and in need of an outlet. We were studying poetry one term and he responded well to the poems, and enjoyed having a go at writing. So after class one day I gave him a notebook and told him that he could try writing his feelings down. Soon he was approaching me with reams of poetry that he'd written; it was raw but beautiful. My conversations with him started to take a more positive turn. I didn't have the same life experiences as him – I wouldn't patronise him by claiming to identify with that – but we could share a common language which was literature, in this case poetry. He didn't last at the school sadly – too many troubles for poetry to fix overnight – but I have hope that wherever he is and in whatever moment there will be a poet there.

Case study 2

More recently, I taught a pupil who has Asperger's Syndrome and experienced significant personal tragedy; we studied war poetry and this was initially difficult to negotiate as he struggled with the idea of discussing death. Yet by the end of term we had carved a path through this together and he had both written a sonnet to express 'the Pandora's box of feelings [inside his mind]' and had also spoken movingly to the whole class about what it meant to experience this kind of personal loss. For him the subject allowed him to express his emotions and build a sense of himself in relation to his classmates.

Case study reflections

- Which purpose was the curriculum motivated by here?
- Which purpose(s) was I perhaps motivated by?
- Which purpose (s) could be assessed here?
- Which purpose(s) was/were achieved?

So perhaps another angle to take, is to ask if we should prioritise the purpose of education for its own sake – to meet what Barack Obama says is the goal of most parents: 'to make sure your children are a little bit smarter than you are' ('Running Wild with Bear Grylls', 2015) – and hope that this will in its own way address the other purposes but accept that schools cannot take responsibility for all of these within their curriculum.

This makes more sense when thinking about what form of curriculum you are designing: intended, implemented or enacted (see p 5). I finally understood this when I read Dylan Wiliam's criticism of the 'over-simplification' of trying to find one aim or purpose and assertion that the curriculum should be 'child-centred', 'subject-centred' and 'society-centred'. He expands on this by saying that curriculum 'should regard emotional development and intellectual development not as alternatives but as strands in a rope, which mutually strengthen each other.' (*Principled Curriculum Design*, Wiliam, 2013). It's a reasonable argument which makes sense to me if I think about it in relation to the idea of the enacted curriculum. It's here that I see the natural way in which dialogue between teacher and pupil opens up the possibility for questioning of knowledge, for addressing the mono-cultural nature of much of history and literature, to engage with some of the big moral and ethical problems. It is through these relationships between the teacher and the class and between pupils that both emotional and intellectual development are fostered. What is important therefore is to distinguish between the aims, purpose and outcomes of an intended/implemented curriculum and the natural results of an enacted curriculum. Within the enacted curriculum the ideas around social justice, character and citizenship are natural products of a class' engagement with a strong knowledge base. As such, there is a strong case to be made for the intended and implemented curriculum to be designed solely around intrinsic academic value and to have an accompanying assessment system which can truly measure this.

Further reading

Gibb, N (2015), 'The purpose of education' (www.gov.uk/government/speeches/the-purpose-of-education)

'Dangerous conjectures' (horatiospeaks.wordpress.com/2016/01/01/dangerous-conjectures)

Fordham, M. (2015) 'What are schools not responsible for?' (clioetcetera.com)

Chapter 4 takeaway

Teaching tip

Find your purpose

Explore the different approaches to understanding a curriculum's purpose and consider what your natural bias is and whether you have changed your mind about purpose at any point. Once you know what you think, discuss with others on your team to see if your views align.

Pass it on

Have a look at the Education Select Committee inquiry and express your views on their findings by tweeting #edselect
Sign up to events and debates where these type of issues are discussed, this will allow you to hear a range of views and to share your own.

Share and tweet

Share your thoughts on curriculum purpose by tweeting some of the bloggers/writers in this chapter or by including #edselect or #BloomsCPD

CPD book club recommendation

Frank Furedi, *Wasted: Why Education isn't Educating*
(see Bibliography and further reading)

Bloggers' corner

Michael Fordham has a good collection of blogs which reflect on a school and a curriculum's purpose, as well as the impact for assessment. His blog is: clioetcetera.com/

To do list:

☐ Determine the ultimate purpose – the aspect that you are completely responsible for and would be a dereliction of your duty not to fulfil.

☐ Discuss your ideas around purpose with your leadership team – are you all on the same page?

☐ Now consider what must stay or go in the curriculum to achieve this purpose.

☐ Tweet out your ideas and questions about purpose by using the hashtag #BloomsCPD

☐ Check out blogs by Michael Fordham (@mfordhamhistory) on a school and curriculum's purpose, as well as the impact for assessment: clioetcetera.com.

☐ Read *Wasted: Why Education isn't Educating* by Frank Furedi.

5 Getting to grips with the key researchers

So now you're ready to get your teeth into thinking about curriculum design and assessment. There must be some research out there that can tell you what the best thing to do is, right? Well yes and no. Anyone looking for a magic bullet in research will find themselves sorely disappointed; the complexity of education including the different contexts in which we teach means there are few simple answers. However, research can be a really helpful tool in that it can direct our ideas, provoke thought about what has worked in other places and also help show what doesn't work. Recent work of bloggers and grassroots movements such as ResearchEd has provided room not only for research but also for critical voices.

In this chapter, I will explore some of the research on curriculum design and assessment that I found useful in my work on this topic. This is by no means an exhaustive list and I've simply dipped into the ideas they present. You should be able to glean a sense of this and determine where you want to explore further reading. I have a set of values which influenced my reading:

- belief in a knowledge-driven curriculum, based around academic subjects
- belief in the power of assessment, including testing, which is driven by the curriculum.

But I want to give you a chance to think through the different options you face when designing curriculum, which means I've tried to include some writers who I might not necessarily agree with, but who are important in terms of their approaches to curriculum and assessment because of what they offer/challenge us to think about. As one of my pupils said to me recently: 'I have never learnt anything from someone I agree with.' (Oh the wisdom of youth!) There's a mixture of old and new; researchers, philosophers, psychologists and academics. From each, I have drawn out some of the themes that have been key to my understanding of curriculum design, namely:

- content
- sequencing
- expectation
- assessment.

It's a chance to learn from the thinking that has come before and even that which is brewing as we speak; creating some sense of a framework for you to use within your own schools.

E. D. Hirsch on core knowledge curriculum

Name: E. D. Hirsch

Twitter handle: @ckschools

Website: www.coreknowledge.org

What to read: *Cultural Literacy: What Every American Needs to Know*; *The Schools We Need and Why We Don't Have Them*; *The Knowledge Deficit* all by E. D. Hirsch

---

Why Hirsch?

In Andrew Pollard's criticism of the draft programmes of study in his blog, 'Proposed primary curriculum: what about the pupils?' (2012), he described how the primary curriculum had been directly influenced by one man: 'The voice that has really counted from beginning to the end has been that of an American educator, E. D. Hirsch.' As the designer of the 'core knowledge curriculum' in America, Hirsch has had a big influence on the curriculum in a number of charter schools there, and has now influenced the development of primary curriculum in the UK as well as secondary curriculum in schools such as Pimlico Academy, the Ark Academy chain and many of the new free schools.

Key ideas

Hirsch's ideas centre around the notion that all pupils are entitled to knowledge and that curriculum should be based around an idea of 'minimal content' that pupils should be required to know. For Hirsch this needs to be a curriculum which runs across schools and that has specific prescribed content rather than an 'over-reliance on large-scale abstract objectives'. This means named knowledge content such as literary texts in English, assigned to particular year groups. Across schools, pupils would study exactly the same content at exactly the same time (allowing for easier transfers between schools).

Core knowledge curriculum

Hirsch is the creator of the core knowledge curriculum, which is a list of facts, terms and knowledge points that acts as a minimum entitlement for all pupils and is therefore expected to be learnt by heart by pupils. He critiques the idea of critical thinking or analysis as being 'higher order' than learning facts, as in order to be able to think critically you need a deep background of knowledge. This is not to say he dismisses any teaching of procedural knowledge [skills] but that he believes this should come from the knowledge rather than being taught as a generic set of skills that could be applied across subjects. Hirsch is particularly persuasive when talking about this idea of domain knowledge when it comes to reading. He argues that reading is not a skill but is something (once pupils have been taught the basics of decoding words) that is based around your knowledge of the domain, such as the vocabulary. He uses as an example the idea of a broadsheet newspaper and how much knowledge is needed to be able to access this: 'General wide-ranging education is the only way to become a reader' (2016). Equally, when looking at an article on basketball, a group of novice readers performed better than more expert readers because they were lovers of basketball and therefore could understand the specific basketball terminology and access the article.

Purpose

He explores the 'egalitarian nature of knowledge' in his arguments in which he clearly sees a social justice purpose of education levelling the playing field. Hirsch also argues against some of the contemporary thinking about the idea of individualised education in which children can use critical thinking to explore knowledge that they find for themselves (such as through looking up information on the internet). 'You cannot become an instant expert. [Google] rewards those who already have knowledge.' Schools therefore have a moral responsibility to teach a knowledge-driven curriculum because we 'can't rely on an invisible hand' to help those who have less access to this knowledge because of their social background.

Pedagogy and curriculum

Much of this can be achieved by the focus on how to memorise this content: 'the best approach to achieving retention in long-term memory is "distributed practice".' This has implications for both curriculum and assessment design: curriculum has to be designed around spaced out practice with opportunities for topic reviews every 30 days, including use of assessment tools such as quizzing, Q&A and drill practice to memorise this knowledge. Assessment that is not based on the precise curriculum being taught to pupils (such as a reading age test), Hirsch describes as an unfair assessment of both the school and pupil.

Criticisms

Criticisms of this approach question whether the prescribed knowledge is the best knowledge to be teaching – and whether the knowledge that matters change with the times. Equally, Hirsch is accused of atomising knowledge - taking it away from subjects and making knowledge more of a checklist of facts, which could limit academic challenge.Other criticisms include whether this type of curriculum preserves a certain order and pushes out other voices. Some critics have gone further and argued that it preserves the status quo and enforces a mono-cultural approach to education, such as the articles listed below on the next page by teacher Tait Coles and by Jane Manzione. By enforcing a unified curriculum including prescribed content at each key stage, are we taking away the authority and autonomy of teachers? What about individual teachers having passion for certain aspects of their subject which might not be found in a core curriculum?

Key questions

Content

- What is the essential knowledge that you think your pupils should have?
- Should this knowledge be prescribed nationally?
- Is prescribed factual knowledge the same as the knowledge of an academic discipline?

Sequencing

- Do you think you should sequence the curriculum on a year by year basis?
- Do you believe in the importance of making connections across subjects and if so, how should this be organised?
- How should you use knowledge about memory to sequence your curriculum?
- How can you use quizzing and other assessment to support memorising of knowledge?

Further reading

Coles, T. (2014), 'Critical pedagogy: schools must equip students to challenge the status quo' (www.theguardian.com)

Manzione, J. (2015), 'Whose knowledge is it anyway?' (schoolsweek.co.uk)

Facer, J. (2015): 'Just one book: curriculum' (readingallthebooks.com)

McInerny, L. (2012), 'Things to know about E.D. Hirsch and the "common cultural literacy" idea (lkmco.org)

Kirby, J. (2013), 'What can we learn from Core Knowledge and E.D. Hirsch?' (pragmaticreform.wordpress.com)

Michael Young on powerful knowledge

Name: Michael Young

What to read: *Knowledge and Control*, Young, M.; *Bringing Knowledge Back In: From Social Constructivism to Social Realism in the Sociology of Education*, Young, M.; *Knowledge and the Future School: Curriculum and Social Justice*, Young, M., Lambert, D., Roberts, C. and Roberts, M.

What to watch: 'The attack on knowledge: Interview with Michael Young' (www.cambridgeassessment.org.uk)

Why Young?

Michael Young, Emeritus Professor of Education at the Institute of Education, is an important figure in curriculum and assessment design because of his research and writing on the use of knowledge within the curriculum. Originally Young argued against the knowledge focus of schools, instead looking towards Freire's ideas about authentic dialogue in education (see p 76), but he has since become a critic of this approach. Young now argues 'that freedom from the existing curriculum without access to knowledge leads nowhere.' (Young, 2014) Firmly positioned on the left of the political spectrum, he presents a slightly different approach to the teaching of a knowledge-led curriculum.

Key ideas

Like Hirsch, Young agrees that knowledge is an entitlement for all pupils, identifying the purpose of schools as: 'to enable all students to acquire knowledge that takes them beyond their experience' because 'access to this knowledge is the "right" of all pupils as future citizens.' (*Knowledge and the Future School: Curriculum and Social Justice*)

In his book, *Knowledge and the Future School: Curriculum and Social Justice* written with David Lambert, Carolyn Roberts and Martin Roberts Lambert, the authors assert that the idea of curriculum itself as central to schools has lost its impact, and has led to an over-emphasis on attainment of pupils for the sake of the grade rather than because of the powerful intrinsic value of education: 'Occasionally you wonder what children are meant to make of our obsession with achievement and assessment rather than the *stuff* they are learning.' (*Knowledge and the Future School: Curriculum and Social Justice* Young M., Lambert D.)

Young argues that there is a fear surrounding knowledge, which we need to overcome, and that the very concept of a curriculum means there is a body of knowledge beyond what we can learn in the everyday. He also highlights a particular problem with a fear of the 'struggle' that comes from teaching knowledge and for pupils attempting to learn knowledge. It is this struggle both to access the knowledge but also cope with the potential challenges to one's own views and sense of self that he sees as a vital part of a curriculum: 'real knowledge challenges not only what we know but sometimes our sense of who we are' (*Knowledge and the Future School: Curriculum and Social Justice*). He argues that there is a danger that the fear of this 'struggle' leads us to labelling pupils as 'non-academics' rather than dealing with the fact that whilst it might be more difficult for some, there is a huge problem of dumbing down the curriculum and lowering expectations rather than attempting to find ways for every pupil to rise up to the challenge; a potential problem of the social justice movement.

Powerful knowledge

The big difference here, from Hirsch, is the emphasis on 'powerful knowledge' which is the knowledge that enables this idea of pupils moving beyond their experience. This highlights the importance of subject expertise: having confidence in the idea of what is the 'best' type of knowledge. Young criticises the idea that this is a dry, purely didactic approach to education but rather that the 'transformative aspect happens after the powerful knowledge is taught.' (Young, M., Lambert, D., *Knowledge and the Future School: Curriculum and Social Justice*)

Knowledge is also subject-specific and Young states the importance of these boundaries between subject areas of knowledge to give identity to pupil, teacher and subject. Christine Counsell, Cambridge University, has also written a number of papers about the importance of subject disciplines with a focus on history. See her blog post on this: thedignityofthethingblog.wordpress.com/2016/01/11/genericisms-children/.

For Young, the key considerations are: selecting the 'powerful knowledge' and sequencing knowledge to promote progression and pacing. He believes this should all be prescribed in a National Curriculum, which all schools should subscribe to – including independent schools. Where Young differs from Hirsch and Gove is in the idea of knowledge as 'fallible and open to question'. For Young, a knowledge-led curriculum cannot simply be about learning a selection of facts, because whilst facts are a part of knowledge so is the ability to question this knowledge 'and the authority it is based on'. He directly challenges the Govian version of a knowledge-driven curriculum, which seems to be based on the idea that because it was taught in the 19th century it therefore has value. Instead the curriculum should teach children to 'think the unthinkable and think the not yet thought'. Indeed, to achieve this, Young thinks that curriculum needs to be taken out of the hands of politicians and be given back to the experts in the subject field; to re-assert the professionalism of teachers. Hoorah!

Criticisms

One of the criticisms is that Young's ideas centre around the belief that the pursuit of knowledge is the main aim of a school. This takes us back to the discussion on a school's aims and purpose (see Chapter 4).

Another criticism comes about when looking at Hirsch's viewpoint; he prescribes a list of unquestioned knowledge as resting within subject disciplines, with the potential for subject experts to challenge and refine this knowledge. This then also leans into pedagogy: can a knowledge-led curriculum be unlinked from a mastery approach, or from factual recall and pedagogy based around memory?

Key questions

Content

- Does knowledge need to be more than learning facts?
- What is the powerful knowledge of your subject?
- Should a school's curriculum be designed to make pupils question knowledge?
- Is it important to have clear subject boundaries?

Sequencing

- What are the key concepts that a subject is based upon and how do you build and sequence units of work to grasp these concepts?

Assessment

- Are all forms of assessment effective?
- Are all qualifications of equal standing?

Further reading

White, J. (2012), 'Powerful knowledge: too weak a prop for the traditional curriculum? (www.newvisionsforeducation.org.uk)

Kirby, J. (2013), 'Why we shouldn't close down the skills–knowledge debate' (pragmaticreform.wordpress.com)

Stock, P. (2015), 'Miltonic Vision Part 1: Trivium 21C, Threshold concepts and the power of "powerful knowledge"' (joeybagstock.wordpress.com)

Playfair, E. (2015), 'What is powerful knowledge?' (eddieplayfair.com)

Paulo Freire on questioning the traditional curriculum

Name: Paulo Freire

What to read: Freire, P. *Pedagogy of the Oppressed*

Why Freire?

You can't get far into a discussion about curriculum without Freire's name springing to the surface. Often a point of conflict within discussions about curriculum, Freire's essay *Pedagogy of the Oppressed* has had an indisputable impact on thinking around curriculum.

Key ideas

In direct opposition to the ideas of E. D. Hirsch, Freire argues in *Pedagogy of the Oppressed* that there are two approaches: the banking form of teaching and the problem solving form. He rails against the idea of depositing facts into pupils' minds; he calls this the 'banking model' of teaching, arguing that it assumes that pupils know nothing when they enter the school and that the teachers own the knowledge. Freire sees this as creating passive learners who will not be able to question what is being taught because of an unequal relationship with the teacher – who is the font of knowledge. He argues that we should be constructing our curriculum around 'problem posing education' which encourages critical thinking about the world within which we live. Therefore instead of pupils memorising knowledge, they should be encouraged to enter into a dialogue with their teacher and thus become critical thinkers. His argument centres around the idea that any more traditional form of education is a form of oppression, which allows a minority to enforce their world view onto the children that they teach. It is the teacher filling pupils with their own narrative by using techniques such as memorisation, which makes students mechanical and unthinking.

Freire argues this is a deliberate attempt to oppress because the more time spent sorting through the knowledge pupils have learnt, 'the less they develop the critical consciousness'. He argues that the teaching of knowledge in this way and the subsequent curriculum is designed to deliberately stop people thinking, or questioning the status quo and that as memory is not thinking: 'in the name of the "preservation of culture and knowledge" we have a system which achieves neither true knowledge nor true culture.' (Freire, *Pedagogy of the Oppressed*).

Criticisms

One of the criticisms of Freire's argument is that it is a political argument – not one based on any quantitative proof – that is misused by those in education to criticise explicit instruction. Greg Ashman comments in his blog 'Why educational theory is flawed': 'When you look at the case that Freire builds, it is clear that it is political; it is what Freire reckons about education based upon his revolutionary political beliefs and his experiences of teaching illiterate adults.'

There is also an argument that in order to be able to argue critically, you need to be able to base this on knowledge. Young would challenge Freire's ideas at this level: you cannot achieve freedom from oppression without first having the knowledge;

to know something you must be taught the facts and how to critically evaluate these. This is a position also supported by cognitive scientists such as Willingham, who sees knowledge as the building block for skills such as creative thinking (see p 79).

Key questions

Content

- Should you include any form of critical thinking in your curriculum design?
- Will the curriculum be based around the idea of learning facts or will it be based around tackling problems?
- To what extent should you consider diversity and representation within the curriculum?
- Should pupils have a choice in what they study?

Assessment

- How will your assessment allow for dialogue and critical thinking?
- What are the emotional impacts of testing?

Further reading

Ashman, G. (2015), 'Why educational theory is flawed' (gregashman.wordpress.com)
Smith, M. (1997, 2002), 'Paulo Freire: dialogue, praxis and education' (infed.org)
Coles, T. (2014), 'No input, no output' (taitcoles.wordpress.com)

D. Willingham on memory

Name: D. Willingham

Twitter handle: @DTWillingham

Website: danielwillingham.com

What to read: *Why Don't Students Like School?: A Cognitive Scientist Answers Questions About How the Mind Works and What it Means for the Classroom*, Willingham, D.

'Allocating Student Study Time: "Massed" versus "Distributed" Practice' www.aft.org/periodical/american-educator/summer-2002/ask-cognitive-scientist

---

Why Willingham?

One of the most interesting developments when it comes to curriculum design has been an increasing interest in the use of cognitive science and the link between memory and thought. Willingham has been one of the most influential writers on this subject and the implications for curriculum and assessment design.

Key ideas

We have a limited working memory, but an expansive long-term memory. If we can therefore learn techniques to transfer what we're trying to learn from working to our long-term memory, we allow for an opportunity to know more and to also make much of our thinking processes automatic rather than needing the work that comes with retrieval. This will allow pupils to move onto thinking about more complicated concepts and also ensure that they remember what they have learnt, beyond the test. His work has been influential (alike to Carol Dweck's *Mindset* (see p 95) in its consideration of how the correct level of challenge can actually be motivating. Willingham says it is wrong to argue that knowledge is boring or that curriculum should be designed to be engaging or entertaining and that this has led to a focus on activity over content. In contrast to Freire, he asserts in his book, *Why Don't Students Like School?*, that 'memory is the residue of thought'; it is about providing work that will make pupils think. Willingham identifies how the difficult process that is thinking, can be eased by making some of the process more automatic.

Teachers should aim not to reduce or dumb down content but to structure their teaching so that pupils are given sufficient challenge and taught the appropriate background knowledge before engaging. Much of this has more ramifications for the implemented curriculum than it does at the level of intended curriculum; focusing on the structuring of lessons such as the development of appropriate questions and the use of memory aids within the classroom to lessen the strain on working memory.

Willingham's arguments also highlight the importance of sequencing teaching of knowledge; he argues that pupils need to be taught specific knowledge and to revisit this through spaced practice before they can be creators of knowledge. He argues against the idea of aiming to teach primarily through creative tasks because pupils need to aim for 'knowledge comprehension' before they can become experts; it is not through acting like experts that they will become expert, but by building the expert knowledge. Willingham cites evidence on the cognitive science of learning and thinking, which suggests that pupils are simply not cognitively ready for this stage of thinking about knowledge. The implications for the curriculum here are a clearly sequenced curriculum in which interleaving and spaced practice are features of the design and which includes a number of retrieval techniques through assessment such as quizzes.

Curriculum content

On the subject of curriculum content, Willingham subscribes therefore to an idea that curriculum content should be based on knowledge that 'yields the greatest cognitive benefit'. His findings support the idea that creativity and critical thinking or any other form of thinking skills must stem from a body of knowledge: 'trying to teach students skills such as analysis or synthesis in the absence of factual knowledge is impossible ... Factual knowledge must precede skill.' (*Why Don't Students Like School?*, Willingham). However this does not mean he is an advocate of simply teaching lists of facts. He states the importance of links between memory and thought; we remember things that make us think. Like Hirsch (who is a fan of his book), he is also an advocate of teaching background knowledge (what Hirsch refers to as 'domain knowledge') in order to teach reading. His argument also covers some of the criticism about knowledge teaching encouraging the propagation of the dead, white, male cultural history; he argues that it is this culture which continues to inform much writing whether in history, science, politics or literature and therefore pupils will need to be taught this background knowledge themselves so they can engage with this writing.

Criticism

Cognitive science is a very new field of science as Willingham himself confronts in the introduction to *Why Don't Students Like School?* when he questions why cognitive science hasn't had more of a hold in teaching (we've learnt most of what we know within the last 25 years). There is therefore still plenty of uncertainty about its findings, even amongst scientists themselves: 'While it is possible for neuroscientists to make progress in the physical brain, the great question is still the causal, water-into-wine relationship of the physical brain and body with subjective mental events' (Susan Greenfield, 2011).

Equally the very different conditions between the lab and the classroom, often captured in the debate about whether teaching is an art or a science, mean teachers and leaders can be reluctant to take some of the scientific findings to heart. This is something Willingham engages with himself, arguing that the values based nature of education makes it difficult to be treated scientifically but that 'once you've defined the goals, science might be able to help you achieve the goals.' (Interview with D Willingham, *Trivium 21c: preparing young people for the future with lessons from the past*, Martin Robinson).

Key questions

Content

- Should our choice of knowledge content be informed by thinking about cognitive needs?

Sequencing

- Should we design curriculum and assessment around spaced practice?
- How can we sequence the curriculum to ensure pupils remember it?

Expectation

- How can we ensure the curriculum provides appropriate challenge without overwhelming pupils?

Assessment

- Should we use more quizzing, including multiple choice questions in order to help pupils remember curriculum content?

Further reading

Kidd, D. (2013), 'Myths about education: an alternative view' (debrakidd. wordpress.com)

Kirby, J. (2013), 'What can science tell us about how pupils learn best?' (www.researched2013.co.uk/310)

Robinson, M. (2015), 'Memory' (martinrobborobinson.wordpress.com/2015/05/05/ memory)

Dylan Wiliam on formative assessment and sequencing the curriculum

Name: Dylan Wiliam

Twitter handle: @dylanwiliam

Website: dylanwiliam.org

What to read: Black, P & Wiliam, D., *Inside the Black Box* Wiliam, D. 'Planning assessment without levels – article by Dylan Wiliam' (thehub.walthamforest. gov.uk); Wiliam, D. (2013), *Redesigning Schooling – 3: Principled curriculum design* (www.ssatuk.co.uk); Wiliam, D. (2014), *Redesigning Schooling – 8: Principled assessment design*

Why Wiliam?

Wiliam has been a strong voice on curriculum and assessment for a number of years since his publication of *Inside the Black Box* written with Paul Black and Bethan Marshall in 1998, which focused on the importance of formative assessment, also known as assessment for learning (AfL). More recently Wiliam was part of the expert panel that advised Gove in advance of the new curriculum (although it is noteworthy that he did not continue to work on the programmes of study), and produced two significant pamphlets for the schools, students and teachers network (SSAT) on how to design curriculum and assessment.

Key ideas

Inside the Black Box had a 'school-led vision' and called for a way to provide strategies within classrooms to improve standards, rather than teachers simply being given policy and being told to embed this. The focus was especially on formative assessment, which they concluded was an important way to adapt teaching and learning to match the needs of pupils and therefore drive forward their understanding. Wiliam's argument was that the pressure on teachers to cover a statutory curriculum takes time away from developing formative assessment and therefore the curriculum should be reduced. (Incidentally, this was something which we saw in the curriculum revisions of 1999 and 2007.)

Much of the criticism of high-stakes testing such as GCSEs and how it dominates teaching and assessment originates from this work. For Wiliam and Black this high stakes testing, including ranking pupils, encourages pupils to 'look for the ways to obtain the best marks rather than at the needs of their learning.' Consequently this encourages pupils to avoid hard tasks and be fixated on looking for a 'right answer'. (1998)

Content and sequencing

In his work for the SSAT on curriculum, Wiliam advocated for a curriculum design which involves teachers and is designed backwards from the end point. Whilst he is clear to state that he offers guidance rather than answers, he provides some strong arguments from Lawrence Stenhouse (notable for his work on his curriculum design) and others on the importance of subject teaching, alongside creativity and critical thinking.

Wiliam also looks at the ideas around sequencing a curriculum, exploring the different approaches that schools take, from using chronology (although he discredits this) through to the concept of the 'big ideas' of a subject. This is based on an understanding of the 'logic of the subject'. He argues that curriculum will work differently for different schools and must be often renewed and reviewed.

This concept of the 'big ideas' of a subject also drives Wiliam's ideas for assessment systems, as he suggests that these should be the focus for assessment – warning readers that these must be located in the understanding of the subject, not equated with GCSE specifications. Whilst working as part of the expert panel advising on curriculum and assessment reform, he and others on the panel reached the conclusion that 'all assessment should be assessment for learning' (*Redesigning Schooling – 8: Principled assessment)*. As such, assessment should be used to make inferences about children's grasp of the curriculum. He describes this engagement with curriculum as a 'learning progression' or 'pathway', with assessment as a checkpoint along the way. These checkpoints can be based around threshold concepts, (read more about these in the next chapter), which might include what David Perkins, Senior Professor of Education at Harvard University, calls 'troublesome knowledge': the parts of the subject content which pupils might struggle with the most. Assessment may be sequenced to fit with this curriculum and also at staging points in a child's schooling, such as at the end of a key stage.

Test design

Wiliam also has useful points to make about how we draw conclusions from the tests we set, which has huge implications for test design and analysis of results at department and whole-school level. You have to consider 'the extent to which a test measures what it claims or purports to measure.' (2014*)*. This is also important when you think about the types of assessment you want to use as sometimes the inferences you might make from one test won't tell you much about what pupils have actually learnt. A multiple choice quiz for instance might allow you to infer what factual knowledge a pupil has learnt, whilst an essay might mean you can infer more about their ability to articulate themselves in writing. This is particularly important when it comes to thinking about how the type of assessment might affect the validity of the inferences made; a wordy maths problem might tell you more about pupils' reading abilities than about their knowledge of maths.

On the subject of test design, Wiliam looks at the different ways a test can be marked – either by 'degrees of difficulty' or 'marks for style' or the 'support model' (2014) in which pupils can only get a top grade A, all other work is returned ungraded with feedback on how to improve until they all reach grade A. Wiliam also sings the praises of well-designed multiple choice questions and challenges the idea that they cannot show higher order thinking; he gives examples of questions which do just that. He suggests that the problem may not be to do with the type of test but the understanding of the 'construct of the subject' – a historian who sees history as being made up of facts and chronology would see a multiple choice question as a suitable way to test this knowledge whilst a historian who sees history as about analysing concepts and sources would prefer the inferences that can be made from an essay question.

Whole-school assessment

In terms of Whole-school assessment, Wiliam is keen to assert the importance of record-keeping/marking/progress measures being linked up with supporting learning. He advocates for systems which have a specificity that allows pupils and parents to know how to move learning forwards and that enables teachers to adjust teaching and learning accordingly. This also has useful implications for target setting – here Wiliam points out the uselessness of predicted grades, which stifle progress rather than encouraging it because they are often unreliable and encourage low expectations. Schools must always be thinking about how inferences made from assessment and the reporting of these improve learning.

Assessment maps

Finally, he reminds us as leaders of schools that assessment is an important tool to ensure pupils are indeed on track, not in terms of progress measures, but in relation to the knowledge of the subjects they study and to inform us as to whether pupils are actually learning, which is our ultimate responsibility. It is wrong to blame testing, but rather we should look at the quality of tests and the use of reported detail and data. Wiliam suggests creating assessment maps (not dissimilar to the assessment flow chart in Chapter 1) which can demonstrate how assessment is used to fulfil the wide ranging criteria of a school. Assessment, after all, shows what a school values.

Criticisms

Many people, including Wiliam himself, have been critical of the way in which AfL has been oversimplified and turned into a gimmick in classrooms – more about the look of assessment than genuine assessment.

Wiliam doesn't take a complete stance on many aspects of curriculum and assessment, preferring instead to give guidance and principles for people to choose from. For those with a more strident view about education, this may seem too much of a compromise.

Wiliam's argument for the potential reduction of curriculum content in favour of creativity and thinking skills is also a challenge for those who see content, in terms of knowledge, being central to a strong curriculum.

Key questions

Content

- Should curriculum content be different, based on the different needs and aims of schools?
- Is a subject-based curriculum important?
- Should creativity and critical thinking be important components of a curriculum?

Sequencing

- How is curriculum best sequenced in order for pupils to grasp the construct of the subject?
- Could you structure your curriculum around the 'big ideas' of a subject and considering the troublesome knowledge?

Expectation

- How can you ensure your use of target setting does not limit pupils, or worse create a culture of low expectations?

Assessment

- How do you ensure that all assessment is AfL?
- Can you make valid inferences from your assessment?
- How do you ensure that your assessment gives specific and precise feedback about how pupils can progress in their learning?
- Is it a school leadership's responsibility to have an assessment system which checks and monitors pupils' knowledge of the curriculum?

Further reading

'The Secret of Effective Feedback' Dylan Wiliam: www.ascd.org/publications/ educational-leadership/apr16/vol73/num07/The-Secret-of-Effective-Feedback.aspx

'What can we learn from Dylan Wiliam and AfL?': pragmaticreform.wordpress. com/2013/03/30/afl/

'Dylan Wiliam's defence of formative assessment': www.learningspy.co.uk/ assessment/dylan-wiliams-defence-formative-assessment/

'Principled curriculum design: the English curriculum': www.learningspy.co.uk/ english-gcse/principled-curriculum-design-teach-english/

'Dylan Wiliam on assessment': http://thinkedu.net/blog/dylanwiliam/

Daisy Christodoulu on assessment after levels

Name: Daisy Christodoulu

Twitter handle: @daisychristo

Website: thewingtoheaven.wordpress.com

What to read: Christodoulu, D. (2015), 'Guide to my posts about assessment' (thewingtoheaven.wordpress.com); Christodoulu, D. (2013), 'Research on multiple choice questions' (thewingtoheaven.wordpress.com)

Why Christodoulu?

Daisy Christodoulu became a particularly influential and controversial figure after the publication of her book, *Seven Myths of Education* which took a critical approach to the 'progressive' practices of the current UK education system. Her later work on assessment, as part of the commission on assessment without levels, has become integral to all discussions about designing assessment.

Key ideas

Much of Christodoulu's work on curriculum is influenced by researchers such as E. D. Hirsch and Willingham, but with a UK focus. It's no secret that Christodoulu is an advocate of the traditional knowledge-driven approach to curriculum including use of assessment to support this curriculum and pedagogy that is focused on direct instruction and memory. She argues that this goes against the general trend of UK education, which has become overly focused on teaching skills and cross-curricular work and therefore has been 'dumbed down'.

However it is Christodoulu's work on assessment, most of which she has revealed through a series of blogposts, which is particularly useful to readers of this book. When it comes to whole-school assessment systems after levels, Christodoulu notes that many schools still fall into the traps of criterion based assessment including the 'adverb problem' where a range of adverbs are used to assess how pupils are achieving: think about the comparisons between 'confident' writing and 'sophisticated' writing – these essentially fall down on teacher judgement, which is not impartial. Teachers may also set different tasks or have a different understanding of what these criteria mean. Equally, assessment systems which define pupils as 'reaching' or 'exceeding' targets may fall into the same trap as levels, in which there is an appearance of a common dialogue but it is actually vague and 'can't be relied on to deliver accuracy or precision about how pupils are doing'. ('Problems with Performance Descriptors', D Christodoulu thewingtoheaven.wordpress.com/2015/05/22/problems-with-performance-descriptors/).

Instead she advocates for a norm based assessment system, in which pupils are marked against a model of what is expected from them at their age and against other pupils in their cohort. This involves looking at a range across groups and comparing/moderating papers. For essays, there is an online project called 'No More Marking' which allows teachers to upload pupil work and to make comparisons between them. Essays are put up one against each other and the teacher simply decides which one is better, this then loads up another essay and eventually you get a ranked selection of essays. Of course you still need to add feedback to help pupils improve, but by ranking them against each other you get a clearer and fairer idea of where their work stands in relation to each other. You can read more about this by following @nmmarking and through David Didau's blog posts: http://www.learningspy.co.uk/tag/comparative-judgement/.

She also suggests using questions as a way to assess – by creating question banks with statistics coming from the percentage of questions that a pupil is able to answer. She draws on Wiliam's work, in his SSAT pamphlet on assessment, about how questions can be designed so that they are 'tightly defined'. Christodoulu is an advocate of using multiple choice questions; she explains how these can be used to help us ensure pupils remember what they learn by using them frequently as a low stakes assessment tool in lessons. They allow us to quickly determine what pupils know and where the misconceptions lie. By using online systems, you can even create self-marking quizzes which then generate spreadsheets of data about a class, showing common patterns which allow the teacher to adjust their teaching and learning.

Christodoulu also tackles the idea of progress measures and the fact that (based on Goodhart's Law about government regulation of financial assets) as soon as 'a measure becomes a target it loses all value as a measure.' ('Assessment: High Stakes, low improvement', *Changing Schools*, ed. R Peal). She notes that this is what has happened with some of the GCSE measures such as five A*–C including English and maths; as soon as a school is aware of this, they often attempt to game the system, e.g. with the use of intervention work at the C/D border line, or the flipping between different exam boards, which then makes the measure meaningless.

This also links back to curriculum, because curriculum is currently driven by assessment, which means that it becomes content free and focused on teaching to the test rather than using assessment to move pupils forward and ensure that we place the value on the curriculum that we are teaching.

Criticisms

Some criticisms include the concern that effective multiple choice questions are difficult to construct and that short answer questions and essay questions allow for the expression of more complex knowledge. And also that much of this work is based on the relatively new and therefore not entirely reliable field of cognitive science, with Christodoulu's use of examples being not far reaching enough to be declared valid evidence.

Being a firm follower of E. D. Hirsch's and D. T. Willingham's work has meant Christodoulu has also come under the same criticisms about the focus on knowledge and treating education as a science. Debra Kidd has written a detailed blog post about this in response to Christodoulu's book *Seven Myths About Education*.

Key questions

Content

- Is a knowledge, fact-based approach to curriculum the best means to ensuring a good education for all pupils?
- Does a knowledge-rich curriculum require including direct instruction, rote learning and prescribed knowledge?

Sequencing

- Should cognitive science evidence on memory influence the sequencing of your curriculum?
- Could you use sequencing strategies such as interleaving and spaced practice to help pupils remember what they have learnt?

Assessment

- Can criteria based assessment be replaced effectively by closely defined questions including multiple choice?
- Is norm-referencing the best way to check standards and progress?
- Should your assessment system include frequent low stakes testing driven by the curriculum?

Further reading

Quigley, A. (2014), 'Multiple choice questions: a) use regularly b) don't use' (huntingenglish.com)
Kidd, D. (2013), '7 myths about education – an alternative view' (debrakidd. wordpress.com)

Tim Oates on curriculum and assessment reform

Name: Tim Oates

Twitter handle: @Cam_Assessment

Website: cambridgeassessment.org.uk

What to read: Oates, T. et al (2011), *The Framework for the National Curriculum: A Report by the Expert Panel for the National Curriculum Review*; Oates, T. 'Opening the door to deeper understanding' (cambridgeassessment.org.uk)

www.cambridgeassessment.org.uk/insights/national-curriculum-tim-oates-on-assessment-insights/

What to watch: 'National Curriculum: Tim Oates on assessment' (www.youtube.com/watch?v=-q5vrBXFpmo)

Why Oates?

One of the biggest impacts on curriculum design and assessment, particularly at Key Stage 3, came as a result of the coalition government's launch of a review of the National Curriculum, with an expert panel led by Tim Oates looking closely at the existing curriculum, including assessment, in the context of international comparisons. Whether or not you agree with the findings, there is no denying the significance of the outcomes which led to the re-writing of the National Curriculum, the reform of GCSE qualifications and, perhaps most notably, the end of National Curriculum levels.

Oates then went on to draft the programmes of study for the National Curriculum and to advise on assessment. You don't have to go far in the blogosphere to find a reference to Oates on assessment. His video explaining some of these ideas ('National Curriculum: Tim Oates on assessment') is particularly useful.

Key ideas

Curriculum

The report by the expert panel (led by Oates) reviewing the National Curriculum highlighted two areas which were common components of curriculum in 'high performing jurisdictions' such as Singapore: curriculum control and curriculum coherence.

> 'A certain degree of curriculum control is necessary (that this need not be associated with 'top down' control or control exercised exclusively by the State) and that this control should be directed towards attaining 'curriculum

coherence.'' (Oates, T. et al (2011), *The Framework for the National Curriculum:*
A Report by the Expert Panel for the National Curriculum Review)

Curriculum control can be both direct and indirect; from controlling the types
and quality of teacher qualifications through to prescribed content of curriculum
material. Curriculum coherence specifically relates to the design of curriculum
in that it is about the structure of curriculum in relation to year groups and
progression for cohorts.

With these ideas of control and coherence at the fore, the conclusion drawn was
that a curriculum would benefit from including a list of the 'essential elements
of subjects' (something which is clear in the draft programmes of study),
which would ensure stability and consistency rather than the constant review
and update which makes demands on teachers to create new resources and
approaches.

Another key observation from the report was about focusing on depth of learning
as opposed to breadth of learning based on international comparisons where
pupils are assessed as to how they have mastered key concepts in knowledge and
skills rather than moving along at a fast pace through levels.

Oates and the panel also argued in favour of agreed knowledge rather than
contextually relevant subject material. When it comes to context they identified
the need for content to be prescribed by the curriculum and context to be in the
power of the teacher, with this also being the argument for motivation as the
responsibility of the teacher not the curriculum content.

Assessment

Levels were initially introduced as a way to move students beyond the labelling
of being a certain grade and see them progress, but Oates notes that levels have
reverted to become the very thing they were trying to get away from; students
now label themselves with a certain level and this is 'dysfunctional in terms of
learning'.

Oates also refers to the way in which schools have adopted a system of 'undue
pace' with their use of levels; suggesting students should move quickly up the level
ladder, rather than assessing whether they have secured the key ideas, concepts,
skills and knowledge. Oates points out the lack of validity in the assignment of
a level based on one piece of work or one test – you ARE level 3 because of this
one piece of work that you have done, which does not account for the rigour of
the test or for the variety of work students may have completed throughout the
year. Furthermore, he suggests that the use of Assessing Pupils' Progress (APP)
assessment and 'best match' to verify what level a pupil has gained allows for

pupils to be given certain levels without any assurance that they have fully grasped key concepts, knowledge and ideas. Without security in all of the ideas or content, it is inappropriate for students to be 'moved on' a level. Moreover, he suggests there is an incoherence to levels when we consider pupils being at the 'threshold' of a level; this implies that there are different meanings to a teacher assigning a certain level compared to what the government or another school may think this level means.

Finally, he notes that levels present an idea of 'children's ability', where levels suggest that children are at a fixed point in their ability and that when they do not grasp a certain aspect of the school content, this is to do with their fixed ability rather than the teacher finding a way to present this material so that they can indeed grasp it. Oates highlights the promise of a school system that believes ALL students can achieve at the highest level dependent on the effort that they put in and on how the material is presented to them.

Assessment thus should focus on whether children have secured the concepts, ideas, skills and knowledge rather than on marking them with a level; it should expect that all children can achieve everything. Oates does say that the new National Curriculum is also 'chock full' of skills alongside knowledge and that these should be assessed.

In fact, Oates argues that: 'There is too little assessment. The reason for that is that we don't have enough assessment of the right kind.' Assessment should be probing of the big ideas in the curriculum and should be 'supportive of learning'. It should look at 'secure and deep understanding' not 'undue pace'.

More generally Oates points out that in successful schools, children produce a lot of work. They are making claims, producing hypotheses, producing more written work, diagrams and pictures on paper. This is 'fundamental' to assessment and education in general.

To fully embrace the development of meaningful assessment, Oates argues that schools will have to become experts in assessment and think hard about the questions they are posing to students and which questions probe the ideas that the child is required to understand. Oates recommends the use of examination questions 'to probe their understanding and stimulate discussion.'

Criticisms

One of the main criticisms against a prescribed curriculum – a list of specific content – is that by prescribing all content, you take away from the teacher's chance to innovate and be involved in the creative experience of designing curriculum. This type of curriculum makes teachers into 'deliverers' of a curriculum. Also there is still much disagreement about what the content of this curriculum should entail, even amongst the expert panel. A number of panel members were critical about the praising of E. D. Hirsch's approach to the curriculum.

Amongst those who are advocates of the knowledge rich curriculum, there is a criticism that the focus on knowledge is not represented in the current examination system which means that it's difficult to feel confident in teaching a knowledge-driven curriculum without fearing that you won't properly prepare pupils for their exams.

Michael Rosen also critiqued the report in relation to the strength of the evidence used and wrote directly to Tim Oates with his concerns, to which Oates replied. Their conversation and Rosen's criticisms can be found on Rosen's blog.

Key questions

Content

- Can the knowledge content of an intended curriculum be agreed upon at a national level?
- What are the pros and cons of a prescribed curriculum? Would this work within your school context?

Sequencing

- Should we set out a year-by-year specific sequence of learning?
- What are the implications of this within individual subjects?

Assessment

- What forms of assessment would best support the examining of key ideas, skills, concepts and knowledge within a subject?
- How can you create an assessment system which formatively feeds back to pupils about how to secure deep understanding, whilst also creating a tracking and reporting system?

Further reading

Rosen, M. (2012), 'Tim Oates lengthy reply to my request for evidence' (michaelrosenblog.blogspot.co.uk)

Ron Berger on expectations and varied forms of assessment

Name: Ron Berger

Twitter handle: @RonBergerEL

Website: elschools.org

What to read: Berger, R. *Ethic of Excellence*

What to watch: Berger, R. 'Austin's Butterfly' (vimeo.com/38247060)

Why Berger?

Berger is well known for his work on pupil feedback and the use of specific critique and re-drafting to produce work of 'excellence'. Both his book *Ethic of Excellence* and related video 'Austin's Butterfly' (a clip of Berger working with primary school pupils in America to use specific critique to improve a pupil's (Austin) drawing of a butterfly), went viral amongst the teaching community.

Key ideas

Whilst Berger has some interesting thoughts on curriculum, including the use of real-life contexts to motivate pupils, it is his work on feedback and critique which has had the most traction. Both the book and video mentioned focus on expecting more from your pupils and achieving this through detailed verbal feedback and the use of re-drafting. Berger also emphasises the importance of using model exemplars both for pupils and teachers. In the video, Berger works with a group of pupils to look at a series of drafts that Austin completes based on critiques he has received from his classmates. In this frankly adorable clip, the pupils demonstrate their ability to be guided to make precise critiques that would help to produce improved work. The final draft elicits gasps of admiration from the pupils as they notice how much Austin's drawing looks like the original model. They also demonstrate an awareness of the importance of the drafting process. Berger sees the use of exemplars, learning to be an expert critic – using 'critiques [which] are specific and focus on one quality at a time.' (Berger, *Ethic of Excellence*) as the best way to encourage excellence. This is a way in which pupils can begin to become self-assessors and get used to self-critiquing as they go along. His advice for critiquing can be summed up as: be kind, specific and constructive. This form of feedback is particularly useful when it comes to thinking about the implemented curriculum including the use of gallery critiques as a part of formative assessment.

Berger is less keen on the use of frequent testing or of 'teacher-proof curriculum' subscribing to the philosophy that 'testing children constantly doesn't make them smarter.' Instead, as detailed in *An Ethic of Excellence*, Berger looks to a more long-term approach to building 'an ethic, a culture, which supports and compels students to try and to succeed.'

Criticisms

Berger's focus on cross-curricular projects and real-life contexts runs contrary to many of the arguments about the importance of direct instruction, teaching background knowledge and focusing on subject disciplines.

Whilst many agree with Berger about the potential damage of a high stakes testing culture, there is disagreement as to whether this should lead to less testing. In fact, many educators have begun to argue that testing needs to be more frequent and that it can be more reliable than other methods of assessment.

Key questions

Expectations

- How do we ensure high quality work from our pupils?
- How can we build opportunities for re-drafting and critiquing work within the curriculum?

Assessment

- Should we use a range of different types of assessment including portfolio work?
- Are standardised tests damaging for our pupils?

Further reading

Quigley, A. (2012), 'A taste of Berger: reading "An Ethic of Excellence"' (huntingenglish.com)

Sherrington, T. (2013), 'Lessons from Berger: Austin's Butterfly and not accepting mediocrity' (headguruteacher.com)

Fawcett, D. (2013), 'Creating a culture of critique' (reflectionsofmyteaching. blogspot.co.uk)

Hall, R. (2013), 'Da Do Ron Ron' (rug62.edublogs.org/2013/01/07/da-do-ron-ron)

Radice, A. (2015), 'National testing should be broader, simpler and more frequent' (thetraditionalteacher.wordpress.com)

Carol Dweck on growth mindset

Name: Carol Dweck

Twitter handle: @mindsetworks

Website: mindsetworks.com

What to read: Dweck, C. *Mindset: How You Can Fulfil Your Potential*

Why Dweck?

Dweck's book, *Mindset: How You Can Fulfil Your Potential*, was one of the big influences for many schools in designing new Key Stage 3 curriculum and assessment systems. Like Willingham, Dweck's approach comes from research in the fields of cognitive science and psychology and whilst it has a wider remit than schools it can also be used as a way of understanding how pupils' learning develops.

Key ideas

Dweck's ideas challenge the concept of fixed ability; arguing that instead it is mindset that limits our potential. Dweck explores two mindsets: fixed and growth – these can be mindsets adopted by people about themselves or others, such as parents and teachers about their children/pupils. The fixed mindset refers to those who believe that they have certain fixed abilities and that they cannot do much to change these, whilst those with a growth mindset embrace challenge and sees this as learning/development; you can learn from failure. Those who adopt the fixed mindset struggle to deal with failure and see this as a setback, meaning they are reluctant to try again.

If all pupils are capable of developing their abilities, then the same curriculum is appropriate for all. This has a particular influence on the enacted curriculum, where teachers have to consider strategies that will help those with more 'fixed' mindsets to embrace challenge. As Dweck says it is about the 'how' of teaching pupils rather than the 'can' I teach them? Dweck gives examples of teachers who have taught high challenge material to pupils who have been assumed unable to cope with it because of their background or attainment; she furthers the ideas about the danger of dumbing down the curriculum 'on the assumption that they can't handle more'. (Dweck, *Mindset*). Dweck's example teachers all work on the belief that any pupil can achieve and that this is done through a mixture of an atmosphere of high challenge and the feeling of being nurtured. In English for example, the lists of literature taught reflect a focus on a demanding curriculum driven by knowledge. The teachers do not reduce the challenge – they adapt their attitude so that the expectation is that all pupils will be able to access this literature. They then operate honestly with their pupils – being clear about where the pupils are, why they are succeeding or failing and how they progress.

Some of this doesn't exactly feel like rocket science – but the reality is that sometimes we do need to be reminded of this way of thinking about learning. Understanding the different mindsets is equally useful for considering assessment; it means that we have to think about the consequences of labelling pupils but also about how we can approach failure as a means to progress rather than a reason to give up. This is particularly useful when thinking about formative assessment and how this can be used to make pupils think about assessment as an opportunity for development and learning rather than validation; important for thinking about our approach to testing and the negativity that can often surround using tests to assess pupils. Tests are often seen as damaging and a way of measuring people in unfair ways – as is evident by the frequency of quoting Einstein: 'Everybody is a genius. But if you judge a fish by its ability to climb a tree, it will live its whole life believing that it is stupid.'

Dweck's research offers us a challenge to this way of thinking – both in the fact that if we don't see ability as fixed, then humans (unlike fish) can develop their abilities if they put in the work. Also it would suggest that it's the way we respond to the exam that makes us carry the belief of stupidity rather than the actual exam itself. This has repercussions when it comes to designing an assessment system: if it is driven by the curriculum and offers pupils an opportunity for growth and to learn from failure, then we might be getting somewhere. Dweck also challenges the idea of basing all our understanding of a pupil on one assessment which links to Wiliam's point that assessment doesn't mean simply measuring pupils at one point, it should be about more than just one moment, but should allow us to make inferences about whether they will be able to apply this learning in other contexts.

Clearly this poses wider problems around national assessments and perhaps hints at the idea of portfolio work or coursework as an option for assessment. Whilst this is clearly not an option at GCSE or A-level, it does pose the possibility of using a range of assessment such as portfolio assessment within schools.

Criticisms

There have been some concerns that after the mass popularity of Dweck's book, some of the key messages became reduced into motivational messages on posters and in assemblies. Alex Quigley, a supporter of Dweck's work, writes persuasively on this in his blog, 'The problem with growth mindset'.

Some argue that genetics does in fact have a role to play in children's abilities to succeed and therefore Dweck's work is an idealistic way of viewing the world, and does not take into account the real problems that may come from disadvantaged backgrounds. You can read more about this in the blog by @DisIdealist.

Key questions
Expectations
- How do we ensure that our curriculum and assessment systems provide suitable challenge and do not limit pupils' potential?

Assessment
- Should we offer a range of assessments such as tests and portfolio work?
- How do you build in honest feedback and strategies for formative development within an assessment system?
- How do you make sure that you are able to make valid inferences from the assessment – do you know what you are assessing for?

Further reading

Quigley, A. (2014), 'The problem with growth mindset' (www.huntingenglish.com)

Didau, D. (2014), 'Grit and growth: who's to blame for low achievement?' (www.learningspy.co.uk)

'The growth mindset: telling penguins to flap harder?' (disidealist.wordpress.com/2014/12/05/242)

Tomsett, J. (2013), 'This much I know about...developing a Dweck-inspired Growth Mindset culture' (johntomsett.com)

Tomsett, J. (2015), 'This much I know about...why we are developing Growth Mindset Learning tools' (johntomsett.com)

Hildrew, C. (2014), 'Becoming a growth mindset school' (chrishildrew.wordpress.com)

What next?

This is just a brief overview of some of the thinking that has influenced me when it comes to considering curriculum and assessment design. But each time you open a book or click into a blog, you open up a wide variety of research and a history of ideas about education. The question you may now be faced with is, 'what do I do with all this?' For some people it works to directly apply research – to build their curriculum and assessment around a particular body of evidence. For others it is more about being informed by the thinking that has come before and using this to consider what the principle features of a school's curriculum and assessment system should be. When designing curriculum and assessment, I have tended to take the latter approach but with a focus on thinking which theory/research matches to our school purpose and have used this as a springboard to consider what this means practically in the context of our school.

In the next chapter, I explore ways in which teachers and schools have used theory/research to build curriculum and assessment systems.

Chapter 5 takeaway

Teaching tip
Prioritise

There is an endless amount of theory and research on curriculum and assessment design, much of which is in conflict. You can easily get dragged into an endless cycle of reading, which can often make you feel more bewildered about your own instincts and knowledge. Instead aim to prioritise the theories and research that make the most convincing case and link to your purpose. From here you can narrow down the key ideas which fight to be part of your design process.

Pass it on

This is another excellent opportunity for blogging about the process of curriculum and assessment design. You might want to post about your thinking as you read and research or you could write specific reviews about the different books/articles/blogs.

Consider setting up a CPD book club at school – this will allow for an informal discussion of ideas and encourage more staff at your school to engage with theory and research in their own practice.

Share and tweet

Many of the people who are currently writing about curriculum and assessment design can be found on Twitter or in the blogosphere. If so, their Twitter handle/Blog address has been included in the chapter. In my experience many of these people are very personable and happy to engage with discussion online. So it's worth getting in contact to see if you can develop your understanding of their work.

CPD book club recommendation

Knowledge and the Future School, Michael Young, David Lambert,
Carolyn Roberts, Martin Roberts.
(see Bibliography and further reading)

Bloggers' corner

Daisy Christodoulu has written a vast range of excellent blog posts on assessment: https://thewingtoheaven.wordpress.com

TO DO LIST:

- [ ] Read through the different ideas and pick out some that resonate to explore in more detail.
- [ ] Make use of the criticism available so that you get a full picture of the given ideas.
- [ ] Identify where any of the theories/research match with your current curriculum and assessment – is this effective?
- [ ] Pick out the key ideas that you would like to use in your curriculum and assessment design.
- [ ] Now narrow this down until you have the essential ideas which will be central to your curriculum and assessment design.
- [ ] Tweet your thoughts on the theory/research by using the hashtag #BloomsCPD
- [ ] Check out Daisy Christodoulu's blog posts on assessment: https://thewingtoheaven.wordpress.com
- [ ] Read *Knowledge and the Future School*, Michael Young, David Lambert, Carolyn Roberts, Martin Roberts.

6 Overview of the main strategies

You're thinking: 'it's all very well talking the talk and giving me a load of fancy theory but how does this actually work on the ground? I can't just waft around chatting education, I want to build something real that will stand strong in the face of the needs of our staff, children, parents, governors and community.' You're right and the hardest step can be moving from theory to practice; it's the point when you have to have courage in your conviction and that's particularly risky when you know that it affects the future of the children in your care, but equally not making the change will be detrimental.

I still remember the day I started teaching my curriculum and the absolute fear that it wouldn't work – a fear that was proved to be groundless because, I believe, of the dedication I had to getting it right by looking at examples from real schools (as well as the process of consistent review; the curriculum will always be somewhat in flux but the design process is about creating a strong framework). I was lucky enough to have the opportunity to visit a number of fantastic schools and departments along my way, but time and cost constraints means this will not always be possible.

In this chapter, I open up the doors of my school and the thinking behind our curriculum and assessment, as well as peering through into other schools which have invested in curriculum and assessment design. Significantly in the wake of mass change in mandated curriculum and assessment at both Key Stage 3 (with the removal of levels) and Key Stage 4 (with the GCSE reforms); many schools have become pioneers. Their sharing of this and consequent discussion has provided a rich variety of resources for school leaders and teachers to plunder before embarking on introducing their own systems. I've picked out elements which follow on from the main themes identified in the previous chapter; looking to see how these work in a real school environment. These aren't blueprints of a system that can be rolled out in any school (although there are many educators who would argue for this kind of approach to curriculum design), but tried and tested approaches which may help you to see how to make dreams into a reality.

Establishing your own goals

- **Research the theory** – if you've read the previous chapters, you should be well-informed by now, but make sure you read advice from all the different education spectrums: from traditional to progressive; knowledge-led to skills-led; subject specific to cross-curricular.
- **Survey** – look at what is going on in your own school; visit other schools and read blogs by other teachers in a similar role and make endless notes about what you do and don't like.

- **Tweet** – try Tweeting out your question to education communities such as @Pedagoo, @staffrm or to #ukedchat, #edchat or a subject specific hashtag such as #engchat.

I found the Twitter community to be hugely helpful and informative. It wasn't that I wanted to take on other people's views or that I didn't have an instinctual vision, but I was so overwhelmed by the amount of ideas I had shooting around in my mind, that I had to step away from them – let them sit in the back of my mind waiting patiently like a Christmas cake which I was occasionally dousing in brandy.

I immediately received brilliant, inspiring support and advice from the teaching community. Freya Odell (@fod3) had recently started as a Head of Faculty and gave me a number of tips and guidance, as well as directing me to her faculty and department's planning. She left me with two important questions which framed her thoughts when designing curriculum:

1. 'What do I have to get into my curriculum?
2. What are the key issues for my school?' (@fod3)

These directed me back to the whole-school guidelines and I therefore knew that my goal for my ideal curriculum had to:

- challenge my students to make outstanding academic progress
- provide them with a deep base of my subject knowledge (as well as teaching the necessary skills to engage with this)
- fill them with a life-long [I said ideal!] love of all things to do with my subject – in my case all things literary and linguistic.

As noted above, I do think it is important to look at advice from educators from across the different education spectrums – even if you are sure on the type of curriculum you will design, it is worth considering the differing approaches. This has become more and more important to me as a curriculum designer over the last couple of years. Whilst our English curriculum is rooted in a traditional body of knowledge, it also has a framework based around philosophical questions. This was inspired by reading some of Debra Kidd's work on linking English and philosophy, which she kindly emailed to me after a conversation on Twitter. Whilst this wasn't going to be the entire basis for our curriculum, it made sense to me to use philosophical and ethical questions as a way to link knowledge together because I think English has a strong philosophical and ethical core. I was also inspired by bloggers such as Joe Kirby and Katie Ashford to think about the types of texts I would be teaching and how I would ensure a strong knowledge focus in a subject which in my own experience has often been treated as a skill.

My discovery through this online world was that seeing theory and ideas in practice and exploring others' journeys was hugely useful to my own design. Here I look at some of the approaches my school (East London Science School) and others have taken to the task of first designing curriculum and secondly assessment, at both whole school and subject level.

Designing a curriculum

Step 1: Determine the purpose

I'm going to take you back to Chapter 3 now and remind you of the importance of being clear about your purpose before you start trying to design the curriculum. As I said in the self-assessment section the 'your' here should represent both you and your school. As a lead on curriculum and assessment design you are working to determine what the whole-school curriculum purpose is, whilst as a subject lead you will be determining the purpose of your subject within the context of a given whole-school purpose.

At whole-school level

- Revisit your ideas around purpose, draw links between the curriculum and the purpose: if you can't find a link, then reconsider the content/structure of your curriculum.
- If you are re-shaping an entire curriculum, this will also involve modelling a curriculum by thinking through the subject allocation on the timetable and how you will dedicate other hours to anything else you would like to cover.
- Consider how the purpose might be fulfilled through the intended, implemented and enacted curriculum.
- Explore ways to make the purpose clear through the expressed ethos and values of the school; it is important that the whole school is aligned with the primary purpose of the curriculum; trying to persuade subject teachers to design a curriculum based around building character is going to be difficult if they believe the curriculum should be focused on pupils getting the qualifications that will prepare them best for the workplace. This doesn't mean they can't fulfil a range of purposes but they do need to be in agreement with the driving purpose of the intended curriculum.

At subject level

- Consider how your subject fits into the wider context of the whole-school curriculum purpose. How could a department for a practical subject like music or art design a curriculum which fits with a whole-school purpose of valuing academic knowledge? Should a science curriculum be designed around the intrinsic value of scientific ideas and discoveries or about exploring real world problems and current scientific topics such as climate change?

- Look at the purpose of your subject, or as Dylan Wiliam calls it: the 'construct' of your subject. This differs from curriculum purpose in that it is situated within the history of your subject – the teaching of English literature for instance has always been tied to a moral purpose, starting out as a means to bring British moral values first to the Empire and then to the working classes and later, in an about turn, as a means to be free from prescribed moral values by exploring personal development through response to literature. This doesn't mean all English teachers now agree on this, but it does shape how many English teachers might be likely to respond to their subject.
- Consider how your understanding of subject purpose is influencing what you teach. Is your department all aligned in their understanding of this?
- As a subject lead you need to be clear on what the driving purpose of the curriculum should be but it is worth discussing any conflicting views to see whether this strengthens or adapts your ideas around the shape of the curriculum.

At East London Science School (ELSS), the school's purpose was already clear from the outset: to teach an academic curriculum for the intrinsic value of education. This meant that the curriculum was based around a model of traditional subject teaching. The focus on giving all pupils an access to a liberal arts education also means that all pupils are expected to study Latin and Ethics (including philosophy). It is through the teaching of these subject disciplines that pupils gain the chance to 'stand on the shoulders of giants' and develop their own critical thinking. It also provides a subject-based approach to ideas often incorporated through PSHE programmes – pupils debate these from a philosophical and historical perspective, as well as through their own reality.

Uniquely the school also runs an enrichment curriculum entitled 'London as our classroom', which sees pupils venturing out into London every week on subject-based trips. It's where the academic life of the pupils expands beyond the boundaries of our school walls and where they begin to see how the knowledge they have been taught has influenced the culture of our city. It's often on these trips that you see the 'transformative' power of knowledge which Michael Young writes about in the book *Knowledge and the Future School*.

These are all firm curricular decisions based on the school's purpose; it impacts on the shape of our days and the range of subjects our pupils are exposed to. Our enrichment curriculum for instance, requires a block from 13.20-16.20 so that pupils can travel to their destination and have enough time there, as well as a two week block where the enrichment curriculum takes over from the regular curriculum.

Step 2. Decide on the key principles

This should be a list of about five-six principles on which you will base your curriculum.

At whole-school level

- Imagine that you have been asked to speak at a global event about your school: what would you say about it? What makes it unique? What makes it great (and I don't mean GCSE results or levels of progress or saying you're 'twenty-first century' learners). You need to be able to explain on this and use real examples to support what you are saying – you should have something you are proud to speak about.
- Use this imaginary speech to make a list/find the list of the key principles of your school.
- Explain how each one of them is exemplified in your curriculum.
- If a principle is not exemplified in your curriculum – you either need to adjust the principle or the curriculum, depending on which you think is more meaningful.

At subject level

- You can do the same tasks as above but for your department: consider what makes it stand out in the school and why your subject matters to the pupils that you teach.
- What are the defining principles of your subject and how are these demonstrated in your teaching and learning?

Example 1

At ELSS our school vision is tied up with our understanding of what makes a good curriculum – it is the core of the school:

1. All children deserve the best education possible.
2. A 'well-educated' pupil must have a good science education.
3. Good teaching is the best way to open a child's mind.
4. The best pupils are open to questioning their own thoughts.
5. Pupils should be encouraged to nurture their talents and develop new skills.
6. We can judge our success by the impact our pupils have on the world.

It really helped that from the offset the school philosophy of subject-based teaching and high academic expectations for all pupils was extremely clear. This meant all developers of subject curriculum had to be aware of the following:

- Pupils are streamed by attainment so that teachers can teach the same curriculum to all but adapt teaching accordingly to ensure access.
- The curriculum needed to set a high bar of challenge but also fill in gaps of knowledge, particularly in elements such as literacy and numeracy.
- The curriculum should be aspirational and inspirational.
- The curriculum should be driven by knowledge.
- Pupils will be tested and ranked on this knowledge each half term.
- Key Stage 3 will cover two years, with pupils making subject choices at the end of Year 8.

At the same time, the school runs the enrichment curriculum: 'London as our classroom'. It's in this curriculum that pupils gain an opportunity to see their subject in the wider world and has more creative and exploratory elements than the traditional curriculum.

Example 2

Take a look at the Michaela school website (http://mcsbrent.co.uk/vision/) and you can clearly see their vision for their curriculum, which can be summarised as:

- All children deserve a broadly traditional and academically rigorous curriculum.
- Children should be taught learning habits such as politeness and obedience.
- Competition is important.
- Knowledge is power.

Example 3

At School 21, a very different type of new school, they lay out their six attributes for success (http://school21.org.uk/about-us/6-attributes) which seem to match their thinking behind their curriculum:

1. Expertise
2. Professionalism
3. Eloquence
4. Grit
5. Spark
6. Craftsmanship

It's easier to see examples of these different principles at new schools, because they have had a unique opportunity to develop something from scratch with a specific vision, however it doesn't mean this is limited to new schools or that it can't be something introduced at a new school. It can be true that some schools are limited to a vision based simply around the qualifications offered.

Example 4

At Highbury Grove, Tom Sherrington has introduced a new curriculum based around the idea of a National Baccalaureate and the three principles of the Trivium:

- Grammar
- Dialectic
- Rhetoric.

This is influenced by Martin Robinson's book *Trivium 21c: preparing young people for the future with lessons from the past* in which he advocates for a liberal arts curriculum which has a strong knowledge base (grammar) but also encourages teaching pupils how to question and argue (dialectic) and to communicate and present their ideas (rhetoric). Tom Sherrington's blog on how this has influenced development of the school curriculum is well worth reading: 'The Trivium and the Baccalaureate: the flesh and bones of a great education' (headguruteacher.com). See also Chapter 9.

Michael Fordham on designing a whole-school curriculum

Name: Michael Fordham
Twitter handle: @mfordhamhistory
Website: clioetcetera.com
What to read: 'A radically traditional secondary curriculum model'

Step 3: Set the expectations

At whole-school level

- Ensure all pupils have access to the same curriculum: support those who need it, but don't lower your expectations of what they can achieve.

- Make sure every member of staff understands what you mean by challenge and has incorporated this into their curriculum.
- Set expected standards of work for pupils and make them accountable for sticking to these.
- Create academic reading lists to be paired with the units of work you are studying.
- Examine how you will timetable the support needed for lower attaining and struggling pupils to ensure they can access the curriculum.
- Set a clear academic agenda, which is rigorous from the start of Key Stage 3, rather than patching up with intervention in Year 11.

At subject level

- Consider what you would need to be a true scholar of your subject; imagine that instead of aiming at an A* at GCSE, you are aiming at a 1st class honours degree. How do you get your pupils to that point?
- Look at how you can raise the bar for your subject and at the same time ensure you teach the functional skills and knowledge needed for pupils to articulate their understanding of the subject.
- Consider the rigour of the resources you are using: a generic photocopy from a revision guide is not going to encourage academic thinking, try to look for relevant journal articles or academic texts and edit them to make them appropriate for the classroom. In Year 8 Latin for instance, our classics teacher uses poetry from Catullus and Ovid, in the original, to teach some of the basic grammar whilst also setting a high demand in terms of vocabulary and literary analysis.

At ELSS, by highlighting that ALL pupils at our school deserve the best education possible, the expectation is set extremely high for the entire school. Classes are streamed by attainment (they move depending on test results in English, maths and science) but the curriculum is not changed – all pupils study the same content. That 'best' education means one which is considered challenging and rigorous means the curriculum must match up to this; it is expected that subjects will go above and beyond the normal requirements for each year group. This is crucial to the curriculum design as it sets expectations for those in charge of their subjects to be experts in their subject and to be confident in determining how they will handle this curriculum with their pupils. Teachers have to have the attitude that all pupils can achieve at a high standard and be willing to push them to achieve this. Whilst this sounds pretty obvious, it actually requires a real shift in thinking. I remember when I first started teaching, I often taught material that was not hugely challenging because I didn't think that pupils could or would engage with it. Yet I've now gone from teaching *Skellig* in Year 8 to teaching *Animal Farm* and have found myself continually amazed at how far the pupils have been able to go with this. We recently started a unit of work on dystopian fiction and my bottom set Year 9s were quick to point out that this was like *Animal Farm*, quoting parts of the book at me to prove their point.

Dweck's work on growth mindset really helped me to understand the reality of how a 'hard work ethic beats natural talent mentality' approach is beneficial for all pupils. It's not a bad idea for staff either: the challenge of teaching a difficult curriculum, is that you need to be at the top of your intellectual game too. When you're having to read serious academic literature to make sure you can keep up with your Year 7s understanding of epic poetry, you know that you are on the right page. Our pupils know they are expected to work hard, they recognise and use our phrases 'above and beyond' and 'aiming higher' in their speeches about the school and they are relentlessly, and for the most part positively, competitive with themselves and others about achieving the highest forms of academic success.

I was also inspired by a visit to KEGS School in Chelmsford in 2014 where despite the relatively unchallenging intake (it is a grammar school) teachers were constantly investing in ways to challenge and push their pupils, whether this be in research projects around poetry by heart or co-construction of lessons with older pupils. In particular, stumbling into the head of English's office and seeing the immense selection of books and journals reminded me that challenge doesn't come from a flashy PowerPoint or an extension question, it comes from a school culture which encourages academia and hard work to flourish.

Tom Sherrington on high expectations

Name: Tom Sherrington
Twitter handle: @headguruteacher
Website: headguruteacher.com
What to read: 'The anatomy of high expectations'

Alex Quigley on high expectations

Name: Alex Quigley
Twitter handle: @HuntingEnglish
Website: huntingenglish.com
What to read: 'Thinking hard and why we avoid it'

Step 4. Determine the big ideas

Having a framework of big ideas is not only useful for designing the curriculum but also as a way to consider how to set about designing an assessment system. For if you know what the key concepts are that your pupils must grasp in order to 'get' your subject then you also know what your assessment needs to be testing.

The 'big ideas' of your subject, according to Wynne Harlen in the paper 'Principles and big ideas of science education' are the thematic ideas which go beyond the core body of knowledge of a subject:

> *'Education not in terms of the knowledge of a body of facts and theories but a progression towards key ideas which together enable understanding of events and phenomena of relevance to students' lives during and beyond their school years.'* (Harlen, 2010)

I take issue with this thinking that core knowledge is not relevant or that in fact that needs to be the driving focus of a curriculum, however I like the idea of trying to consider what the big ideas of your subject might be. My approach to this perhaps can be more closely identified with the idea of 'threshold concepts'. I first became aware of this way of thinking about them when I visited Alex Quigley at his school Huntington and saw how he had used them when thinking about his curriculum. I had unwittingly done the same kind of thing when designing mine – centring the design of the curriculum around key ideas I had about the subject. There is still much debate about what a threshold concept actually is, with some schools approaching these in specific detail and others in a wider thematic way.

It is a good idea to read the paper on this by Jan Meyer and Ray Land entitled 'Threshold concepts and troublesome knowledge: linkages to ways of thinking and practising within the disciplines'. It is worth reading for the opening line alone which is beautiful:

'A threshold concept can be considered as akin to a portal, opening up a new and previously inaccessible way of thinking about something.'

The ideas they propose for determining threshold concepts are that they are:

- 'transformative'
- 'irreversible'
- 'integrative'

and possibly also both:

- 'bounded'
- 'troublesome'.

This means that you are looking for aspects of your subject: the concepts, context and knowledge which unlock the subject for your pupils. These not only transform the way that pupils view the subject but also can not be unknown once you have learnt them.

Jan Meyer and Ray Land on threshold concepts

Name: Jan Meyer and Ray Land

What to read: 'Threshold concepts and troublesome knowledge: linkages to ways of thinking and practising within the disciplines'

At whole-school level

- Use CPD time to help departments determine the big ideas of their subject (see Part 2 for more information about how to run this).
- Map out the different big ideas across the curriculum and make them public: share them with pupils, parents and governors; publish them online. This sends the message that you have clarity about the curriculum and you value the subjects you teach beyond merely getting a GCSE pass.

At subject level

- Use Twitter to find fellow teachers and leaders in your subject area and ask them what their big ideas are or post a blog of your own and debate these with people in the teaching community.
- Make contact with a university and find a subject specialist to speak with about their ideas of your subject in higher education.
- Join a subject association and suggest a meeting/conference to battle out these ideas.
- Do some research about the history of your subject.

In designing my English curriculum, I focused on big thematic ideas and then broke these down into specific areas of knowledge and threshold concepts. The ideas I started with are wider in scope than threshold concepts, but created a good starting point for a picture of the subject. I began with these ideas:

- The chronology of English literature
- Context and literary criticism
- Genre and form
- Grammar
- Rhetoric
- A writer's techniques

Clearly I could have gone into more detail, but I liked the idea of this big picture approach with the more specific detail being part of the process when I set about determining the knowledge that fits within these. These also have changed and will change or alter slightly as I continue to think and read about my subject and particularly in conversation with my growing department.

This year, my department and I refined these ideas to make them more precise and to have corresponding threshold concepts.

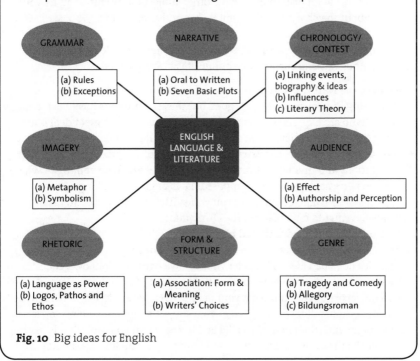

Fig. 10 Big ideas for English

Step 5. Determine the content

Whilst the threshold is the skeleton of your subject, the knowledge within this is the flesh and muscle. Determining what this should be is a harder process because of the vast body of knowledge that there is out there. Indeed it is why we have to in the end come back to the Arnoldian view of teaching 'the best of what has been thought and seen' (based on Matthew Arnold's argument in his book *Culture and Anarchy*). Every subject teacher could fill an entire school timetable with the knowledge and skills that they would like their pupils to know and still be left wanting. So in the end you have to choose the best knowledge, as determined by yourself and other subject experts.

When it comes to the topic of diversity and knowledge, I agree with the importance of being critical of a mono-cultural approach. I want my pupils to see and read and share a multitude of voices, so this is worthy of discussion but we can learn as much from the lack of representation as well as by hearing those voices. Within English this can be explored through the use of literary theory and the pairing of contemporary texts (which tend to have a wider set of voices) with canonical texts, not to forget the opportunities within the enacted curriculum to open up discussion and questioning of the knowledge being imparted and to explore different cultural viewpoints throughout literary history. It's easier to understand this in English than in some other subjects, as literature in its very nature is about the sharing of different voices and experiences.

Determining the key knowledge of the subject is therefore tricky. Other than perusing other existing curriculums online, it is also a good idea to:

- **Analyse the National Curriculum in some detail** – I'm no advocate of everything the government says goes, but these documents have been built by people who are experts in their field and who have spent a great deal of time doing the thinking about what a curriculum should include.
- **Look at responses to the curriculum** – these are often conducted by subject associations and unions or through the media and will help you to see where other experts have picked out supposed flaws or gaps. By taking a broad approach and sweep of opinions, you will start to have more of an idea of what you believe fights for a place in the curriculum.
- **Look over your own educational background** – whilst it's not advisable to base your educational decisions on anecdotal evidence of yours and others school years, it's not a bad idea to consider what knowledge from your own educational background sticks out; where your gaps of knowledge were when you embarked on a university degree and what your unknown knowns (Zizek, 2008) might be. It can also be difficult if you are good at your subject to remember how you learnt some of the information that you did and to know that you can't simply assume this will be the same for everyone else. I find this particularly problematic with

teaching elements such as grammar and spelling; I just remember knowing the rules but have no recollection of how I knew them or was taught them.

- **Browse through university curriculums** – look at how they structure their curriculums and what expectations (including reading lists) they have for pupils wanting to apply to their courses.
- **Have conversations with other teachers or experts in your subject** – whether online or in person, this is an excellent way to argue out the knowledge that should make it into a school curriculum. This could include speaking to experts in ITT provision or through subject associations or via the education conference circle. It's not even a bad idea to debate it with friends outside of education – especially those who have come from different educational backgrounds.

At whole-school level

- Make time for teachers to invest in subject CPD – this could be within their departments, giving them access to relevant journals, sending them on subject specific trainings such as those run by the Prince's Teaching Institute (www. princes-ti.org.uk/) or sending them out to other schools in order to see how the subject knowledge is being developed in different departments.
- Centre the curriculum around the key content – each unit of work in our school is designed around five key areas of knowledge and each lesson should be guided by these areas.

At subject level

- Sit down with your department and use the big ideas and threshold concepts to help you consider what knowledge is needed to grasp these ideas.
- It is useful to imagine saying goodbye to your pupils post A-levels: what would you need them to know at that point for you to feel that you had taught them successfully?
- Reading about your subject is also key – you might want to revisit material from your training. One of my colleagues has also found the Oxford 'Very Short Introduction' series to be useful for engaging with different academic theories and ideas about your subject.

Step 6. Determine the sequence

In Chapter 5 there was a number of suggestions about how one might want to sequence the curriculum, based around ideas concerning memory and also about building an understanding of your subject.

Threshold concepts can be a really useful way of sequencing content, as David Didau demonstrates in his blog: 'Using threshold concepts to think about curriculum design', where he explores interleaving threshold concepts throughout different units of work over the year.

David Didau on sequencing the curriculum

Name: David Didau
Twitter handle: @LearningSpy
Website: learningspy.co.uk
What to read: 'Using threshold concepts to think about curriculum design'

Chronology is another way of thinking about sequencing a curriculum. It is particularly helpful for the arts and humanities but perhaps less so for maths or science, although there is something to be said for an understanding of how scientific ideas have developed from ancient times to today. In fact, if approaching the study of a subject as an almost history of ideas, probably most curriculums can be sequenced to some extent in this way.

At ELSS, in biology, for instance, our science team have structured the curriculum around 'evolution' and Darwin's work in particular, including human evolution. This lends itself naturally to a chronological approach, which in turn compliments other subjects such as history and classics. Additionally, in English, we've taken an approach which blends threshold concepts and chronology together: there is a sense of chronology throughout the year and in the units of work but this is not entirely fixed – pupils move between the different eras and each year we start at different points. History meanwhile is taught completely through a chronological approach. There has definitely been a benefit when these dates align so that an era of history matches the era of literature being taught or similar for links with classics or RE. Learning about the enlightenment in ethics and science also strengthened Year 8s understanding of Romantic poetry. Some schools have worked on making these links a planned part of sequencing the curriculum. In his blog, 'What makes a great school curriculum?', Joe Kirby describes a curriculum in which English for instance should be 'dovetailed' with history.

Joe Kirby on sequencing the curriculum

Name: Joe Kirby
Twitter handle: @joe_kirby
Website: pragmaticreform.wordpress.com
What to read: 'What makes a great school curriculum?'

At my school, being a science specialist school, we've begun considering this sequencing at a whole-school level by looking at the ways in which the sciences and maths could be taught in conjunction with each other, for instance thinking about which subject takes responsibility for teaching graphs, or revisiting material with an awareness that it has been studied in another subject previously, e.g. the study of the atom in physics and in chemistry respectively. On the blog post above, there is an interesting discussion in the comment session about the evidence for chronology having any impact on memory, to which Willingham responds with the idea of 'causality' as being a useful tool for memory and that chronology can be considered to be aiming towards this.

Curriculum mapping (which I will explain in more detail in the next chapter) is also an important strategy to help consider sequencing as it relies on building back from the intended outcomes or end goals to the start of a child's academic journey at a school. Therefore it makes you think about the building blocks of knowledge needed to reach these outcomes.

Interleaving is another element which can be considered when designing curriculum. This is where you move, you break up and revisit content over the year rather than teaching content in sealed off units of work. We do this by revisiting threshold concepts each term and using assessments which include content from previous terms, including an end of year examination which tests pupils on key material from the whole year.

At whole-school level

- Decide how you want to sequence curriculum: should it be based on ideas behind memory or the construct of the subject, or a combination of both?
- Consider whether you need different approaches for different subjects.
- Decide whether you want to build in sequencing which runs across different subjects and how this will work without negatively impacting on the authenticity of the subject.

At subject level

- Determine the natural sequencing of your subject
- Use curriculum mapping (see Chapter 7) to help you understand the natural progressions of your subject.

Step 7. Review

It has been three years since I started teaching the curriculum that I designed in English and it has changed during that time – not significantly, because it was built on quite firm foundations and principles, but enough to notice. The more you read, the more you implement a curriculum and the more you discuss it with colleagues and other experts, the more you find to review and critique. I see this as a positive part of curriculum design; that you are always able to tinker with it to make it just that bit better.

Reviewing can really only take place once you have begun to teach the curriculum or established the curriculum within a school. This is especially true because the review should be about evaluating the impact of the curriculum on the pupils.

Key considerations

- **Purpose** – does the curriculum drive towards achieving your school's purpose? Is this true across the curriculum?
- **Principles** – does your curriculum match your school's vision and principle? Can you draw direct lines between the two? If not, why?
- **Expectations** – are pupils being significantly challenged by the content of the curriculum and does the curriculum build sufficient background knowledge to allow all pupils to access the challenge?
- **Big ideas** – does each subject have a clear picture of the big ideas and can they explain this to other staff, pupils and parents?
- **Content** – look at examples from other schools and compare them with your curriculum: is there anything essential missing?
- **Sequencing** – do pupils remember what they have been taught? Why/Why not? Is there a sense of building knowledge and understanding of the subject? Does the curriculum link together effectively through use of chronology, threshold concepts, interleaving or another focus?

At whole-school level

- See the curriculum review CPD session in Part 2 for a guide to running whole-school reviews (p 245).
- Ask yourself to what extent your assessment system offers the opportunity to make valid inferences about the strength of the curriculum.

At subject level

- Take time in fortnightly department meetings to reflect on how the curriculum is being enacted in your classrooms. At the end of every half term, make sure you put in time to check if anything in the curriculum needs to be reviewed or refined.
- Consider how you could use assessment to ascertain the strengths of your curriculum.

Designing an assessment system

Meaningful assessment is vital for understanding how successful the curriculum is and can also be a way of ensuring pupils make significant progress with the curriculum. In fact if there is one thing that you get out of this book, I hope it is the realisation that curriculum should drive assessment and not the other way around. This is much easier at Key Stage 3 when assessment is in the hands of schools, clearly when it comes to public examinations there are some restrictions but I believe you can still work within this system AND ensure the curriculum drives.

Step 1: Determine the purpose

With the curriculum driving assessment, the purpose of assessment seems simple: to check how much pupils have learnt of the curriculum and to help them move forward in their learning. As Dylan Wiliam says in his work on 'Principled Assessment Design' – all assessment should be AfL.

Of course the reality of external summative exams means this cannot always be the case. You'd be hard pressed to find a school or teacher who didn't think getting successful results for their pupils was a key part of their job. Schools also rely on these successes to attract parents and to soothe inspectors – the accountability is seductive. The need to prove that you can achieve successful results and that you can show 'progress' means that schools are reliant on having assessment systems which can display this.

Yet this doesn't have to become meaningless, if it remains driven by the curriculum purpose. Having determined your curriculum purpose, you are also determining the purpose of your assessment as it shapes ideas around the types of qualifications you will offer and the expectations you have for your pupils. Your curriculum will hopefully be richer than that offered by an exam specification and consequently your assessment will be worth more.

Measuring what you value

I agree with Daisy Christodoulu and Dylan Wiliam – as explored in Chapter 5 – who both assert that an assessment system highlights to everyone concerned with the school, what it is that the school values and that therefore if we get lured into valuing the target we take away from the whole purpose of the curriculum. Educational history has taught us of the danger of focusing on assessment over curriculum.

The key thing is to focus on the essence of the subject and the eventual outcomes. Students of literature should become literary critics and writers; students of science should become scientists – or these must at least be our aims. Whilst not every pupil who studies literature will become a writer nor every pupil who studies science a scientist, the subject teaching has to allow for this, in fact its aim has to be to engender it, with any other consequences being subsidiary benefits. In order to do this, you must use the ideas and principles of your curriculum to inform your assessment and you must ensure that the format of the assessment is true to your understanding of the construct of your subject. Ideally this should mean that you can use a range of assessments, as long as you are clear what kind of inferences you can make from them.

At whole-school level

- Consider the idea that we value what we measure and therefore a whole-school assessment system sends a strong message about what the school values. What do you value?
- Focus on the curriculum purpose and look at whether your current assessment system is helping to fulfil this. If you are focused on teaching character, do you also need to assess this in some way? Can you do this? What types of assessment and qualifications should you offer to achieve this?
- Be realistic about the complex purposes of your assessment system: it must combine a drive for curriculum purpose and also meet the needs around monitoring and accountability.
- Map out the different purposes and draw links between them or ways that you could link them together.

At subject level

- Explore what different aspects of the subject you want to assess (the essential content that pupils need to remember).
- Think about what you are trying to assess and what assessment formats will allow you to make the most valid inferences e.g. if testing knowledge of historical chronology, a quiz on dates might be a more useful way to gauge how much pupils can remember, rather than setting an essay task.
- Decide the purpose of an assessment before setting it and communicate this with teachers and pupils – this will ensure you are not setting meaningless assessment tasks.
- Determine the purpose of assessment in your subject: to check understanding/ help with memory/gauge understanding.

At ELSS as our purpose is to teach an academic curriculum for the intrinsic value of education, it is unsurprising that assessment is driven by our rigorous curriculum. Assessment has to help us ascertain how much knowledge pupils have retained from this curriculum and how to help them progress. At whole-school level, this means that testing pupils regularly in the specific academic knowledge is important: we have half termly tests, and mid-term multiple choice knowledge tests as a way of celebrating the fact that we value knowledge. Previously, instead of the mid-term, we were marking and recording an extended piece of work, however this was overly vague and led to a burden of marking which did not have a significant impact on pupil progress. The mid-term test instead allows us to pick the precise factual knowledge that we want pupils to remember and to show them that we value this by assessing it and giving them instant feedback about what knowledge they need to learn.

Similarly in the English department we considered the purpose of the subject and determined that essays needed to feature as a component of our end of term tests because we value extended analytical writing, but we also include short answer and multiple choice questions where appropriate to gauge specific knowledge such as literary chronology. When it comes to a dramatic unit, such as a Shakespearean play, there is a drama component in which pupils have to perform a scene off by heart, as we value the art of performance and of memorising speeches and poems. Whilst in the Sciences, practicals are a key component of the curriculum - as the subjects are guided by the purpose of creating scientists and therefore need to conduct laboratory work. This vision from the Principal of the school, when it comes to the practical element of Sciences has led him to look into creating specific lab books so that this work can be effectively assessed and monitored.

The inferences we have made from this combination of assessment has made for interesting discoveries. Pupils who have been performing well but not excellently in their end of term tests often scored below par on their mid-term multiple choice knowledge test, suggesting that this means they are confident and articulate writers but their weaker factual recall is stopping them from achieving the highest results. Conversely looking at data for pupils who achieve well in the multiple choice tests but not so well in the end of term test helps to reveal struggles with literacy and/or analytical writing. Equally, we often see pupils perform to a high standard in drama exams when weaker in writing and vice versa. This makes a significant difference to how we can target our teaching, feedback to help pupils to improve.

Step 2: Decide the key principles

Ensuring meaningful assessment can be difficult when under pressure, leading us into teaching to the test or, in a frenzy of panic, to assign grades for the sake of grades, rather than thinking about why we are marking something or if that is indeed the best work to be marking. Letting the curriculum drive doesn't necessarily mean making assessment low-stakes, it means designing an assessment system which is principled.

At whole-school level
These principles should be based around the following:

- ensuring assessment is meaningful
- measuring what you value
- being able to make (and feed back) quality inferences about what pupils have learnt (testing, monitoring, reporting and formative assessment).

Ensuring assessment is meaningful
When beginning to look at developing assessment after levels, Michael Tidd posted an excellent blog giving seven questions which you should ask about any new assessment system. These were:

1. Can it be shared with students?
2. Is it manageable for teachers?
3. Will it identify where students are falling behind soon enough?
4. Will it help shape curriculum and teaching?
5. Will it provide information that can be shared with parents?
6. Will it help to track progress across the key stage?
7. Does it avoid making meaningless sub-divisions?

(Tidd, M. '7 questions you should ask about any new 'post-levels' assessment scheme')

Later the DfE released its own set of principles (2014) which limited these to three areas of effectiveness:

1. Give reliable information to parents about how their child, and their child's school, is performing
2. Help drive improvement for pupils and teachers
3. Make sure the school is keeping up with external best practice and innovation.

These are pretty vague, but they are useful to bear in mind when thinking about the different requirements of assessment within schools.

Notably what both these sets of principles prompt schools to think about is the idea of assessment as an important tool to ensure pupils succeed. Negativity surrounding assessment originates from the misuse of assessment and the frustrations about types of assessment which do not help pupils to learn or force schools to measure aspects which they do not value. Assessment which is designed without thinking about pupil learning and school values is indeed meaningless and worthy of criticism. However this doesn't mean that assessment itself, even in the form of a test or examination, is the problem. Clearly we are in need of some form of national qualifications, but also assessment, both formative and summative, is essential to ensuring that your curriculum works, that your pupils remember the valuable content you teach and to enable you to have a good knowledge of the academic strengths and weaknesses of your pupils and thus help them to improve.

These questions/principles also highlight the fact that an assessment system has to be meaningful for a number of different groups of people and for different purposes. This makes it seem extremely complicated but in reality it simply means making sure you're assessing what matters and that you are able to feed this back to pupils, parents, teachers, governors and the wider world so that they can understand it and (for the first four groups) use it to improve. This is meaningful because it is centred around your pupils and how you drive towards achieving your curriculum purpose.

Top tips for whole-school assessment

1. Make sure that the curriculum drives all your assessment.
2. Set high expectations with your assessment – don't place limits on your pupils.
3. Use a tracking and monitoring process that offers useful inferences for teachers, pupils and parents.
4. Ensure that your assessment system allows you to check basic knowledge and skills as well as high order knowledge.
5. Make sure that the system is clear and easy for teachers, pupils, parents and external visitors to understand.
6. Use model examples and norm-referencing (ranking pupils against one another) to set standards.
7. Only measure what you want pupils to learn.
8. Avoid wordy criteria and levels/sub-levels of learning.
9. Ensure all formative assessment has clear, specific advice about how to improve.
10. Frame assessment positively: encouraging an expectation that with hard work from teachers and pupils, everybody is capable of success.

At department level

- Model your department assessment principles on the whole-school assessment principles.
- Aim for consistency between the way you report to pupils and the whole-school systems: embrace the shared language.
- Know what principled assessment means in your subject and fight for that when it comes into conflict with whole-school demands. If you don't think

a certain format of assessment or reporting allows you to maintain the principles of your subject, then it is worth battling out in a meeting with leadership.

In 2014, the DfE awarded an assessment innovation fund to a handful of schools to develop their assessment systems. Nothing much more has been heard of them since – they were supposedly going to be reviewed by the commission on assessment without levels – but the schools chosen and their assessment principles are still available online. One of the schools was Durrington High School, their deputy head, Shaun Allison, describes the purpose and principles behind their assessment system: 'The key goals of any assessment system should be simple. It should celebrate what students already know, whilst building their aspirations towards excellence and supporting them to achieve this, through high expectations and quality feedback.' (2014) Allison has blogged about the design of their assessment system and written there about the 'consistent principles' which have allowed for 'flexibility across all subjects'.

ELSS assessment principles

- Assessment is driven by curriculum

We create our own tests and assessments based directly on the important knowledge and concepts of our subject curricula. This means we design tests and assessed work around the five areas of knowledge studied during a term and the end of year exam covers knowledge from throughout the year. Reporting and monitoring is based on overall scores but also on the specific areas of knowledge. Pupils immediately understand the specific areas of curriculum that they need to work on harder to grasp. (This also helps teachers consider how they need to direct their teaching.)

- Testing promotes learning

We are strong advocates of testing and see it not as a way to simply measure pupils, but to gain a nuanced understanding of their knowledge and their strengths and weaknesses and to help them improve.
We therefore test every six or seven weeks and have an end of year examination. Our half termly reports ensure that everyone involved, including parents, knows what pupils can do to achieve more highly.

- Aim higher

We hold high aspirational expectations for all our pupils – they are all measured in regard to whether they have reached our aspirational school target (aiming for nine A*), not in regards to a modified target based on their starting point.

- Be honest

We're a big advocate of honest conversations about pupil progress – or lack of progress. Regular testing, ranking and class moves means pupils and parents have a clear understanding of pupils' strengths and weaknesses. This same honesty is applied to teachers: class average test scores are compared across subjects and underperformance of pupils addressed with individual departments and/or teachers. Both pupils and teachers have reviews to examine these results and look constructively at how to make improvement.

- It has to work

Because we invest so thoroughly in assessment as the tool to help us evaluate our pupils' knowledge of the curriculum and our teaching of the curriculum, we have to make sure the assessment we choose works for pupils and teachers. This addresses Michael Tidd's point about whether the assessment is manageable. Over a half term, teachers are expected to assess one piece of extended work (prep work), one mid-term multiple choice test and the end of half term test. We've made these our priorities and replaced another piece of extended marking with the mid-term test so that this is manageable, meaningful assessment for the teachers.

Step 3: Set the expectations

One of the key aspects of any assessment system is determining how pupils will progress through to an end goal. Different measures have been given to schools at different points such as: expected progress Key Stage 2 to Key Stage 4; five A*–C grades GCSEs/equivalents (including English and maths); C grades in English and maths; Progress 8; EBacc. Sadly the pressure and fear that exists within school leadership has meant that these nationally prescribed benchmarks have often become the set expectations for pupils which has led to game playing – time invested in moving Year 11 pupils from Ds to Cs or playing around with the qualifications offered to meet whole-school grade targets. The recent story about a school where pupils are asked to carry around their target grades at all time (http://www.telegraph.co.uk/news/2016/04/17/school-tells-a-level-students-to-wear-target-grades-around-their/) is evidence of this system being taken to the extreme. We can easily see how this culture of target and predicted grades can lead to limited expectations for pupils.

It clearly is in conflict with, for instance, Dweck's work on growth mindset and with any justification for a rigorous academic curriculum – if pupils are just not able to reach this standard, then teaching it would be elitist/wrong. For Willingham the answer lies in arguments around memory – you have to look at the transfer from working memory to long-term memory; differences in ability can be seen as simply different capacities of working memory.

At whole-school level

So how do you track and monitor progress but ensure you don't limit expectations?

- Consider which data is available to which groups of people.
- Set high aspirations through the test/assessments you set.
- Move away from labelling pupils and instead focus on specific feedback.
- Have honest conversations with pupils about their progress.
- Use ranking/norm referencing.

At department level

- Use moderation to ensure that you are all maintaining the same high standards.
- Choose exemplar work to demonstrate expected standards.
- Share and model examples of excellent work with teachers and pupils.
- Don't apply grades to every piece of work – concentrate instead on useful targets.

ELSS

David Perks, the Principal of my school, is fond of saying: 'If we aim the bar higher, the pupils will jump higher.'

- We achieve this by setting an aspirational school standard for all our pupils, regardless of their starting points. This standard, if achieved, would result in a top grade at GCSE but also, perhaps more importantly, signifies a sophisticated knowledge of the subject curriculum as determined by the subject expertise of our teachers and leaders.
- In departments, this high challenge standard is informed by pupil work from the previous year; looking at the best work available to use as a measuring bar for others and also through looking at the expectations for an A-level pupil in your subject.
- Pupils all embrace the chance to aim for green and the fact that there are no limits set for them means you can be in the lowest set and still

---

know your teachers are pushing you to reach the highest grades, even if it will take you longer to get there.

- We do have data about how pupils are progressing in terms of expected GCSE grades, but this is not shared with pupils and not used by teachers.
- Teachers are held accountable to progress towards the school standard which is more demanding, for all pupils, than the nationally prescribed benchmarks.

Ranking

- At ELSS, pupils are ranked in each subject and across their year group in terms of their English, maths, science(s) aggregate average. This informs which class they are placed in. Each class studies the same curriculum but teachers can use different strategies and approaches to target the differing needs of pupils within different classes. Ranking means pupils know they will not compete with only those at the same starting point, they are all being held to the same expectation.
- In Sally Coates' book *Headstrong*, in which she writes about being a headteacher at Burlington Danes, she describes how high expectations 'means securing the best possible outcomes for all students' and identifies regular assessment as one of the features which helps achieve these outcomes. This includes using ranking to 'mirror public exams' and 'to raise motivation amongst pupils through the transparency of the system, and create a competitive spirit.'
- Chris Hildrew writes about comparative judgement and norm-referencing in his blog 'Refining assessment without levels.' He draws on work from Daisy Christodoulu and Tom Sherrington to explore how GCSE grades are awarded and how we can apply this to our own assessment systems. Inspired by growth mindset, he describes how his school will use comparative judgement to create a rank order, 'Students' relative positions at these subsequent assessment points will then allow judgments of progress: if you started low but move up, that's good progress. If you start high but drop down, we need to look at what's happening.' This avoids the low expectations of set target grades.

Step 4: Determine the big ideas

Once you've determined the purpose and expectations and finalised your key principles, you need to consider what this looks like in reality: what are the big ideas that make up your assessment? This includes the type of assessment you will run across the school and how consistent you need to be in this assessment, as well as how you intend to report and monitor the results.

At whole-school level
Testing

- Determine how frequently you want to test pupils. This decision will be informed by how useful you think tests are for helping pupils learn and what impact they have on your pupils. Consider whether they are best placed to run every half term or term or at the end of year.
- Will the tests be low stakes (results just used to inform learning) or high stakes (used to make decisions about pupils or teachers)? Read more about the differences here: edglossary.org/high-stakes-testing/
- Consider how important consistency across the school is when it comes to tests, for example, should they all be the same format? Obviously consistency is good for ensuring a whole-school clarity about the purpose of assessment, but it's also worth considering how this impacts on different subjects. This is particularly relevant to practical subjects such as art and music.
- Plan to schedule tests at key checkpoints in the pupils' learning. This might be at the end of a year, or a key stage.
- Ensure you find ways of testing content from throughout a year, rather than just at the end of a unit, to make sure pupils remember all the important knowledge they have studied.

Assessed work

- All schools will assess work over the year, as well as testing. Whether or not to include this as part of your assessment system is the big question. Most schools tend to operate a system in which departments determine what work they assess and this is monitored through marking reviews (which isn't necessarily recorded) and some kind of termly data entry. With levels, this often meant an obligatory rise of a sub level every half term. Consider what the best measurements are for creating a more meaningful record of pupil achievement.
- Consider using quiz scores to demonstrate how successfully pupils are able to recall key knowledge and concepts.
- Explore meaningful ways to record assessment of extended work – such as using comparative judgement to grade work or grading based on a specific knowledge/skill area so that pupils can be clear about how to improve.

Projects

- If projects form a part of your whole-school curriculum, you will want to reflect upon whether they should be part of your assessment system. Not including them could mean they lose their value, but including them could be reductive.
- Be clear about what you are assessing the project for: the blurred subject boundaries that often come as a consequence of project work mean it can be difficult to ensure pupils know what they are supposed to be demonstrating. A model of a historical building for instance, could be assessed in terms of the creativity of the model, the aesthetic qualities, or the historical accuracy. Determine what learning you want the pupils to display and assess this, making sure you inform pupils before beginning the project!
- Decide whether this can be assessed with the same system that you use for tests and assessed class work or if it needs its own reporting/monitoring option.

Reporting and monitoring

Like it or not, reporting and monitoring of assessment is a big part of a school assessment system. It has, quite fairly, got a bad reputation as a bureaucratic exercise but this doesn't have to be the case. Reporting and monitoring can be extremely beneficial for pupils, teachers, parents and school leaders.

- Consider what you are reporting: look at how specific the feedback is and how this helps inform pupils and parents about how they can improve.
- Ensure that your monitoring gives a meaningful representation of pupils' achievement – consider using ranking and aspirational school standards to help identify where pupils are falling behind.
- Look at the way your reporting and monitoring sets expectations for pupils.

At department level

Formative assessment

As I said in Chapter 1, assessment happens all the time in schools – every decision by every teacher may count as some form of assessment. But do those assessments always ensure progression in learning? Here is a list of some of the main types of formative assessment that you should aim to use in class, or encourage others to use in theirs, to support the aims of your curriculum.

Gallery critique

As Ron Berger talks about in his book, *Ethic of Excellence*, gallery critique is a great way to get pupils sharing their work and self- and peer-assessing. It encourages pupils to push themselves to achieve because they know they will be displaying their work in front of their peers. This involves displaying work around a room for a class to critique; you can use sticky notes or big pieces of paper for pupils to add their comments, specifically focusing on how to help each other improve their work. It's also a good way to encourage a culture of editing and re-drafting of work. Read the superb post by Andy Tharby on gallery critique to understand more about how to put this into action.

Andy Tharby on gallery critique

Name: Andy Tharby
Twitter handle: @atharby
Website: reflectingenglish.wordpress.com
What to read: 'Adventures with gallery critique' 2014.

The two main teaching strategies that make for excellent pedagogy are explanations and questioning. Both of these are techniques which a teacher should be constantly aiming to improve and hone, because they are the most effective means of ensuring pupils learn and respond to the curriculum Although Toby French @mrhistoire has written an interesting challenge to the cult of questioning: https://mrhistoire.com/2015/07/01/is-questioning-yet-another-cult/. Clearly questioning has an important role as an assessment tool and there are a range of different types of questions that are helpful for this, but here I want to examine two key forms of questions that can be deliberately designed to fit into your curriculum. These are hinge questions and probing questions.

Hinge questions

These are questions that you use in the middle of a teaching sequence to assess whether your pupils have grasped the content of the lesson. They usually take the form of a multiple choice question, which simply requires pupils to raise their fingers to show their answer choice. This allows teachers to quickly assess who has understood and therefore either re-visit the knowledge or move on. Harry Fletcher Wood has collated a number of posts, from his own blog and from other teachers, about the subject of hinge questions and how to go about designing a good question. These are well worth a read.

Harry Fletcher Wood on hinge questions

Name: Harry Fletcher Wood
Twitter handle: @HFletcherWood
Website: improvingteaching.co.uk
What to read: 'Hinge questions hub'

Probing questions

When using probing questions it is almost as if you are completing an interrogation of learning. I've always enjoyed the process of this type of questioning pupils as it's here that you often challenge them out of their haze and force them to really start thinking about the content being covered. A probing question should do this: it should move pupils beyond repeating a basic answer and make them actually begin to qualify their answer. It can at first feel as if you are putting a lot of pressure on pupils, but once you build a relationship with your classes, it allows for a very effective way to assess where there is a lack of understanding rather than just laziness or lost focus. Read more about this type of questioning in Tom Sherrington's blog, 'Great lessons 1: Probing'.

Tom Sherrington on probing questions

Name: Tom Sherrington
Twitter handle: @headguruteacher
Website: headguruteacher.com
What to read: 'Great lessons 1: Probing'

Quizzes

These are not the last day of the Christmas term style of quiz but useful recap quizzes that help you quickly revisit key lesson content. They help identify the precise detail that pupils need to remember and can also be useful revision tools. The best form of quiz needs to be quick to complete, precise in the content it is testing and have immediate or close to immediate feedback. In her blog, 'How should I revisit past content?', Bodil Isaksen explores the use of this as part of a way of 'making learning stick'.

Bodil Isaksen on quizzes

Name: Bodil Isaksen
Twitter handle: @BodilUK
Website: blog.bodil.co.uk
What to read: 'How should I revisit past content?'

Exemplars and shared marking

Finally, I think it's an important part of the assessment process to show pupils examples of good work from their peers. We so often explain the success criteria for a task but never show what that would look like in reality. This can also involve taking an example piece of work and either marking it publicly or discussing the feedback that has been given. This helps pupils to understand what you want to see from their work; what you are looking to assess. Seeing what their peers can achieve also makes them want to raise their game, which is never a bad thing.

ELSS: The big ideas

We have a rigorous testing system at my school: the half-termly tests form part of our general assessment system, which is driven by the curriculum, NOT the other way around. The tests are one key way in which to build our understanding of how best to support all the children at our school to achieve excellence.

We don't use levels, instead after each test pupils are flagged as red, amber or green to identify how far they are on their way to securing key areas of knowledge as decided by subject leaders' curriculum maps (see Chapter 7) and are ranked by percentage against their cohort. These results are sent home to parents each half term.

RED	AMBER	GREEN
Below the school standard (in need of extra support/ re-visiting of subject knowledge)	Close to achieving the school standard (given targeted areas of knowledge to secure)	Working at the school aspirational standard (on track to achieving highest result at GCSE)

Fig. 11 Red, amber, green (RAG) rating system

As the tests are designed based around our curriculum, there is a high challenge – developing each year until a green would be equivalent to at least nine A* standard at GCSE by the time the pupils reach Year 11. Pupils also get a RAG on each of the five areas of knowledge in each subject, so that they can see the specific curriculum areas which they need to improve.

Results inform conversations with the pupils

We then use these results to inform conversations with the pupils, which happen after every test cycle, and to make individual targets with pupils to help them progress. Framed like this, the tests become a positive way to interact academically with our pupils. The focus on the areas of knowledge, means there is a specificity to the reports which parents get each half term: they know that a pupil is particularly struggling with understanding the process of photosynthesis in biology or that they can't remember their reflexive verbs in French. It's manageable for teachers, they simply give them a RAG rating in each area and it makes sense to pupils. Teachers spend 20 minutes or so of a lesson reviewing the test to help pupils identify where they've gone wrong. All the material is then tested again at the end of the year in their final exam.

Results inform departments looking to improve teaching and learning

This is also helpful in terms of the data it provides for departments when looking at how to improve their teaching and learning – last term in English, for example, it was clear that we had not spent enough time consolidating the dates of poets and their poetry, as pupils struggled with this area of knowledge as a cohort; whilst their understanding of themes, techniques and poetic vocabulary was much stronger. We are also becoming experts in test design.

Progress and accountability

Senior leaders use comparative judgement across subjects, by analysing test data at class and individual pupil level and comparing these to English, maths, and science averages. Departments are challenged to explain if classes and pupils are below average and what they are doing to ensure pupils reach the school standard. The frequency of testing means we are highly aware of how pupils are progressing and the specific areas they need to improve. The tests themselves are excellent evidence of our high expectations for our pupils and how we push them to excel. Use of ranking also means that if pupils move up or down the rankings significantly, we are being given another indicator about their progress. Finally, at senior leadership team (SLT) level we also use reading ages and MidYis data in comparison with our school standards, these help us to identify pupils who are significantly underperforming, determine why and deal with it fast.

Enrichment curriculum

Our enrichment curriculum is assessed through project and portfolio work. This is reported separately from their academic subjects, although we still give it a RAG rating so that pupils can see whether they are meeting our expected standards. We share good examples in assemblies and in form classes so that pupils know the expected standards. This works because of an understanding of the inferences we are trying to make about their knowledge of the curriculum; with our traditional subject-based curriculum, we need to infer what knowledge they have (most written tests, even in the arts, include short answer, multiple choice and extended writing questions to allow us to see this learning in different contexts) whereas in the enrichment curriculum we want to see how they have taken on knowledge to inspire creation and thought of their own. Sharing and displaying good project work here means we have model examples which demonstrate what you can create over six weeks.

Step 5: Determine the content

This one is pretty simple in my mind: does your assessment actually assess pupils on the key content of your curriculum and how effectively does it do this? This applies to both whole-school and department level, and requires the following:

- Identify the key content (concepts, ideas and knowledge) from your curriculum that need to be assessed.
- Identify the best forms of assessment to test this content.
- Feed back specific information to pupils, parents and teachers about how close pupils are to grasping this content and how they can improve.
- Ensure formative assessment is mapped into the curriculum so that it is the key content that is being assessed.

- At ELSS, we use our curriculum maps to direct all our assessments; these have been mapped back from Year 11, so that we know we are teaching the key content in preparation for GCSEs but it goes far beyond this and ensures the teaching of the key content of that subject as determined by teachers. This is then broken down into areas of knowledge and the tests are designed around this key content, as are the mid-term tests and the assessed extended work. We have begun to develop ideas around threshold concepts, so that these can be assessed and revisited in assessments throughout the year.
- At Durrington School, subject teachers are expected to identify threshold knowledge and threshold skills in each unit of work, which they use to create their assessment. Shaun Allison, deputy headteacher, describes this, on his blog, as the best way to ensure that they 'Focus on and assess what matters'. They too use curriculum maps to ensure progress towards GCSE. (classteaching.wordpress. com: 'Assessment without levels')
- At Huntington School, this same process of curriculum mapping is in place with a strong focus on the big ideas (threshold concepts) in each subject to create examinations. Alex Quigley, Director of Teaching and Learning, also describes how they are beginning to build banks of student work to set comparative standards based directly on their curriculum. (www.huntingenglish.com: 'Moving beyond National Curriculum levels')

Step 6: Determine the sequence

When it comes to how to sequence assessment, it makes sense to think about how you are assessing the build in the curriculum and to consider when you want to assess for progress. There's a danger in trying to see rapid progress; even Ofsted has moved away from the crazy idea that you could see this type of progress within 20 minute observations. The problem with progress when it comes to assessment, is that you imagine pupils will always be making linear progress and it also does not take into account the different units of work studied – it is possible to be excellent at algebra and really struggle with geometry; this could mean a high test score one half term and a low score the next half term. This doesn't necessarily suggest a fall back in progress; you would rely on teacher judgement at this point. You'd also hope that challenge would be increasing incrementally, which potentially might mean pupils seem to go backwards before taking a big leap forwards. For some schools, sequencing involves the concept of 'mastery' – pupils must show in their assessment that they have mastered the key concepts, ideas and knowledge before moving on. Others adopt a spiral curriculum, in which pupils revisit concepts, ideas and knowledge throughout their time in school, but the challenge and contexts change; again this must be reflected in assessments which build challenge and revisit work. This is similar for those designing a curriculum around threshold concepts and interleaving.

At whole-school level

- Look closely at your curriculum sequence and mirror your assessment to match the needs of this sequence.
- Map out your assessment over the year and pick the key points within a year, or over a key stage, where you will assess pupils formally.
- Determine how you will build assessment over a year and how your formative and summative assessment connect together: formative helping pupils to develop towards their summative assessment.

At department level

- Consider the content that you want to revisit over the year and design assessments which support this.
- Refine your formative assessment, so that you ensure it assesses material that is crucial and that the feedback helps move pupils forward.
- Map out your formative assessment over a half term, using quizzes and questions to revisit content and to interleave curriculum material.

Step 7: Review

Key considerations

- **Purpose** – does your assessment help fulfil the curriculum purpose? Does it help pupils to move forward in their learning?
- **Principles** – do you have a strong set of assessment principles at both whole-school and department level? Are these principles being honoured in your approach to assessment and are they known across the school?
- **Expectations** – does your assessment system give room for every pupil to achieve highly? Are you placing any caps on the expectations you have for pupils? How are you helping pupils achieve these expectations?
- **Big ideas** – do you have a coherent set of ideas about how to put the principles of your assessment system into action? Are these big ideas consistent across the school and do they achieve your purpose? Are these being successfully communicated to pupils, parents and teachers?
- **Content** – is your assessment driven by your curriculum?
- **Sequencing** – have you mapped out your assessment so that you have a clear picture of how it works across a year or a key stage and how it helps pupils to retain knowledge of the curriculum?

At whole-school level

- Hold regular review meetings with staff to evaluate their data and pupil achievement.
- Review tests regularly to ensure they match the demands of the curriculum and are set at an appropriate level of challenge.

At department level

- Complete regular moderation of pupil assessment to ensure that you have a shared understanding of expected standard.
- At a mid-point in the year conduct a review of your tests and adjust the challenge accordingly.
- Share and review the impact of formative assessment through observations and completed class work.

Chapter 6 takeaway

Pass it on

Consult with others

One of the biggest mistakes leaders make is trying to put a new system into practice without consulting with those who will implement the system. It's worth gathering a group of colleagues to review or trial approaches before you put them into place. Or if you've decided on a curriculum and assessment system at leadership level, ensure that you discuss this with middle leaders so that they're clear about the purpose and principles before attempting to introduce this to their departments. No matter how great your ideas are, if they're not communicated clearly to staff and not made manageable, they will not work. It's also an opportunity to get a range of different perspectives which you might not have thought about.

Discuss with colleagues from other schools

It's now so easy to connect with colleagues from other schools, both online and in person. Discussing your ideas with others in similar situations is invaluable and can both give you confidence in your design and also help you articulate your thinking to those outside of your school.

Share and tweet

Tweet your ideas about creating a new curriculum and assessment system by using the hashtag #BloomsCPD

CPD book club recommendation

Ron Berger, *An Ethic of Excellence*
(see Bibliography and further reading)

Bloggers' corner

Read Bodil Isaksen's posts on assessment: blog.bodil.co.uk

TO DO LIST:

- [ ] Look at some of the example schools in more detail – read their websites and blogs and see if you can try to arrange a visit to see them in action. Look at what works and see if you can apply this to your own school.
- [ ] Try to follow the design plans chronologically and make sure you let the curriculum drive your assessment.
- [ ] Be vigilant about the design's link to your school purpose – don't do anything for the sake of Ofsted!
- [ ] Tweet your ideas about creating a new curriculum and assessment system by using the hashtag #BloomsCPD.
- [ ] Check out Bodil Isaksen's blog posts on assessment.
- [ ] Read *An Ethic of Excellence* by Ron Berger.

7 Putting it into practice

Now the real fun starts: it's time to hit the ground running with some practical ideas to kick-start your new approach to curriculum and assessment. In this chapter I will look at ten ways in which you could start to use your ideas around curriculum and assessment both at a whole-school level and within the classroom. The activities are again grounded in the curriculum themes providing a solid base from which to launch. With each activity are some top tips and thinking points to make the process run smoothly.

1	Big ideas: mapping your curriculum
2	Content: areas of knowledge
3	Sequencing curriculum
4	Expectations: raising the bar
5	Subject expertise: bring the knowledge
6	Talk about it
7	Assessment maps
8	Quizzing
9	Assessment for excellence: modelling high quality work
10	Test design and review

Fig. 12 Ten ways to put your ideas into practice

When I was a child, I decided to put into practice what I had learnt about excellent forward rolls in PE. I decided to give this a go in my bedroom; it was big enough so that I could have the long run up that I needed and I would land on my bed, which was surely better than any gym mattress. So I leapt through the air, into the forwards roll, onto the bed and then crashed my feet right through the window. Miraculously I managed not to get a single scratch on me, nor fall the two floors to the concrete below – despite having smashed the window to pieces. The moral of the story is that one shouldn't necessarily take what you've learnt in theory and run into practising it full force without taking the time to test the waters, measure and evaluate. If I had for instance tried a seated roll on my bed first, I would have become aware of the fact that my feet would hit the window.

The same goes for applying your learning, thinking and research straight onto a whole new school-wide curriculum and assessment system without taking the time to test it in small increments. Now that you have an awareness of the research and theory behind curriculum design and assessment, coupled with some practical working examples, it is time to start slowly putting this into practice at your school. You will be treading the first steps of the path towards introducing a new approach to curriculum and assessment. Whilst it seems that this is immediately easier for members of the senior leadership team (SLT) responsible for these areas, much of these can also be implemented at department and even classroom level to start.

1. Big ideas: mapping your curriculum

This is a task which can be done at senior level or in departments but requires the guidance of a subject specialist.

- The first job is to determine the philosophy of the specific subject: answering the question 'What is your subject about?'.
- Determine what the 'big ideas' of your subject are and what you consider to be your 'subject construct'.
- Now identify the key areas of knowledge or concepts that you believe it is essential for your pupils to have a grasp of in order to really 'get' your subject by the end of their time in school. Try to imagine a world without examinations; consider not what they need to know to get a good grade but what they need to know to be confident scholars in your subject.
- Map backwards – starting from the end of Year 13 or the end of Year 11 all the way back to Year 7. If you know what your end goal is, you can work out how you will build towards this point. It's easiest if you divide your subject into different areas and work out how you might become an expert in each of these areas over the years. For example in history, to have a good grasp of the Second World War, pupils will need to have a knowledge of the First World War and the impact of the Treaty of Versailles. Chronology is a key component of designing a successful history curriculum, but which are the essential aspects you need to know? For instance do you need to have an understanding of Ancient Greek history in order to have a grasp of modern history and politics?
- The final step is to ensure that you build pupils' knowledge successfully over the year. There's a lot to consider, such as the sequencing and interleaving as mentioned in previous chapters. So I'd suggest starting with the basic core areas of knowledge and working from there – remember you can keep reviewing your maps; it doesn't have to be a finalised version.

2. Content: areas of knowledge

This is again an approach that can at first be taken when looking at one unit of work, before attempting to use this across the curriculum. It's a different approach to usual planning, as most units of work don't delve into specific detail about what knowledge needs to be learnt.

- Experiment with detailed and less detailed areas of knowledge: you could for instance say that the author of a text was an area of knowledge – you will then need to break down for pupils the type of things you expect them to know about this author, or perhaps leave this to be interpreted; looking to see how pupils engage with the given author. Or you could be more specific: naming the dates of the author's life and a number of key facts about them that you want the pupils to memorise. It's worth looking at the knowledge organisers, a structure created by Joe Kirby at Michaela School, and used by a number of different teachers as a way to potentially prescribe specific knowledge that pupils need to know. I've found them to be a really useful way to reach clarity about what you really want pupils to learn, and to force you to really think about the details of your subject. They also serve as a handy revision resource.

Joe Kirby on knowledge organisers

Name: Joe Kirby
Twitter handle: joe_kirby
Website: pragmaticreform.wordpress.com
What to read: 'Knowledge organisers: specify subject knowledge in meticulous detail'

- At ELSS, our areas of knowledge are split into five different areas per half term. It is these that we use to assess our pupils, so they also are key for revision and for giving specific feedback about how to improve learning. Here are some examples of what these look like for Year 7 in one half term. All of the curriculum (except for our Enrichment programme which has a loser structure, inspired by the subject learning in the day) is structured around this knowledge. Some of the subjects chose to focus on more procedural knowledge, whereas others were more factual.

Subject	Areas of Knowledge (Year 7 - Half Term 1)
Art	**Ancient ways of communication** 1. Aboriginal culture and religion 2. The process of dot work and meaning of dreamtime 3. Impact of Aboriginal art today: Emily Kamye Kngwarreye 4. Japanese calligraphy 5. Buddhism and Buddhist art
Biology	**Cells and living organisms** 1. The seven life processes 2. Structure and functions of animal and plant cells 3. Structure and function of specialised cells 4. Levels of organisation within the organism 5. Structure and function of single-celled organisms
Chemistry	**Particle theory** 1. The atom 2. Particle arrangement in solids, liquids and gases 3. Changes of state 4. Expansion and contraction 5. The diffusion of particles and concentration gradients

Classics	**Introducing Ancient Rome**
	1. Introduction to Latin and the logical analysis: the subject and the object
	2. Feminine, masculine and neuter nouns and the plural formation (nominative singular and plural of the first and second declension)
	3. Present tense of the verbs to be and to have
	4. Roman gods, members of the family and Roman numbers
	5. Epic: 'The Iliad, Book I'
Computer Science	**Web Design**
	1. Simple HTML document
	2. Changing the text style and background
	3. Complex tags and attributes
	4. Introduction to code editors - Dreamweaver
	5. Building Interactive webpages
English	**'Beowulf' and the history of language**
	1. The features and history of an epic text
	2. The socio-historical context of 'Beowulf': Anglo-Saxon warrior culture, re-ligion and values.
	3. The plot of 'Beowulf'
	4. History of English language
	5. Word classes, tenses and sentence basics.
Ethics	**Truth**
	1. How do we know the sun will rise tomorrow? (Defining truth)
	2. Darwin's theory of evolution
	3. The Big Bang and the age of universe
	4. Karl Popper and refutation
	5. Questions science can and cannot answer
Geography	**Place**
	1. History of Geography
	2. Geography of London
	3. Geography of the UK
	4. Geography of Europe
	5. World Geography
History	**Introduction to Chronology**
	1. The Black Death
	2. The Peasants Revolt
	3. The Hundred Years War
	4. The Wars of the Roses
	5. Henry VII
Maths	**Number**
	1. Long multiplication and division (number calculations)
	2. Order of operations (BODMAS/BIDMAS)
	3. Factors and Multiples (Highest common factor and lowest common multiple)
	4. Data: Frequency tables and charts (bar charts and scatter graphs)
	5. Algebra: Graphs (linear graphs and quadratic graphs)

Modern Foreign Languages	Family
	1. Vocabulary to describe the family
	2. Federico Garcia Lorca and family.
	3. Present tense verb to be "estar" and "ser" and "tener"
	4. Possessive adjectives
	5. Plural forms of nouns and adjectives
Physics	Space and the Universe
	1. Know the order of planets in the solar system including gas giants, terrestrial and dwarf planets
	2. Know that planets rotate on their axis and how day-night on the Earth is caused
	3. Know planets orbit the Sun and for the Earth with its tilted axis this causes the seasons (know the equinoxes and solstices)
	4. Know the phases of the moon including shape and timing
	5. Know there are different types of telescope (Hubble Space Telescope, refractor and reflectors)
RE	Islam
	1. The history of Religion
	2. The history of Islam: Suuni and Shia
	3. Al Fatiha
	4. The Pillars of Islam: Shahadah (Belief), Salah (Prayer), Zakah (Charity), Sawm (fasting), Hajj (Pilgrimage)
	5. The Mosque
Sports	Rowing
	1. Equipment: Bow, Bow ball, Stern and Fin
	2. Manoeuvrability using one blade to turn the boat and the other blade to stabilise the boat
	3. Enter boat from the pontoon using the rigger to balance the boat
	4. Leg Drive pushing off the foot plate to create power within the stroke
	5. Recovery (restarting the stroke, coming back towards the catch position)

Fig. 13 Year 7 areas of knowledge for one half term

3. Sequencing curriculum

In the previous two chapters, it has become clear that the sequencing and ordering of curriculum is an extremely important feature of curriculum design. Here are some approaches you could take at whole-school and department level.

- Hold a meeting with subject leads in linking subjects (such as maths and physics, or English and history) and look at how well their curriculums are sequenced alongside each other. Tease out the links between the subjects e.g study of the Romantic poets in English and learning about the French Revolution in history or about the Enlightenment in science. Map how these can be sequenced to compliment each other.

- Create a clear assessment structure for the year, this will help the sequencing of the curriculum, in particular when it comes to revisiting knowledge.
- Work with a strong subject lead to trial use of interweaving within their curriculum: this might be trying to map it out, or looking at ways to revisit content within a term. Present your/their findings to SLT.
- Within departments, look at what pupils need to know in order to have a secure knowledge of the topic. This should mean that they won't forget it; that they will be able to take this knowledge forward and build upon it. Trial one of the sequencing suggestions such as use of chronology, use of quizzing and use of threshold concepts: evaluate the impact.
- Devise an activity or test which gives you some indication of your pupils prior knowledge. In their book, *Making Every Lesson Count: Six Principles to Support Great Teaching and Learning*, Shaun Allison and Andy Tharby describe how Andy opens a sequence of lessons on Sherlock Holmes by asking pupils to write down everything they already know about the character, which as there has just been a TV series about him is a fair amount, although not all of it accurate when considering the book. This initial activity allows you to address misconceptions and plan which areas of teaching you will need to focus on.
- Plan to start every lesson with a recap/quizzing activity and study information more than once but in different contexts.

4. Expectations: raising the bar

There are a number of things you can do to raise expectations at whole-school level and within your classroom about the type of content you expect your pupils to tackle.

- Design the content of the curriculum with aspirations beyond the year group you are teaching. A GCSE class shouldn't be limited to a GCSE specification – consider introducing content from A-level or university, if it makes sense for the study of the subject.
- Consider how your curriculum will allow opportunities for pupils to engage with challenging ideas, concepts and knowledge.
- Plan to start a lesson with a challenging extract from a text or a philosophical problem. Discuss this together and praise those who struggle with the quest to find the answer or to understand the message. It's important to show that the struggle (the mental working out) is an essential and exciting part of learning.
- Consider how you and your staff are developing your own subject knowledge, including reading around the subject. It's all too easy to be just one step ahead of the class, rather than deeply embedded in the curriculum.

- Plan for opportunities in the extended curriculum which encourage learning outside of lessons, such as a debating club, a reading group or inviting external speakers who are experts in their field to talk to pupils.
- Design reading lists for your subject to encourage pupils to find out more in their own time.

5. Subject expertise: bring the knowledge

This is one for an SLT or department meeting to encourage teachers to engage more with the knowledge of their subject and therefore begin to build confidence amongst staff that they can take responsibility for their subject curriculum.

- Ask each person to present to their colleagues a key concept or topic from their subject – they should be prepared to explain why this is crucial to their subject and is worthy of study in school.
- Treat it as an exciting way to share inspiring subject knowledge amongst staff – the aim should be to enthuse the other teachers about this concept/topic.
- At the end of the sequence of meetings, evaluate whose presentation was the most successful in inspiring you about their subject and use this as a model for other staff when they are thinking through their curriculum.

6. Talk about it

One of the best ways to ensure curriculum becomes a core focus of teachers at your school is to talk about it more frequently. We naturally assume that whatever we are being asked to do, or whatever comes at the top of a meeting agenda is the topic of primary importance. However, it is often the case that it is just an immediate problem. This can lead schools to become overly focused on behaviour management and pedagogical tricks rather than over long-term concerns such as curriculum.

- Ensure curriculum is mentioned near the start of every meeting, either by feeding back on some aspect that is being developed or by sharing good practice in the school or suggestions for further reading through blogs or education books/articles.
- Ensure departments are given time to discuss their curriculum and their assessment systems on at least a fortnightly basis. This could include presenting some reading they have been doing on their subject, some subject development CPD or reflections on their use of assessment tools within their classroom. Use staff meeting minutes to help broach conversation on their findings with yourself and the subject lead.

- Invite some curriculum and/or assessment experts into your school. Encourage them to present their ideas and then debate their thinking in a Q&A with your staff. It helps to prepare staff beforehand by sending them some prior reading or thinking points. At the start you might need to prompt some staff members in particular to start the questioning, but this will quickly open up and allow the rest of the staff to feel they can test their ideas.

7. Assessment maps

Dylan Wiliam suggests the use of assessment maps to plot out the different types of assessment that you can use in your subject. These maps could include the types of assessment you want to use and the purpose behind the assessment.

- Separate formative and summative assessment.
- Under each of these, note down the forms of assessment you use.
- Next, map out the different inferences that can be made from each type of assessment.
- Cross-reference this with your curriculum: do your assessments allow you to measure everything you need?
- If not, then look for a space and type of assessment that will fulfil this need.
- Try mapping out when assessment will take place over the course of a year to get a realistic view of how and when you will assess.
- Add to the map how you will report back specific feedback to interested parties.

8. Quizzing

It could be that you decide to create a quiz rather than a test, based on the ideas around quizzing and memory in the previous chapter. This is a particularly useful exercise for individual teachers within their classroom or at department level when creating shared resources.

- There are some excellent online resources to use as a segue into designing your own quizzes or as a platform for tests you have designed. Both Socrative (www.socrative.com/) and Quizlet (quizlet.com) have a variety of different quiz options and include pre-made quizzes as well as the option to create your own. They also provide some fun options such as 'Space race' and 'Memory games' for pupils to use as a revision tool.
- Ensure any quiz you create is low stakes by planning for it midway through a topic and re-visiting it later in the unit of work.
- Encourage self-and peer-quizzing by setting pupils up with accounts if you are using an existing platform or getting them to produce quizzes for each other based on specific content.
- Experiment with a range of questions from multiple choice, to short answer and true/false.

- Consider what you want to do with the information that you glean – how will you use it to inform your teaching and learning? One of the benefits of online quizzing is that it enables you to collate data and explore trends in learning/ common misconceptions.

9. Assessment for excellence: modelling high quality work

Modelling high quality work can be important both within the classroom and amongst teachers in a department. You could also ask subject leaders to present model exemplars of their subjects to the leadership team as a way of explaining expectations for their subject.

- Within the classroom, this is a great way to use pupils' work to help model how to move forward. Use a visualiser or a camera to share pupil examples of high quality work (this can be recent work from within the class or work from other classes or previous years). It helps if the work is written by someone the pupils know and who is of a similar age, as this empowers them to believe they can also achieve at this standard. Be clear on your standards and expectations by showing what this looks like in reality – it's much more tangible than success criteria. This can also work with filmed examples in practical subjects: I've previously recorded pupils performing drama scenes and poetry by heart to demonstrate what it is possible to achieve with hard work.
- Consider also using exemplars where pupils have missed the point. One of the vice principals at my school uses this to give feedback to a whole class by targeting one pupil's work and demonstrating to the whole class where it needed to be developed. This encourages constructive conversation around feedback and lets pupils see the honesty of your marking. It also can be used as the start of a re-drafting process as seen in the wonderful example of 'Austin's Butterfly' from Ron Berger (see Chapter 5).
- At department level, you can ask each of your teachers to bring an exemplar from their class. This will allow for a shared discussion around what makes a good piece of work and can also ensure that you are clear about the expectations you set for pupils. This used to be a strong feature of coursework moderation, however the time pressures around this and the high stakes nature of GCSE grading reduced the constructive elements. Whereas focusing on one piece of assessed work, which should be brought to a department meeting and can be from a range of classes, makes the process more collaborative, it also ensures that there is an understanding of what excellent work at Key Stage 3 should look like.
- Often SLT have a patchy grasp of what work should look like other than in their specialisms. This can lead to an overly bureaucratic focus on marking or

appearance of work over actual content. This is also true for heads of year who often have the time to look at pupils books but are ill-informed about what they should expect to see. It's such a missed opportunity to hold pupils to account for the quality of their work and to create a shared vision of curriculum amongst staff. By asking subject leaders to present model exemplars to SLT or to pastoral teams, you allow everyone to have an ownership over pupil work.

10. Test design and review

This could be a test that is designed for a whole year group for the end of term or it might be a test that you design for your own class. The key thing is that it should be driven by your curriculum.

- Look at how you can ensure the test allows for the full range of pupils' current abilities. This might mean some opportunities for recalling of the knowledge that you consider the minimum pupils need to know that term; this could include multiple choice and short answer questions including testing of subject-specific vocabulary, followed by questions which allow pupils to demonstrate extended knowledge such as long answer or essay questions.
- Consider what it is that pupils need to know from the term and how you will know that they have truly grasped this within the test. For instance, if you were looking at a physics paper do you need pupils to just know that to calculate speed you have to use the equation speed = distance/time or do you need them to be able to apply this equation to a given problem? Do they need to be able to know the equation automatically and then apply it or do they just need to apply it?
- Using your knowledge about assessment and its different purposes, determine what inferences you will gain from the test and consider how the questions could be adapted to ensure you are able to make valid inferences about their knowledge of the given subject.
- Examine closely how the examination is weighted – does it measure what you value in the curriculum?
- It is a good idea to consider how to feed back information to your pupils – reviewing tests can be a constructive alternative to marking work.
- Create a pro-forma sheet to use with pupils, so that their responses are structured.
- Consider how you want pupils to learn from their test results; is it best to make notes as you mark and then give generalised feedback to the whole class, this might be identifying a particular question/topic that they struggled with and where they went wrong? Or perhaps it is better to lead a class to complete a review together or have pupils complete individual reviews?
- Plan for how you will help pupils to identify what they need to do in order to move forward in their understanding: what will be the measurable outcome of this? Another test result, a conversation with you, another piece of work?

Chapter 7 takeaway

Teaching tip

Build the foundations

When you have spent a while thinking about and developing work on curriculum and assessment, it is tempting to rush everything through at the same time out of a passion for your work. However it will all fall apart if you don't take the time to consider how you can build a new system in your school. This is particularly important if you are working in a school which has existing systems in place – throwing out one assessment system and replacing it with another overnight will be disastrous. You need to remember that your staff have to buy into this for it to work, so they have to feel confident that it has been developed with due thought and that they will be trained properly on how to put it into practice themselves. This chapter allows you to build up to this point: the maps are for example a great way to engage all staff in the process of thinking about curriculum and assessment design.

Pass it on

Try it out and feed back

Trying some of these ideas out whether in your classroom, at department or leadership level, will give you plenty to discuss with colleagues. This means you will be ready to run some CPD trainings (see Part 2 for more details) or to share more informally in meetings or in the staff room. You could even pair up with someone and either work on something together or try different ideas out and then feed back to each other about their effect. Designing a test, asking one of your department to sit the test themselves, and then drawing out inferences together is a good example of both passing your learning on and developing your learning.

Share and tweet

Share your reflections on the strategies you have tried or your questions about ideas posed in this chapter using the hashtag #BloomsCPD

CPD book club recommendation

Shaun Allison and Andy Tharby, *Making Every Lesson Count: Six Principles to Support Great Teaching and Learning*.
(see Bibliography and further reading)

Bloggers' corner

Read Joe Kirby's blogs on knowledge organisers and curriculum design: pragmaticreform.wordpress.com

To do list:

❏ Pick one or two of these ideas to start the process of changing the curriculum and assessment within your school.

❏ Make sure you are always keeping in mind the overall purpose, and the key ideas you have gleaned from your research.

❏ Evaluate how purpose, theory, research and your own expertise work together when it comes to putting the ideas from this chapter into practice. (Use the next chapter to help you review this.)

❏ Tweet the results of using these strategies and what you have learnt by using the hashtag #BloomsCPD.

❏ Check out Joe Kirby's blogs on knowledge organisers and curriculum design: pragmaticreform.wordpress.com.

❏ Read *Making Every Lesson Count: Six Principles to Support Great Teaching and Learning* by Shaun Allison and Andy Tharby.

STAGE 3: EVALUATE

8 Evaluating progress

You've tried some ideas out; perhaps in your classroom or in your department or even at whole-school level but are you ready to scale up? Now is the best time to take stock and reflect on what you have learnt so far before taking the big jump. That isn't to say that once you launch, you won't often come back and edit and tinker with what you're doing, but right now you need to have the confidence in your design to ensure you have something which is firm enough to only need tinkering not replacing. As such, you also need the confidence to say: 'no we need to go back to the drawing board' if you feel there are major holes in your plan. The only way to determine this is to take an honest and critical look at what you have tried so far. This will require you asking questions of yourself but, more crucially, asking for honest feedback from colleagues and pupils.

It is really important for you to have trialled some different activities and approaches before moving on to the questionnaire, so that you can have fully benefitted from the processes outlines in the book.

How and why to complete the questionnaire

You will remember the questionnaire process from Chapter 3, but here is a reminder.

Quick response approach

If your preference for the self-evaluation is to go with your gut only, then simply fill in the quick response section after each question with the first thing that comes into your mind when you ask yourself the question. Do not mull over the question too long, simply read carefully and answer quickly. This approach will give you an overview of your current curriculum and assessment design practice and will take relatively little time. Just make sure you are uninterrupted, in a quiet place and able to complete the questionnaire in one sitting with no distractions so that you get focused and honest answers.

Considered response approach

If you choose to take a more reflective and detailed approach, then you can leave the quick response section blank and go straight onto reading the further guidance section under each question. This guidance provides prompt questions and ideas to get you thinking in detail about the question being answered and is designed to open up a wider scope in your answer. It will also enable you to look at your experience and pull examples into your answer to back up your statements. You may want to complete it a few questions at a time and take breaks, or you may be prepared to simply sit and work through the questions all in one sitting to ensure you remain focused. This approach does take longer, but it can lead to a more in-depth understanding of your current curriculum and assessment design practice, and you will gain much more from the process than the quick response alone.

Combined approach

A thorough approach, and one I recommend, would be to use both approaches together regardless of personal preference. There is clear value in both approaches being used together. This would involve you firstly answering the self-evaluation quick response questions by briefly noting down your instinctual answers for all questions. The next step would be to return to the start of the self-evaluation, read the further guidance and then answer the questions once more, slowly and in detail forming more of a narrative around each question and pulling in examples from your own experience. Following this you would need to read over both responses and form a comprehensive and honest summary in your mind of your answers and a final view of where you feel you stand right now in your marking and feedback practice.

This is the longest of the three approaches to this questionnaire but will give you a comprehensive and full understanding of your current curriculum and

- I have done this self-assessment before.
- I only want a surface level overview of my current understanding and practice.
- I work better when I work at speed.
- I don't have much time.

Quick

- I have never done this self-assessment before.
- I want a deeper understanding of my current understanding and practice.
- I work better when I take my time and really think things over.
- I have some time to do this self-assessment.

Considered

- I have never done this self-assessment before.
- I have done this self-assessment before.
- I want a comprehensive and full understanding of my current understanding and practice and want to compare that to what I thought before taking the self-assessment.
- I have a decent amount of time to dedicate to completing this self-assessment.

Combined

Fig. 14 How should I approach the self-evaluation questionnaire?

assessment design practice. You will be surprised at the difference you see between the quick response and the considered response answers to the same questions. It can be very illuminating.

Rate yourself

The final part of the self-evaluation is to rate yourself. This section will ask you to rate your confidence and happiness in each area that has been covered in the questionnaire, with a view to working on these areas for further improvement. Read the question and on a scale of 1-10, mark how confident you feel about answering the question, either with regards to your own practice or with regards to the level of curriculum and assessment in your school. The table below shows how the scale works: the higher the number you allocate yourself, the better you feel you are performing in that area.

Rating	Definition
1	Not confident at all.
2	Very unconfident.
3	Quite unconfident.
4	Mildly unconfident.
5	Indifferent.
6	Mildly confident.
7	A little confident.
8	Quite confident.
9	Very confident.
10	Extremely confident.

Fig. 15 Rate yourself definitions

Curriculum design and assessment reflection questionnaire

QUESTION 1: Which new approaches to curriculum and assessment design have you considered or tried?

Quick response:

_____

_____

_____

_____

Questions for consideration

- How has your thinking on curriculum and assessment developed since reading this book?
- Which approaches most appeal to you and why?
- Which approaches would you still like to try?

Considered response:

_____

_____

_____

_____

_____

_____

_____

_____

Rate yourself

QUESTION 1: Which new approaches to curriculum and assessment design have you considered or tried?

| 1 | 2 | 3 | 4 | 5 | 6 | 7 | 8 | 9 | 10 |

QUESTION 2: Have any of the approaches to curriculum and/or assessment that you have implemented had an impact?

Quick response:

_____

_____

_____

_____

Questions for consideration

- Who have they impacted: school, teachers, pupils?
- How did they create an impact?
- Which approaches created the most impact?
- Was the impact positive or negative? Why?
- Was the impact expected or not?

Considered response:

_____

_____

_____

_____

_____

_____

_____

_____

_____

_____

Rate yourself

QUESTION 2: Have any of the approaches to curriculum and/or assessment that you have implemented had an impact?

| 1 | 2 | 3 | 4 | 5 | 6 | 7 | 8 | 9 | 10 |

QUESTION 3: How do you know about the impact? Could you prove it?

Quick response:

_____

_____

_____

_____

Questions for consideration

- Is the impact measurable?
- Have you gathered feedback from the pupils/teachers involved?
- Is there anything other than your new approach which could have also created this impact?

Considered response:

_____

_____

_____

_____

_____

_____

_____

_____

_____

_____

_____

Rate yourself

QUESTION 3: How do you know? Could you prove it?

1	2	3	4	5	6	7	8	9	10

QUESTION 4: What educational theories, research, ideas or case studies do you now have an interest in and how does it inform and influence your practice?

Quick response:

_____

_____

_____

_____

Questions for consideration

- Which piece of educational research theory, or idea has particularly influenced your own work on curriculum and assessment design?
- Has this made you more or less inclined to engage with further writing on this subject?
- Have you recommended any particular reading to your colleagues as a consequence?
- Have you considered doing your own research or writing up your ideas about curriculum and assessment design?
- Do you feel you have been able to challenge your own bias and approach ideas critically?
- What do you think you could do to extend your knowledge in this area?

Considered response:

_____

_____

_____

_____

_____

_____

Rate yourself

QUESTION 4: What educational theories, research, ideas or case studies do you now have an interest in and how does it inform and influence your practice?

1   2   3   4   5   6   7   8   9   10

QUESTION 5: Was it easy to explain your new curriculum/ assessment ideas?

Quick response:

_____

_____

_____

_____

Questions for consideration

- Was there clarity about the ideas when you explained them to others?
- Did the ideas resonate with other members of your team?
- If there was any confusion or disagreement, what do you think the reason for this was?
- Have any of the responses to your ideas made you re-consider them?

Considered response:

_____

_____

_____

_____

_____

_____

_____

_____

_____

_____

_____

Rate yourself

QUESTION 5: Was it easy to explain your new curriculum/ assessment ideas? Did people understand them?

1	2	3	4	5	6	7	8	9	10

QUESTION 6: What do your colleagues think about the new ideas? Consider both the positives and the negatives.

Quick response:

_____

_____

_____

_____

Questions for consideration

- How do you know what others thought: what type of feedback did you receive?
- How much conversation and discussion have you had with colleagues in the lead up to introducing your ideas?
- Were there different reactions from different colleagues? If so, why?
- Which ideas garnered positive responses and vice versa?
- Do you have measurable feedback from the work that you have completed so far?
- Have you reviewed the work yourself?
- Have the curriculum approaches you have used matched well with the school's purpose? Could you use this to inform leadership and governors?
- Have the assessment approaches that you have used given you formative information to feed back to pupils and parents?
- What would you adapt going forward, considering the responses?

Considered response:

_____

_____

_____

_____

_____

_____

Rate yourself

QUESTION 5: What do you think others thought of the new ideas? Consider both the positives and the negatives.

| 1 | 2 | 3 | 4 | 5 | 6 | 7 | 8 | 9 | 10 |

QUESTION 6: What did you learn from implementing individual strategies and approaches from the previous chapter?

Quick response:

_____

_____

_____

_____

Questions for consideration

- How did these strategies/approaches inform your thinking about curriculum and assessment design?
- Did your curriculum purpose remain clear when implementing these strategies/approaches?
- Did your thinking and research transfer to the practical approaches?
- Did you know more or less about your pupils' knowledge and how to help them improve?
- What would you change going forward?

Considered response:

_____

_____

_____

_____

_____

_____

_____

_____

Rate yourself

QUESTION 6: What did you learn from implementing individual strategies and approaches from the previous chapter?

| 1 | 2 | 3 | 4 | 5 | 6 | 7 | 8 | 9 | 10 |

QUESTION 7: What do you now see as your strengths and weaknesses in curriculum and assessment design?

Quick response:

_____

_____

_____

_____

Questions for consideration

- Have you strengthened your areas for improvement since the first self-evaluation?
- Are you clear about where you have gaps in your knowledge and how you can improve?
- Have you requested relevant training where appropriate?
- Have you considered how you can share what you have learnt with other colleagues?

Considered response:

_____

_____

_____

_____

_____

_____

_____

_____

_____

_____

Rate yourself

QUESTION 7: What do you now see as your strengths and weaknesses in curriculum and assessment design?

1   2   3   4   5   6   7   8   9   10

QUESTION 8: Is your vision about what you want to achieve coming through in the practical aspects of delivery?

Quick response:

_____

_____

_____

_____

Questions for consideration

- Can the vision be fulfilled in all of the different curriculum areas in your school?
- Do you have an idea of how you could embed this across the whole school and how long this would take?
- What input do you need from other staff in order to make this work?
- What are the CPD requirements for the vision to be fully realised?

Considered response:

_____

_____

_____

_____

_____

_____

_____

_____

_____

_____

_____

Rate yourself

QUESTION 8: Is your vision about what you want to achieve coming through in the practical aspects of delivery?

1	2	3	4	5	6	7	8	9	10

QUESTION 9: What has been the biggest problem or tension you've had to face since starting to introduce some of these ideas into practice?

Quick response:

_____

_____

_____

_____

Questions for consideration

- Are there any aspects of your vision that don't work in practice?
- Are you clear about which ideas are a foundational part of your curriculum and assessment design?
- Are you clear about which ideas you need to jettison or further develop?

Considered response:

_____

_____

_____

_____

_____

_____

_____

_____

_____

_____

Rate yourself

QUESTION 9: What has been the biggest problem or tension you've had to face since starting to introduce some of these ideas into practice?

1	2	3	4	5	6	7	8	9	10

QUESTION 10: Are you clear on the direction you need to take now when it comes to curriculum and assessment design?

Quick response:

_____

_____

_____

_____

Questions for consideration

- Have you created an action plan for taking this forward?
- Have you identified elements of curriculum and assessment design that need more focus?
- Are you in communication with the rest of your leadership/department team about the process?
- Have you reached consensus at whole-school level about the approach(es) you will take going forward?

Considered response:

_____

_____

_____

_____

_____

_____

_____

_____

Rate yourself

QUESTION 10: Are you clear on the direction you need to take now when it comes to curriculum and assessment design?

1	2	3	4	5	6	7	8	9	10

The results

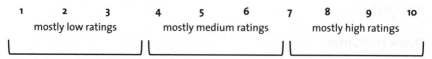

Fig. 16 How did you rate yourself?

Mostly low ratings

You still have some way to go in terms of being ready to embed a new curriculum and assessment design within your school. You would benefit from spending some more time following the different 'To do' sections of each chapter, as well as reading some more of the suggested books and blogs. Work with another member of your team, or an online colleague, to support you in this process.

Mostly medium ratings

You are starting to build a firm understanding of the direction you want to take and have begun to see a positive impact from the approaches you have put in place. You have clearly taken time to read and research the design before attempting to embed this in your own school. Now look at the areas of the questionnaire on which you received a low score – evaluate why this is and what you can do to help you improve. Make sure you are really clear on what is not working before you further embed your design. Ask a colleague to help you out and identify any training needs for yourself and your staff.

Mostly high ratings

You have made a strong start to designing and embedding a new curriculum and assessment. You're now on the path to expertise in this field and are ready to share your knowledge with others. This doesn't mean it is time to stop learning – you will always be able to strengthen and develop your knowledge – but it does mean you can be confident in your ability to lead on these areas. Check out the training plans in Part 2, to begin training others on curriculum and assessment design.

Now what?

As well as reflecting on your own curriculum and assessment design journey, it is important to gather feedback from others involved. No matter how great your ideas are, this will only work as a team effort and requires you getting a closer idea of the impact on your colleagues, pupils and department/leadership teams. Armed with this and your own reflections, you will be ready to launch your curriculum and assessment in full. Here are some ways to gather that much needed information.

Feedback from colleagues

- Survey staff anonymously about the school's approach to curriculum and assessment. Ask them in particular whether it is manageable and if it is effective for excellent teaching and learning.
- Consider the needs of your staff and how well the system that you have designed fits with staff ideas about effective teaching and learning. Bodil Isaksen wrote a fascinating blog about how her current school's assessment system matches her own needs as a teacher in comparison to her previous school which missed the mark (if you excuse the pun). It is well worth a read: 'Just say no to junk data: assessment at Michaela' (blog.bodil.co.uk). In it, she shows two Venn diagrams comparing what her school demands from assessment and what she wants. At her previous school, she found there was no overlap, whereas, at Michaela the Venn diagram completely overlaps.

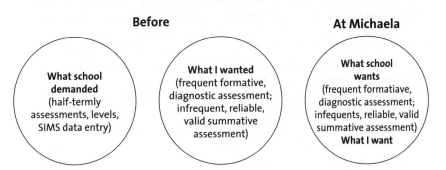

Fig. 17 Bodil Isaksen's Venn diagrams of assessment

Bodil Isaksen on assessment

Name: Bodil Isaksen
Twitter handle: @BodilUK
Website: blog.bodil.co.uk
What to read: 'Just say no to junk data: assessment at Michaela'

- It is worth asking staff to complete their own Venn diagram of their needs in relation to those of the school, this can be useful both for curriculum and assessment. It's important that you also get feedback about how well they think that they have been supported to engage with curriculum development, as this is often quite a difficult ask for teachers who have not been used to this freedom.

Feedback from pupils

I don't want to turn this into the 'Can you tell me what level you are' ridicule of the previous assessment/Ofsted game but it is important that pupils:

- know what they are learning
- can demonstrate their knowledge
- are able to identify what good work looks like in their subject.

You need measurable outcomes. These could be found through speaking to the pupils or by looking at their work.

- Evidence of drafting and re-drafting – if you can see that pupils are taking the time to edit and re-draft their work, you know that the expectations of quality of work are high and that they are embracing the growth mindset.
- Pupils are more secure in their knowledge – obviously a key part of knowing whether you have been successful is whether your pupils know any more than they did before. You can quickly grasp this by questioning pupils in and out of lessons and also through looking at mid-term assessments such as quizzes.
- Data – it gets a bad name because of its association with progress measures and GCSE intervention and can also be seen as a reductive way to understand learning, however it can also be a useful tool to help you make inferences about how pupils are moving along in their learning. Obviously if you have just created a new assessment system it might be difficult to make comparisons with previous data, however the curriculum-rich nature of your assessments should ensure some useful and interesting data to interrogate.
- Books being taken out of the library – if your pupils are reading more, without any obvious incentive, then your curriculum is definitely having a positive effect. Pupils reading is a sign of a thirst for knowledge and a scholarly attitude.
- Academic culture – I really love this blog post from Michael Fordham: 'Ten signs that you teach in an academic school' (clioetcetera.com). I think all of these are a product of getting the curriculum right and empowering staff to engage with this. It makes everyone sit up and take notice of the content of their subjects rather than a fixation on behaviour and pedagogy.

Michael Fordham on academic schools

Name: Michael Fordham
Twitter handle: @mfordhamhistory
Website: clioetcetera.com
What to read: 'Ten signs that you teach in an academic school'

Whole-school/department review

Use this table to run a Whole-school/department review about the actions taken so far. These should help to inform the process of embedding and developing your work, as outlined in the next chapter. An example approach has been written for you in the first row.

Activity/approach	Focus point	Impact	Action steps
Curriculum map	Department curriculum	Department successfully mapped out their curriculum from Year 7–Year 11. Teachers now have a better grasp of the progression of the subject. Some disagreement about the use of chronology.	Share work in CPD session for subject leads. Review use of chronology at end of next HT. Assess the pros and cons of using this structure.

Fig. 18 Whole-school/department review

Chapter 8 takeaway

Teaching tip

Be your own worst critic

It is so tempting at this point to look at the positive impact your curriculum and assessment design has had/will have. However it is important that you remain critical and see where adjustments need to be made. This can be difficult, particularly if you have invested a lot of your own time and thought into the design, but it is vital in the long term. Listen to the feedback you get from others and ensure that you move forward with your design only when you are confident that it can indeed be a success.

Pass it on

Present your vision

At this point it is important to be really clear on your vision for curriculum and assessment design in your school/department. By presenting on this vision you will be able to refine your own thinking and respond to any challenges. Find opportunities to present on this within your school and at external Teachmeets or education conferences.

Blog your journey

I'd suggest that you also keep blogging and tweeting about your journey – this will help others who are also working on curriculum and assessment design. You can set up your own blog using platforms such as Blogger and Wordpress, or you can contribute posts to a collective blog such as Staffrm. You could create a series of blog posts based around the different stages of your learning and thinking about the design process.

Share and tweet

You can share any of the blogs you write by Tweeting about them. It's also worth re-tweeting some of the blogs you have read whilst researching, so that they reach a wider audience of teachers. Include the hashtag #BloomsCPD.

CPD book club recommendation

For an interesting take on developing whole-school approaches, read: *Headstrong* by Dame Sally Coates, (see Bibliography and further reading)

Bloggers' corner

Alex Quigley has a number of interesting posts about curriculum and assessment on his blog: www.huntingenglish.com

TO DO LIST:

- [ ] Reflect on what you have learnt and create an action plan for how you will take this forward.
- [ ] Ensure you have taken a broad range of feedback and reflections – consider what you should change or develop in the curriculum and assessment design as a consequence.
- [ ] Tweet your thoughts, writing and reflections by using the hashtag #BloomsCPD.
- [ ] Check out Alex Quigley's blog posts on curriculum and assessment: www.huntingenglish.com.
- [ ] Read *Headstrong* by Dame Sally Coates.

9

Embedding and developing the practice

Now that you have tried out differing approaches and strategies and learnt from the process, you will hopefully have a firm idea of what you want curriculum and assessment to look like at your school. It is now time to take the leap, to have courage in your conviction, release your vision and embed your curriculum and assessment framework within departments, faculties and at whole-school level.

This is possibly the most nerve-wracking stage, as by standing up for something new you are also asserting that it will have a positive impact on your pupils. In fact, not only that it is positive but that it will be transformative. How you do this, in terms of presenting to your team and also involving pupils and parents is particularly important at this stage. More detailed plans of training you can offer staff will follow in Part 2 but this chapter will consider the challenges this may pose and how you can begin to address these.

Be brave

It is perhaps even more difficult for those implementing a new system into an already established school. However, in this chapter I will explore the ways you can do this to ensure it is accomplished in a measured way that will not alienate the school community. However, it will always require bravery – to change something based on your belief that it is for the greater good requires fortitude and strength of character. It requires you to fight for your principles. However, rest assured: watching the children I teach be absorbed by a curriculum I've designed; seeing 13 year olds, who would have previously been consigned a C grade at GCSE as their highest expectation, write fluent essays on Brutus' hamartia and perform whole speeches from memory, is something truly startling. And it makes it all totally worth it.

Undoubtedly this journey will have its rocky moments and therefore requires an unwavering conviction, but also the ability to continually reflect and review. In these ways it is not dissimilar to the practice of being a classroom teacher, where no matter what the evidence, enacting new ways of teaching is always gutsy as you are aware that what you do will affect the lives of those pupils in front of you. As a leader, this responsibility extends into a wider range of pupils. You will need the support of your colleagues in order to make this work.

Working as a team

No leader is an island. One of the benefits of many of the new schools is the ability they have to recruit people who sign up to the leadership's vision. If this is successful you already have a team behind you who understand, at least on a philosophical level, what you are trying to achieve. Working in an established school, particularly one that is considered successful, means you have to potentially work harder to win the hearts and minds of those in your team. This means opening up the discussion to the rest of the staff so that they have a vested interest in making this work. At the same time, you have to be clear as a leader about what you are and are not willing to negotiate. Being overly open to debate can also lead to staff believing that they control the journey.

Some of the best examples of demonstrating strong leadership and also involving your teaching staff in the process are evident in the blogging network. I refer you again to Tom Sherrington's blogs on his new headship at Highbury Grove where he is implementing a new curriculum based around Martin Robinson's work on The Trivium (see p 61). His series of three blogs (see below) are excellent resources for understanding this process:

- In 'The Trivium and the Baccalaureate: the flesh and bones of a great education' he explains how he is working to use the Baccalaureate as the framework for the curriculum, alongside developing the Trivium as the 'enacted content' of the curriculum.
- In 'Proposals for our new curriculum' he goes on to explain some of the discussions that are had, not only with teachers, but with governors and parents about the proposals. This is particularly important for schools that have been in existence for a while; new schools can hope that they attract parents who like what they have to offer, whereas old schools already signed parents up for something different.
- In 'Our comprehensive curriculum for all' he then explains how this has all come together to make a complete curriculum.

Tom Sherrington on implementing a new curriculum

Name: Tom Sherrington

Twitter handle: @headguruteacher

Website: headgururteacher.com

What to read: 'The Trivium and the Baccalaureate: the flesh and bones of a great education'; 'Proposals for our new curriculum'; 'Our comprehensive curriculum for all'

High expectations for all

It is important to keep in mind the high expectations you should have for all your pupils and to interrogate both your curriculum and assessment to make sure it has the necessary rigour to ensure everyone can aim high and the necessary support to allow everyone to achieve this aim.

Embedding and developing this in practice

- First of all demonstrate to your team/department/whole school the rigorous review you have made of the curriculum – get them on board so that they too see the need for change and where the challenges lie in achieving this change.
- As a school leadership team you have to set what the expectation will be – this might be a statistic or it might be a more general philosophy about the ultimate expectation for all pupils.
- Make sure you have identified where pupils are falling behind from this expectation and determine why this is. Does the curriculum allow them to reach this point or are lower attaining groups being fed a reduced curriculum? If the curriculum is suitably demanding, what do you need to change in teaching to ensure that all pupils are able to access this? Implement the changes needed and review within a couple of terms to assess impact.
- Be sure to have looked in detail at your Key Stage 3 curriculum – how is this preparing pupils both for the rigour of GCSE examinations but also to gain a grasp of your subject? Is there material that is for instance saved for curriculum in later years but that makes more sense to be studied earlier. Our languages team, for instance, have chosen to cover a range of tenses in their teaching of grammar in Year 7 rather than simply sticking to present tense as this then allows pupils to engage with a wider range of texts and ideas.
- Find examples of teachers and departments that you think are embracing this level of high expectations. Make them case studies for INSET days and pair them with other teachers/departments to help others develop.
- Live these high expectations out in your own subject curriculum and share examples of pupil work that demonstrates what they are capable of. In the grind of the day-to-day, it is easy for staff to let their expectations drop or to lose faith that it can be achieved. People (staff and pupils) need reminding of the successes and need a celebration of them to keep them on track.

Mapping out and reviewing curriculum

In order to get a good overview of the whole curriculum, each department needs to be able to provide a map of their curriculum. I describe the basic process of this in the previous chapter but it is a process that will take time for departments to develop. This is where you can incorporate all the work on big ideas, subject content and sequencing into one place. It will also need to include reviews and checks along the way, to ensure that it matches your school vision. Here it is really useful to direct teachers to subject-specific blogs on the process of thinking about the curriculum. You can find a list of these on the blog Education Echo Chamber: educationechochamber.wordpress.com/2015/08/08/list-of-uk-education-blogs-version-12/

History	Harry Fletcher-Wood: 'A "superior rival" to the draft history curriculum' (improving teaching.co.uk)
Science	David Perks: 'Primary Curriculum Review: Primary Science Curriculum' (www.cre.org.uk/docs/primary_science_curriculum.pdf)
Maths	Bodil Isaksen: 'Seven principles of maths at Michaela' (blog.bodil.co.uk) Bruno Reddy: 'Design your own mastery curriculum in maths' (mrreddy.com)
English	Alex Quigley: 'A new English curriculum' (huntingenglish.com) Joey Bagstock: 'Miltonic vision part 1: Trivium 21C, threshold concepts and the power of "powerful knowledge"' (joeybagstock.wordpress.com)

Fig. 19 Subject reference

By way of an example, the maps of our English curriculum that I developed last year are included as Appendix 1, page 269. I like the visual nature of them as it makes them easy to follow. My next task is to refine them with my department and then to try to produce a map that will fit on one page as an overview of the subject. As English teachers are notoriously wordy, this might be a bit of a stretch, but luckily we have an INSET day coming up which is dedicated to this very purpose!

Embedding and developing this in practice

- It will be easier if one department can lead on this: providing a model exemplar for other departments to follow.
- Obviously this can be complicated because of differences between subjects in terms of how a curriculum might look. Having these arguments about what it should look like are important though, as they will allow subject leads to develop a sense of ownership over their curriculum but also to understand how it must fit within the bigger picture. It also requires teachers to take time to really think through the nuances of their curriculum, as they know they will have to defend and argue it at a whole-school level.
- It's also important to remember that not all teachers will be equipped to do this – you'll need to identify training needs and if necessary bring in other subject experts to support this in operation.

Developing your assessment system

One of the biggest tasks we had when designing our assessment system (see our RAG rating system, Chapter 6) was trying to explain how it worked. We could be clear about how we used the curriculum maps to choose what we needed pupils to know and that we could use our testing system to check on this. However we were at a bit of a loss as to how to demonstrate progress, particularly as we did not want to use levels or to create minimum target grades. In the end we used the challenge of the test to ensure that a third were questions which were of an inspirational standard – setting a subject demand beyond GCSE – so that we could make inferences about the pupils' achievement. The questions themselves offer a unique way of setting standards. By close analysis of our RAG ratings, including the percentages achieved and the rankings of pupils, we are able to see how pupils are performing and the end of year tests help demonstrate whether there has been progress throughout the year, as they revisit knowledge from the previous terms.

We've also ensured that we've kept all the test papers, with pupil responses, both physical copies and scanned into our computers. The work speaks for itself, as do the challenge of the questions. Our confidence in these has grown as we've constantly pushed ourselves to refine questions and to raise the bar of expectation higher each year.

It's this process of constant revisiting and rethinking that helps to develop a decent assessment system. We're always talking about assessment and what this tells us about the pupils, as well as running training sessions at a whole-school and department level. We're aiming to run an assessment INSET day later this year to bring these together again as a staff so that there's no chance of anyone being unsure about what this means at our school.

Embedding and developing this in practice

- Create a bank of tests or questions that are suitably challenging, and use these and the pupil responses to set and evaluate standards.
- Revisit learning at the end of the year in the form of a summative test.
- Run training sessions for staff about assessment and include opportunities to discuss examples of tests and questions.
- Keep a continued dialogue about assessment with pupils and staff – always ensuring that it links back to curriculum and the inferences it helps you make about learning.
- Revisit the questions posed in Chapter 6 about what you need to think about when designing an assessment system (p 118) and look to see how your assessment system fits to these.

Further reading

Department for Education, 'Schools win funds to develop and share new ways of assessing pupils' (www.gov.uk/government/news/schools-win-funds-to-develop-and-share-new-ways-of-assessing-pupils)

'Assessment without levels: Using SIMS to create a new assessment system' (assessmentwithoutlevels.com)

Explaining yourself

One of the most important parts of developing any new system is being able to articulate this to others. If you can't explain what you are doing in a way that means people can both easily understand it and see the reasoning, you have either created something overly complicated or it doesn't quite hang together.

To test this out:

- Try explaining your systems to a number of different groups of people, in particular: pupils, parents and governors.
- Open evenings are a good time to see whether this works, it's also an important opportunity to see whether your staff can articulate your vision.
- It's worth running a quick session with staff to see whether they feel comfortable with talking through your curriculum and assessment. Any hesitancy is guidance that either you have not articulated this clearly to your staff or that you perhaps need to take a closer look at what you are doing.

This might mean running some more CPD sessions for staff to engage them fully with what curriculum and assessment means.

We cannot know everything, or be complete experts on curriculum or assessment but there is something to be said for spending the time thinking and researching these topics. It prepares us to embrace all the challenges and twists of the journey to come – there is no predicting how approaches to curriculum and assessment will change but you can weather yourself for it by creating your own pocket of certainty. It is about being brave enough to have control as a school over the direction of your curriculum and assessment. As Amy says in *Little Women*: 'I'm not afraid of storms, for I'm learning how to sail my ship.'

Chapter 9 takeaway

Teaching tip

Believe in your team
Schools are full to the brim of teachers and leaders who want to be involved in developing and improving the education their schools provide. Make the most of this passion and range of expertise, even that which seems critical, in order to bring the curriculum and assessment design to life.

Pass it on

Write an article
Consider writing up your work into an article – there are some excellent publications that are always looking for practising teachers and leaders to write about what they have achieved. The biggest publications like the *TES* and *Schools Week* might already have people lined up to write, but it's worth approaching them with your ideas. You could also try approaching smaller magazines like *UKED* or *Teach Secondary* or subject specific magazines/journals such as *Teaching History* or *Teaching English*.

Share and tweet
Share the impact of your work by tweeting about the embedding of your curriculum and assessment design using #BloomsCPD

CPD book club recommendation

Curriculum Design edited by Michael Golby, Jane Greenwald and Ruth West (see Bibliography and further reading)

Bloggers' corner

Martin Robinson: martinrobborobinson.wordpress.com

To do list:

- [ ] Be brave when it comes to launching your design so that everyone can feel and be inspired by your confidence.
- [ ] Work as a team with other leaders and colleagues to ensure that the whole school is pushing together.
- [ ] Remember to review and evaluate your curriculum and assessment frequently.
- [ ] Tweet about the impact of your work by using the hashtag #BloomsCPD.
- [ ] Check out Martin Robinson's blog posts on meaningful curriculum.
- [ ] Read *Curriculum Design* edited by Michael Golby, Jane Greenwald and Ruth West for an array of different essays on this topic.

Part 2

Train others

1 Preparing and planning your CPD

If you have read Part 1 of this book, you will now have a curriculum and assessment system to hand and will have begun the process of embedding this within your school. To ensure that this is successful, you now need to work to train others to have the same intellectual investment in what you have designed. This also means training others to be able to be involved in the design; to help shape the future of the systems you have put in place. The nature of curriculum and assessment is that it is always in flux – you will need a team around you who have the training to move with this and develop it accordingly. This section assumes that you will be responsible for training yourself or that you will be monitoring training, also referred to as CPD (Continuous Professional Development), even if this is not the case, it should still be a useful way to understand the training process.

CPD: curriculum and assessment

Curriculum involves the whole school and pretty much everything that happens within it including assessment, which as we've seen in Part 1, can also be a driving force of a school. So leading on these at whole-school level is a huge job. For Michael Young it is THE job:

> 'The curriculum defines the purposes of a school and the journey a school wants its pupils to take [...] the head's role as a curriculum leader is crucial.' (Young, 2014)

If you're a headteacher reading this, then you're in the right place, but even if the ultimate responsibility does lie with the headteacher, it's also important to have leaders within the school who can take care of the training of other staff on the subject of curriculum.

Later, I will look more closely at some of the practicalities of running CPD (see p 261) such as: how do you keep adrift, where do you focus your time and how do you resolve where to place resources and training? Before this point though, it's important to think more generally about the attributes of good leadership, because any form of training relies on those who lead the way. Here are some of the points that you should consider.

Vision

There are some leaders who are so inspirational (Sheryl Sandberg immediately springs to mind) that just reading about their ideas makes you want to work for them, but not all leaders will have this instinctive natural ability to inspire. What all leaders can and should have is a vision for their school, which must have curriculum at its core.

This vision should be clear for your forming of a curriculum and assessment system, but its also important to think about how it may come across in terms of the CPD provision you have at your school.

- Are you able to convince others of the vision you have and to engage the staff in committing to developing their practice to enable this vision?
- Do you take the opportunity to re-affirm this in trainings?

It makes sense to use the starts of INSET days by re-telling your story. Consider how you would word this vision and how it might link between curriculum and assessment and the professional development programme.

Aim to link it to your school purpose and consider what your answer would be to the following question:

Question: Why do you run CPD at your school and how does it achieve your school's aims?

The answer needs to be specific and avoid empty rhetoric, for example:

- 'We train you to be an outstanding teacher.' (weak)
- 'We train you to be an expert teacher.' (better)
- 'To inspire pupils with your subject expertise and drive your own professional development.' (best)

Plan for Action

In a speech to Dartmouth graduates Shonda Rhimes, television producer and writer, advises to 'Be a doer not a dreamer.'

'Dreams are lovely. But they are just dreams. Fleeting, ephemeral, pretty. But dreams do not come true just because you dream them. It's hard work that makes things happen. It's hard work that creates change.' (Shonda Rhimes, 2014).

I think this is hugely important. Yes the vision matters – the dream of what you believe can be achieved – yet if you just dream, if you spend endless meetings dreaming about what can be, then guess what? Nothing will happen. Teachers are terrible at this, both dreaming and 'nightmaring' their way through the term. Sometimes getting it right, or at least not messing up can seem overwhelming, it is easier to dream or moan rather than actually taking the initiative to put ideas into practice.

As a leader, you will need to come up with a plan of action to deliver your CPD.

- Give yourself a deadline and share your plans with your team, then make a clear timeline of intended CPD.
- Look at your timetable and block out lessons which you will use for following up on CPD through observations and meetings with individuals/departments.
- Create a timetable of the CPD programme over the year – this will allow you to make sense of what you are hoping to achieve and how you will get there.

It's worth sharing this plan of action with staff too so that they can get a sense of the direction the school is taking. It's not dissimilar to mapping out your curriculum: you work out where you are heading to and plan back from there of what you need to do to reach that point.

If your aim is to publish your curriculum, in order to get there you will have to have followed the following steps:

- Determine big ideas and areas of knowledge
- Training: mapping the curriculum
- Training: modelling curriculum maps
- Training: designing curriculum maps in department
- Training: reviewing the curriculum
- Training: re-visiting big ideas, areas of knowledge and sequencing
- Training: re-map, model and review curriculum
- Publish curriculum.

Be realistic!

These things take their time – it will have taken us three years of work on our curriculum before we reach the point of making it publishable. It is tempting to jump through to the ultimate goal, to the vision and dream of perfection that will follow. However this isn't realistic: long-term change happens incrementally. If you attempt to rush too much you are going to burn out – either yourself or the ideas – and they'll become the new National Strategies, APP, learning styles... Even the most well-researched and meaningful ideas can be destroyed when rushed through in school or made to fit into a range of systems. Joe Kirby writes about this engagingly in his blog, 'What can we learn from Dylan Wiliam and AfL?'.

Joe Kirby on learning from the mistakes of the past

Name: Joe Kirby
Twitter handle: @joe_kirby
Website: pragmaticreform.wordpress.com
What to read: 'What can we learn from Dylan Wiliam and AfL?'

Model it

There is nothing worse than a leader who talks about all the plans for the school and makes demands upon the staff but cannot live up to this expectation themselves. This is tricky; leadership roles are demanding and school life is always busy. This is why blocking your timetable and getting an overview of the year is a good idea.

- Try out some of the takeaway ideas from Part 1 to help determine which goals are manageable. Marking tends to be the worst one of these and SLT with their lighter class loads are often in danger of underestimating the time this takes (a good argument for SLT to keep a decent teaching timetable).
- Make sure you follow through on any policy you implement, including deadlines, as you will get a better grasp of what are realistic expectations.

Kev Bartle on leading by example

Name: Kev Bartle
Twitter handle: @kevbartle
Website: dailygenius.wordpress.com
What to read: 'Heads up 1: Live it. Learn it'; 'Ten commandments for school leaders'

Outcomes

One of the most important principles of CPD as defined by the 'Evaluation of CPD providers in England 2010-2011. Report for Schools Leaders ' (see Introduction, p xii), is the one that reads 'improve outcomes for children and young people.' No matter how much you love your ideas around curriculum and assessment, if you cannot see positive impact on your pupils then it's pointless. Of course we need to realise that like much in education, the impacts made may be evident in the long term; not simply the external outcomes present in qualifications such as GCSEs, A-levels and university entrances, but even longer terms and harder to measure impacts. One of my school's vision statements reads:

> 'We can judge our success by the impact our pupils have on the world'.
> (East London Science School vision statement)

It is this that will be the real guide that we have created something meaningful.

So bearing this in mind, how do you ensure that you can see outcomes in the short term?

The only way we will know it's heading towards our longer term goals is by checking along the way that we are doing our job and our pupils are making the most of their curriculum. This, as you'll have seen in Part 1, applies to your understanding of to what extent pupils are succeeding with your curriculum but it's also important in terms of evaluating the impact of CPD for teachers and pupils.

What should these outcomes look like?

- Measurable – test data, pupil work, improvements in the quality of work and cognitive ability to grasp subject material.
- Specific – trainings should have a specific pupil outcome, e.g. the use of hinge questions to improve checking and re-teaching of key knowledge.
- Linked to purpose – a school with expectations for all pupils to succeed with a challenging curriculum should have training that addresses when this is not successful and how to improve this.
- Part of a wider school culture – pupils should be talking about curriculum and assessment in a positive light; if they are seeking out books to read about the subject and coming to you with re-drafts or work, you know you're on the right path.

Accountability

Another thorny area when it comes to CPD is the issue of accountability and the often blurred line between professional development and performance management. When it comes to curriculum and assessment, the issue is that it's too important to allow staff not to engage. For the most part they will, especially if you've recruited them with the vision already set out. However there comes a needed mix of sensitivity and strength when faced with those who don't want to sign up to the programme.

One approach is to run a variety of tailored trainings, including opportunities for extra optional training for enthusiastic, inspired staff. It's also important to celebrate publicly those who embrace the opportunities offered. As much as possible it also helps to target training and have dialogue with staff about their needs and interests. However there is also a point where you have to draw a line and insist on certain aspects being completed. As a leader you have to realise that part of your role is to ensure that you make your staff accountable for their work. It's about knowing that you are ultimately responsible for the success of the young children in your care and therefore must do everything in your power to build a good education for them, whether this involves supporting staff or challenging those who are not rising to the bar.

John Blake argues persuasively in his blog about the importance of accountability in a school system (even if that's done through Ofsted).

John Blake on accountability in a school system

Name: John Blake

Twitter handle: @johndavidblake

Website: johndavidblake.org

What to read: '"Beware the Ids that march" – to the barricades for Ofsted at Michaela'

Understanding what it means to lead

Being able to embrace all of the these aspects is part of what it means to be a good leader. If you are training others then you are a leader, whether it's in your title or not. The following blogs are great examples of what it means to be a leader.

In this post Jill Berry explains how to get the best out of your staff, for this is the true role of a leader. She emphasises the importance of relationships and communication in order to achieve this. For 'Leadership is what you are, not just what you do' staffrm.io/@jillberry/xOfcXjoQe3

In this post Chris Hildrew shares some leadership lessons from a powerful TED Talk by American Principal Linda Cliatt-Wayman. Her message is clear and strong and sets expectations for the bravery you need to lead, the responsibility this creates and the combined qualities of strength and love needed to support the children and staff to make a real school. chrishildrew.wordpress.com/2015/06/10/leadership-lessons-with-linda-cliatt-wayman/

In this post Ros McMullen gives seven rules for being a leader based on her own experience as a headteacher, including who to listen to and how to interact with your staff. principalprivate.wordpress.com/2014/09/06/my-7-rules-for-leading-when-it-is-hard/

Planning your CPD

Having identified some of the key principles of curriculum and your aims for CPD as a whole, I'll now break down the specific processes that make up the planning of (hopefully) successful and sustained CPD. This will include examples of how other teachers and leaders have set about training others in the fields of curriculum and assessment.

Clarity of purpose and an idea of outcome are both essential elements of the planning stage. This may also involve getting other teachers involved in planning or running aspects of the CPD. Planning a CPD session is not dissimilar to planning a lesson and it is easy to get lured into making the same mistakes:

- Getting carried away with planning activities over actual learning
- Focusing on discovery learning before imparting any knowledge
- Not checking prior learning
- Underestimating or overestimating knowledge
- Not providing sufficient challenge (experienced teachers)
- Not supporting those at the start of their journey (NQTs and new teachers)
- Not making the objective of the session clear
- Thinking that progress can be made in one session rather than over time.

To avoid this, aim to approach your CPD session with these potential pitfalls in mind. Each session – no matter on its length – deserves proper thinking and planning. This doesn't have to mean burning the midnight oil coming up with card sorts and other hooks, in fact just like a great lesson it comes down to planning around some pretty simple points:

1. Identify your aims
2. Know your audience
3. Explain and model
4. Scaffold
5. Practice
6. Feedback, embed, evaluate

1. Identify your aims

What do you want to achieve by the end of the session?

Try to make this a concrete aim that can be realised either in the form of an exit card of sorts or a visible outcome in teaching or assessment/curriculum. It shouldn't be expected that you will complete everything within one session, so pick something specific to achieve within the timeframe, and expect to assess this in a later session. For instance, if you want teachers to learn how to create an effective test question, you should be able to get them to complete a test question by the end of an hour's twilight but the real impact will be seen when you get hold of the complete test that they write.

Differentiating your aims (producing high quality assessment)

Imagine that the aim you want to cover is to identify the criteria of a good test question. You want to have some explanation and analysis of test questions, and your eventual aim would be to put this into practice. The following table shows how you might differentiate the broad aim according to session duration:

Session duration	Aims covered
One hour	Writing a test question
Three hours	Creating a first draft of a test
Whole day INSET	Completing final copy of your test

Fig. 20 Session aims

2. Know your audience

Who is this session aimed at and what do they already know?

It's important to take this into account, and I explore this further when discussing running CPD (p 214). At the start or prior to the session include a check list to work out what people already know and where they need to be pushed in their thinking or given extra knowledge about a subject; this could be in the form of a survey, a hinge question or asking middle leaders to give you a briefing about staff needs.

Another useful approach can be to apply a more business-minded strategy to planning this aspect. As part of a project with the Education Foundation (ednfoundation.org), combining teachers and entrepreneurs, we looked at the use of value propositions to create a vision for a new product to use in the classroom. Whilst the questions have a business slant, they can also be a useful way of considering what your 'users' (in this case teachers) would want out of a training and the impact upon your 'customers' (pupils).

Who are your users?
- ❑ *Subject leads*

What job are they trying to do?
- ❑ *Create a curriculum map*

When and where?
- ❑ *In their department – during an afternoon INSET time*

Why? What's their motivation?
- ❑ *To be able to articulate their curriculum to other staff, pupils and parents*
- ❑ *To build a sequenced set of knowledge to teach pupils*
- ❑ *Motivation: subject passion/expected presentation to other staff*

What obstacles/gaps are in their way?
- ❑ *Some weakness in certain areas of subject knowledge*
- ❑ *Lack of knowledge about how to sequence curriculum*

What are the three best current solution?
1. *Model example from another subject*
2. *Bring in subject expert to guide the process*
3. *Explain the different methods of sequencing: look at examples from other curricula*

Who are your customers?
- ❑ *Year 7 and their parents/guardians*

What are their needs?
- ❑ *To understand what they will be studying*
- ❑ *To remember the content*
- ❑ *To know what they are aiming at – how they will be successful*

How will your product (CPD) fulfil their needs?
- ❑ *Curriculum will be mapped by the end of the training which will demonstrate what they are studying and where they are aiming.*
- ❑ *Teachers will have been helped to sequence so that the pupils can remember the content.*

Fig. 21 A business-minded approach to planning your CPD (Paul Sturrock, http://www.simpleventuredesign.com/)

It's worth thinking about a few key staff who represent different groups (NQTs, experienced teachers, middle leaders) and analysing what they would need or want from a CPD session. By choosing someone specific, you put a face to the group and that makes it easier to plan how you would ensure the CPD fits everyone's needs.

CPD: Designing a scheme of work (SOW) – staff needs

Teacher: *Laura*

Position: *NQT*

Strengths:

Enthusiastic, hard-working and pro-active. Strong behaviour management, particularly good with low attaining pupils.

Areas of need:

How to challenge pupils, how to plan for in-depth engagement with the subject.

Targeting training:

Send links to blog posts on 'challenge', such as:

❑ *http://headguruteacher.com/2013/06/17/the-anatomy-of-high-expectations/*

❑ *https://ragazzainglese.wordpress.com/2013/09/08/aiming-higher/*

❑ *http://www.edutopia.org/blog/pygmalion-effect-communicating-higher-expectations-ben-solomon*

Ask her to look at her SOW (either one she has created herself, or one that she has been given) and identify the challenge in each lesson. Focus particularly on the quality and density of the text resources. Pick one lesson and choose something which seems above expectation of the class e.g. using an A-level text/problem with a KS3 class. Break it down and show how she could teach this. Plan observation of this lesson. Review and re-plan SOW accordingly.

Teacher: *Bill*

Position: *Teacher – 4 years*

Strengths:

Good storyteller, good use of closed questions to check comprehension.

Areas of need:

Learn how to take risks with the subject and create opportunities for pupils to experiment with the given knowledge.

Targeted training:

Focusing on his strengths and developing these to include taking a more risky approach to questions: opening them up to probe pupil knowledge and to make them think about the given knowledge in different ways.

Teacher: *Carrie*

Position: *Head of department*

Strengths:

Strong teaching, good understanding of data, committed to making significant progress within the department.

Areas of need:

To learn how to set the same expectations for the rest of her department and ensure a shared understanding of their subject curriculum, including opportunities for challenge.

Targeted training:

Time spent with leadership on training days to see how to lead other teachers. Training to coach others and time spent on developing strong curriculum maps.

Fig. 22 CPD: Designing a scheme of work – staff needs

Find your experts

This is an important part of your curriculum design. As a lead on curriculum, you can certainly set out principles and provide model exemplars but you can not be responsible for the content of each subject's curriculum. You can never be an expert in each subject, unless you are some kind of superhuman genius, so you need experts to help you. This is worth thinking about if you are recruiting because it is helpful to recruit people who have a confident grasp of their subject not just at the level of teaching but in terms of designing any kind of subject curriculum. If you do not have the luxury of recruiting with this in mind, you still have a number of options:

- Find the experts within your school (these will hopefully already be subject leads, but it is possible that this may be other teachers). Consider not whether they are necessarily experts on pedagogy but whether they are experts on their subject.
- If your staff lack expertise or confidence in their subject then it is worth investing in some subject CPD to help develop their knowledge. This could include making links with other departments or with universities.

At the beginning of the chapter, I quoted Michael Young who commented that headteachers should be leads on curriculum (p 188). I agree with this. It's also important, though, to have other members of the leadership team who are able to be experts and guides – to lead by example. Curriculum design is one of my responsibilities on the leadership team as I lead on teaching and learning, but our team is made up of:

- the Principal – who is the mastermind of the curriculum
- the Vice Principals – who are heavily invested in the overall academic purpose of the school
- Heads of Faculty – each one responsible for overviewing and helping to review subjects in their faculties.

In a classroom, the expert is the teacher leading the class.

In a CPD session, the expert might be you, but it's also possible that there are other members of staff who have an expertise in one of these areas – it might have been that somebody has been embarking on a research project, or someone studied this during their teacher training, or somebody has been implementing something valuable within their classroom. Allow for space for this expertise to be celebrated and shared. It's too often that designers of INSET and CPD look outside of the building for experts, when there are many standing in front of them. Some people aren't that good at drawing attention to themselves; some people are too good at this. Be careful not to fall for the hype.

3. Explain and model

A good session will:

- make the use of this expertise to introduce teachers to some kind of knowledge, whether this be new knowledge or a new way of thinking about something
- it will then get the teachers to take ownership of this themselves; to embed it within their practice.

It is really difficult to get people to understand a concept or new approach without demonstrating how this works in reality; demonstrating what makes a good test question for example, will rely upon looking at a number of real examples of test questions.

To structure a strong session: consider how you would construct a lesson. David Didau's learning cycle is a good example of this: Explain – Model – Scaffold – Practice – and back to Explain (www.learningspy.co.uk). Another way to understand this is: teacher explanation and modelling, guided practice (including questioning and paired work), feedback, independent practice. This leads back into further feedback and teacher explanation in the next lesson to extend knowledge and understanding. When it comes to training teachers, what follows on from independent practice is: feedback, embed and evaluate.

4. Scaffold

Scaffolding when it comes to CPD really means how you break down your thinking and the given tasks so that teachers can find their own way to understanding.

I think that there's room for scaffold and practice to alternate. Sometimes in a training session it does make sense to jump straight into practising and to use the scaffold only if needed. However, there are several reasons why scaffolding can be important.

- To embed understanding – we often take for granted that teachers in our sessions will simply understand what we're talking about from the beginning when the reality is they may not.
- To get teachers on board – there is a tendency for us to assume that teachers, because they are adults, will immediately be on board and willing to embrace the work, but they may need scaffolding to fully understand what you are trying to achieve and why it is a good idea.
- To build confidence – it also gets taken as a given that each teacher will be confident in tackling the tasks suggested and that they can follow your way

of thinking at the same pace as you or as each other. Once you've wrapped your head around an idea, you forget the steps that you took to get there: scaffolding can mean demonstrating the 'show your working out' stage of the modelling process. Seeing how someone else has refined and developed their work (including the mistakes they made) before reaching a final product is both useful and reassuring.

Scaffolding might be as simple as providing a set of steps to follow or a checklist to use when completing the given task. See the training plans that follow to get an understanding of what this looks like.

5. Practice

One of the problems that comes from CPD sessions (particularly twilight sessions which are often restricted to an hour) is the lack of time for teachers to practise anything they have learnt about. As Willingham points out when discussing lessons in his book, *Why Don't Students Like School?*, for pupils to remember anything they learn, they have to have an opportunity to practise work and to have the chance to problem-solve within a lesson. My maths colleagues, in particular, are also often speaking about how important practice is to enable pupils to be successful in their subject. It is the same with CPD. A recent staff session where we did a Year 7 maths test, was a reminder that without practice most of us become pretty rusty. Yet training sessions at school are often treated as one-off lectures or presentations with some opportunity for Q&A without any concerted time to practise.

Even within an hour it is possible to find some time for practising, it just means that you might need to reduce the amount of content. Let's consider for instance the potential of running an hour-long CPD session on formative assessment. It's tempting to present an explanation of why formative assessment is important, perhaps exploring some interesting articles about this, followed by a range of strategies that could be used within the classroom. These might include examples from other colleagues and a set of handouts. The likelihood at this point is that, no matter how much teachers were persuaded at the time of these strategies, they will take the handout away and it will end up being moved from pile of paper to pile of paper on their desk before eventually throwing it out at the end of term. This isn't due to a lack of good intentions but a reality about the busy nature of day-to-day teaching practice.

However, if the session was focused on one formative technique such as the use of multiple choice questions to assess knowledge; it would allow for a 20 minute presentation on multiple choice questions followed by 40 minutes of time to practise creating suitable questions.

Formative technique

Session duration: 1 hour
Session focus: Use of multiple choice questions

Session structure:

Presentation on multiple choice questions	20 mins
Practise creating suitable multiple choice questions	40 mins

Fig. 23 Example plan: one-hour CPD session on formative technique

By the end of the session, teachers would therefore have a classroom-ready resource, which is tailored by them to their specific class. Not only are they more likely to use this but they also have a better understanding of the process of developing these types of resources, which means they are more likely to do this in their own time. Plus they will have the feeling of finishing a CPD session with a complete resource rather than more work to do – this is not to be taken for granted.

Harry Fletcher-Wood has written a number of excellent blog posts on effective CPD, inspired by work from Doug Lemov and his book, *Practice Perfect*, as well as Paul Bambrick-Santoyo's book *Leadership Leverage*. Whilst these are not directly about leading on curriculum and assessment, they do offer some key thinking points for planning a CPD session. Some of his key messages can be summed up as follows:

- Have a clear aim and a 'visible outcome'.
- Cut down on content: ensure you have a very focused idea/area of knowledge to learn about.
- Make time for practising every step: he uses the examples of creating hinge questions and exit cards, from the moment of creation through to their use in the classroom and back to the problems they pose.
- Make time to review and refine.

Harry Fletcher-Wood on effective CPD

Name: Harry Fletcher-Wood
Twitter handle: @HFletcherWood
Website: improvingteaching.co.uk
What to read: 'Practice files: everything is practice'

---

6. Feedback, embed, evaluate

Usually the end of the session will allow a chance for some sort of feedback, whether it is the sharing of some piece of work, a discussion of findings or some form of exit card. However this is just a small marker of the learning from the session, just like in teaching the best feedback comes after pupils (or in this case teachers) have the chance to embed what they've learnt in practice. This is particularly relevant to short training sessions; longer INSETs allow for some dedicated feedback time. So I've grouped feedback, embed and evaluate together as targets for either within the training session itself or as part of the ongoing journey of CPD.

There is nothing worse than expending all your time and energy delivering what you think is top notch CPD, only to see it fall to the wayside. It's one of the hardest parts about running any CPD: seeing sustained progress. You don't want it simply to be another thing people tick off their 'to do' list. Therefore, the best approach to take is to ensure that they don't run as one off sessions but are part of a series of trainings and they do need to have visible and concrete outcomes. There has to be some extent of accountability here unfortunately for it to work, otherwise other deadlines and pressures overtake.

Further reading

Harry Fletcher-Wood: 'Being the 1% – what does it take to make CPD effective?' (improvingteaching.co.uk)
Doug Lemov: 'Harry Fletcher-Wood's checklist for practice sessions' (teachlikeachampion.com)
Alex Quigley: 'Teacher coaching and improving "continuous professional development"' (huntingenglish.com)

Running CPD

Jo Facer recently wrote an excellent blog: 'At what cost?' which asked the reader to reflect on the costs of their approach to teaching: are endless hours of marking and the sacrifice this entails worth it in terms of their impact on pupils; how about intervention sessions or lessons packed with meticulously designed activities? I think the same approach needs to be taken to CPD training; you have to ask yourself 'at what cost?'.

Every time a teacher is in a CPD session they are not doing any of the following worthy activities:

- teaching
- planning

- marking
- reading.

So as tempting as it is to run numerous CPD sessions so that you can share all the wondrous excitement you have for the latest resource you've found or for the blog you've read; unless you know that it's better than doing the things listed above, perhaps you shouldn't be running it or should be targeting it at a specific staff group.

Consider the impact of your CPD

You should plan for the following areas of impact:

- impact on pupils
- impact on teachers
- impact on the school.

Impact on pupils

Determine an outcome for the session which will have a concrete impact on pupils; this could be the use of hinge questions within a sequence of lessons or getting teachers to focus on some 'troublesome knowledge' that they will teach in the term to create challenge.

Make the impact for pupils clear: you can uses examples of where the approaches you have used have been successful or how you foresee them being successful going forward.

Impact on teachers

- What will teachers take away from the training that they can embed within their practice? Notice I say 'embed' not 'use' here – it shouldn't be something which teachers will use once or twice and then forget about.
- What do teachers need?
- How will you be able to see the outcomes (e.g. through observations/data/ conversation/curriculum documents/shift in school culture)?
- To be worthy of embedding or even 'transforming' practice, it needs to be something meaningful; a jazzy resource, or fun trick might look great within the training but does it have any gravity to it? My simple test for this is: could the thought behind your CPD be reduced to a few words on a poster? If so, I would suggest you need to think again.

Impact on the school

- Link up your CPD with your school development plan. If a school target is to create a curriculum in which different subjects dovetail with each other, then it makes sense to have training that responds to this need.

- Take time to assess the impact of CPD on whole-school culture.
- Evaluate the strength of CPD in different departments making sure that you match opportunities across the school.
- Select leading teachers and departments to model where they have successfully taken the school vision forward in their professional development.

Resourcing your CPD

This needs thinking about both in terms of time and money.

How much time can you dedicate to CPD?

If it is going to be 'continuous' then you need it to be running continually throughout the year! Some schools operate early finishes, borrowing ten minutes off the end of lessons on certain days to enable two-hour sessions of CPD, whilst others are more flexible about allowing staff to take days off timetable to visit other schools, attend courses or work on a particular research project. Decide what approach you want to take and then make this clear to staff so that they know how to make the most of it.

How much money can you dedicate to CPD?

This is problematic, especially considering the lack of funds currently available to most schools. It's worth thinking about where you want to invest. For instance, it's worth running trainings in school to avoid costs of courses and external speakers. You could also make links with other schools and relevant institutions to share resources. Again a lot of this links to your school's vision and aims. We invested in an online platform called TeachBoost (teachboost.com) to help record and monitor observations, because we believe in using coaching and frequent observation as a teaching and learning development tool. For other schools, they might be more inclined to invest in online testing systems, so that pupils can complete tests and the data be immediately recorded for staff to analyse.

Different forms of CPD

CPD covers a vast array of different types of training, which all have their strengths and their weaknesses in terms of what they offer staff. If you're in charge of running this training, it means fully grasping the options available and considering how you want to target this to achieve your aims. Here are some of the different approaches to consider:

- individual CPD
- subject-specific CPD
- coaching
- workshop
- lecture or debate

- department training
- INSET day.

Individual CPD

'To be what we are, and to become what we are capable of becoming, is the only end of life.' (Robert Louis Stevenson, *Familiar Studies of Men and Books*).

Too often we pigeonhole teachers into thinking that they should be a certain way or should fit a certain mould, yet a great teacher is usually someone who has found their own way or ways; who brings something of themselves to the table. Sometimes, in the hustle of a school life, we forget about the opportunity to help our teachers develop themselves as individuals; sometimes as teachers we forget this about ourselves.

Over the last few years, it has been my personal CPD journey that has helped me to discover a sense of self as a teacher. I'm a geek at heart so giving my own time over to attending conferences and reading about education seemed like a natural thing to do – it's partially through this interest that I've reached the position I am in now, where I get to lead on the part of school life I find most interesting: teaching and learning. At the conferences I have attended, there are realms of teachers with similar stories to tell: giving up Saturdays and evenings to write, blog, share resources, pursue research and more – each of them clutching at a chance to own their own professional development. People have found friends, jobs and inspiration in this arena.

But it's not only in these networks or publicly that teachers do this – there are many who quietly and assiduously do this on their own. But there's a spirit in these events – a tension which makes you feel as if you're on the edge of something life altering. Each one of the attendees has someone to thank for getting them to this point whether it's introducing them to the world of Twitter, inviting them to a conference, encouraging them to speak at an event or giving time out of school to visit other departments. It is through the support of colleagues and online education comrades that teachers are enabled to follow this path. As a trainer of teachers it could be you who inspires a fellow teacher to pursue their own passions.

Make it work

- Encourage teachers to set up action research projects.
- Encourage teachers to take responsibility for an area of school development.
- Speak to teachers about their personal teaching interests and direct them to useful resources, such as blogs and education books.
- Encourage teachers to attend and speak at education events.

Keven Bartle on personal development

Name: Keven Bartle

Twitter handle: @kevbartle

Website: dailygenius.wordpress.com

What to read: 'The pedagogy leaders project: how our staff drive teaching and learning' (the guardian.com)

Subject-specific CPD

Michael Fordham, who used to be part of the Cambridge PGCE team, makes a good case for subject-specific training for teachers in his blog, '90% of teacher training should be subject-specific' (clioetcetera.com). He argues that most training, even those concerned with the 'skills' of the trade would benefit from being based around the subject. He explores how ideas such as good questioning and formative feedback require an understanding of the construct of the subject and how to apply these techniques specifically in your subject. For instance the type of the questions asked in physics will probably differ from the types of questions asked in English; and even if not, the process of formulating them certainly makes more sense in your subject.

Michael Fordham on subject-specific teacher training

Name: Michael Fordham

Twitter handle: @mfordhamhistory

Website: clioetcetera.com

What to read: '90% of teacher training should be subject-specific'

I absolutely concur with this and think that this can also applied to CPD within schools, particularly when it comes to thinking about curriculum and assessment. During a talk I gave recently at ResearchEd Literacy on teaching an academic curriculum, Phil Stock asked me what we should do about teachers who do not have sufficient subject knowledge themselves to deliver the curriculum. My reply was somewhat blunt: 'It's their job to know it.' At the same time, a school has a responsibility to demonstrate that they value this by encouraging subject-specific CPD either through allocated time within training days or through making subject development a part of the performance management programme. Evidence such as the Sutton Trust report, 'What makes great teaching?', unsurprisingly identifies:

*'teachers' content knowledge, including their ability to understand how
students think about a subject and identify common misconceptions
[and] quality of instruction, which includes using strategies like effective
questioning and the use of assessment.'*

Directing teaching and learning means I'm lucky enough to get to observe lots of
staff at my school and see subject experts in action. I feel a sense of magic when
I witness one of our languages teachers, Luigina Garzone, teach. A linguist and a
classicist, her knowledge is remarkable whether it be tripping from one language
effortlessly into another or making Latin grammar seem like the most vital
thing you must ever learn; it's the combination of knowledge and passion that
demands your attention. Recently she ran a training session for staff on how to
teach challenging knowledge in your subject. Talking to us all in target language
throughout, we all scrambled desperately to complete work and answer questions
that she threw our way. Her tone and her ownership of the subject content meant
she demanded our attention on the work. I've been lucky enough to see her teach
ranges of classes with different ages and ability, the knowledge and demand is
always noticeable; everyone sits up in her classes!

It's this that we want to aim for with all our teachers, and when you demand greatness
from your pupils, you can't get away with demanding anything less from your staff.

Make it work

- Encourage teachers to read relevant research or theory for their
  subject and present this within the department.
- Get staff to invest in subject-specific research projects.
- Have department moderation time.
- Have department/paired planning.
- Focus on curriculum mapping and subject-specific assessment.
- Spur on teachers to blog/present aspects of teaching their subject.
- Encourage teachers to join a subject association.

Coaching

One way to embed practice is to make it part of a coaching programme; this has
the benefit of being something which runs consistently throughout the year.
It's also a way to tie curriculum and assessment together with pedagogy. This is
where you can encourage staff to move from the intended curriculum through to
the implemented and enacted curriculum.

Reading Doug Lemov's book, *Teach like a Champion*, I've always been struck with
his opening advice, which is to stop focusing on all the types of teacher you could

be and instead look at the strengths you already have and work on strengthening them. It's another part of this path of self-identity and professionalism as a teacher; knowing where you can close the gap in your own way. I am not a Blue Peter type teacher; I'd love to be able to create stunning, exciting resources and cool creative visuals that cut straight through to the content I want to teach, but I struggle to draw a straight line, even when I have a ruler – as a child my colouring was always more outside the lines than in the lines! The point being that I could spend hours fretting about this area of teaching and trying to force myself into doing it properly or I could simply look at what I can already do and just make myself better at that. I can tell a good yarn and I ask good questions, so it makes sense to think about how I can use these to drive forward my curriculum.

The difference between coaching and other forms of training is that it should be completely focused on individual needs of teachers and works best to be specific. For example:

- Coaching focus: Improve AfL in lessons (weak)
- Coaching focus: Improve use of questioning for assessment in lessons (better)
- Coaching focus: Improve use of hinge questions to check learning in lessons (best)

Make it work

- Get teachers to work in triads, this allows for more open discussion and a range of observations.
- Ensure you train teachers about how to use coaching approaches (see training plan p 214).
- Make the link clear between the coaching and the curriculum and assessment focus. All results from coaching should be able to demonstrate impact in terms of teaching and assessing the curriculum.

Further reading

CfBT: 'Coaching for teaching and learning: a practical guide for schools' (National College for Teaching and Leadership)

Paul Bishop: 'The new CPD: film lessons and train teachers to be coaches' (schoolsweek.co.uk)

Rachel Lofthouse: 'Opening up a discussion: do coaches and mentors make successful educational leaders?' (blogs.ncl.ac.uk)

Mike Fleetham: '7 tips to making coaching feedback formative' (blog.irisconnect.co.uk)

Alex Quigley: 'Teacher coaching and improving "continuous professional development"' (huntingenglish.com)

Harry Fletcher-Wood: 'Archimedean leadership (2): what are leverage observations? Or, how would Yo-Yo Ma feed back?' (improving teaching.co.uk)

John Tomsett, 'Examples of GROW coaching questions: Goal Reality Options Wrap up' (johntomsett.files.wordpress.com)

Doug Lemov: 'Giving feedback as a coach – Isabel Beck and the secret life of guided discovery' (teachlikeachampion.com)

Workshop

Practical, focused and specific – a workshop is a good way to get to grips with specific aspects of curriculum and assessment design. It's not a time to get embedded in too much research or theory, although it makes sense to frame it within this context briefly at the start. The most important features of a workshop are:

- the use of modelled examples
- the chance for group/paired interrogation of these examples
- dedicated time to practise using this knowledge to create one's own resources.

These can be run as individual hour-long sessions, as a sequence of sessions or put together as part of an INSET day.

Make it work

- Provide clear, precise examples: don't use a whole test paper to teach a good question, but look at three example questions from a variety of papers.
- Make the aims of the workshop clear at the beginning so teachers know what will be expected of them.
- Target the workshop – either aiming it at one particular group such as NQTs, or making it voluntary but with a clear aim, e.g this is a workshop for teachers who would like some help with designing test questions which challenge.
- Preserve the practice time.

Lecture or debate

Schools often waste funds 'buying in' experts when they would be better focusing on those within the school. However, there does come an occasion when bringing in someone particularly knowledgeable can be a good inspiration for staff and can also help to build expertise within the school.

Whilst developing our curriculum and assessment system, we invited in speakers such as Tim Oates and Michael Young. Hearing them speak in person and having the chance to question them about their work was beyond valuable for our staff, and helped cement our ideas. This can also work as a debate or discussion both

A Knowledge Based Curriculum.
Lecture by Professor Michael Young (Institute of Education)
Followed by Q&A
Main Hall, 4.30-6pm (Refreshments provided)

As a school we have centred our ethos around the idea of a knowledge based curriculum and it is therefore something which we will have to defend in the skills dominated field of education. This in turn poses us with some important questions.

What does knowledge mean for us?

Is there a 'core body of knowledge' which we should teach?

Are some aspects of knowledge more important than others?

What does this all mean for the teaching of skills?

Michael Young is an Emeritus Professor of Education and acclaimed academic whose main research interests are 'the sociology of knowledge and its application to the curriculum'[1]. A previous critic of a knowledge based curriculum (his book entitled *Knowledge and Control* (1971) examined the dangers of a curriculum with 'vested power interests'), he demonstrated a change of heart with the publication of his book entitled *Bringing Knowledge Back In* (2008).

His lecture will aim to answer some of our questions, provoke us to think about our ethos and re-frame our ideas about what a knowledge based curriculum means at ELSS.

Be prepared to ask questions and make challenges! The more we interrogate this thorny issue of knowledge, the more prepared we can be to defend our ethos.

Copies of Michael Young's journal articles are available on request before the event.

---
[1] http://www.ioe.ac.uk/staff/LKLB_58.html

Fig. 24 Sample lecture poster

between staff and/or experts. We held a discussion between academics from the Institute of Education about some papers on curriculum and then opened this up to discuss with the rest of staff. Again this offered a chance for a serious battle of ideas.

Make it work
- Include pre-reading to send out prior to the session, this will give staff a chance to prepare thoughts and questions.
- Set out a clear purpose with key questions or ideas.
- Link to the current issues or needs of the school.
- Allow room for staff discussion and Q&A.

Department training

In a recent survey at my school I asked teachers to rank the type of INSET they found most valuable and the majority said it was when they had time with their faculties/departments. It's difficult and scary to hand over the training responsibility to someone else – you have a vision in your mind, the exact idea of what will work, and to put that into someone else's hand feels like passing over your best class to another teacher. Yet it's important for a number of reasons:

1. **Building experts** – by realising that you are not the only person capable of delivering CPD, you lessen the risk of believing your own hype and you also give others the chance to develop expertise. It's no good if the whole of the inspiration for professional development, or for curriculum and assessment, lies with one person. That's not how you make a school culture.
2. **Subject focus** – as with the idea of subject-specific CPD, much of the training around curriculum and assessment makes more sense to be completed in subject departments, as this is where you'll learn whether the school vision for curriculum and assessment works across departments. It's also an opportunity for teachers to try things out and be critical, which if constructive can be useful.
3. **Learning something new** – one of the things that you might find, as a consequence, is that you learn something new about how curriculum and assessment works on the ground level. With thoughtful feedback, the different approaches from subject teams will allow you to see new perspectives and flag any potential problems or areas for review.

This doesn't mean that you have to let go completely; it's about giving others the tools to complete the training and bring back the outcomes. In order to do that you still need to consider how you want it to run.

Make it work

Advice for letting go (but not losing control!)

- Train up subject leads or other interested teachers, so that they can understand and successfully run the sessions themselves.
- Have clear aims to be fulfilled by the end of the session and presented back to you, either in person or in writing.
- Share good practice from the departments who have made a success of the training.
- Be open to learning; it's easy to get on the defensive when a department or teacher challenges your ideas, but you have to be open to the argument even if it means that you might have to go back and review some of your work.

INSET day

This has the most potential of going awry because it tends to result in a 'cater for all' but 'please no one' situation. Yet the amount of time you have to spend on the work in hand, without any distraction or the end of the day exhaustion, is hugely valuable. So this means working really carefully to:

- consider the structure of the day
- include opportunities for targeted sessions
- include choice
- include much valued department time.

By this I don't mean SLT PowerPoint to all, NQT workshop and then unfettered time in the department (which for English somehow always leads to clearing out the stock cupboard!).

Make it work

- Offer opportunities to select a workshop choice during the day or target workshops at specific groups.
- Use role play (in moderation) to have some fun with experiencing what it is like to be a pupil working within the given curriculum and assessment system – this could involve teaching a lesson to a group of staff or setting a test to complete.
- Build opportunities to hear a range of teacher voices by having different people lead sessions (just remember to discuss their sessions with them clearly before the day so that there is a coherence and unity to the day's message).

- Avoid sessions which are presenting/re-hashing material that staff already know or that can be delivered in a briefing or email.
- Don't let sessions run over one hour, unless it's practical time with departments or in paired/individual projects.
- Include opportunities for sharing work produced throughout the day, so that staff can see the potential for successful outcomes.

Events

These could be conferences, debates or TeachMeets and can be run as either internal or external events, but they demonstrate the idea of CPD as something that goes beyond just doing your job. Whilst this won't appeal to everyone, the idealism will touch some and that's all you need for a movement. It also offers a chance to celebrate the great work of the school, either amongst staff or with a wider audience.

Public events also allow you to give something to the wider education community and to put your ideas to the test. It's the ultimate opportunity to take your curriculum and assessment model out beyond the echo chamber of the school and see if it can stand its ground.

Make it work

- Create a clear purpose for the event – is it for sharing good practice or is it debating ideas around curriculum and/or assessment?
- Decide on a specific focus/themes for the event so that you can achieve your purpose. This could be a title or question which frames the event or a specific set of debates/presentations.
- Take time to think about the format you want to use: a Teachmeet offers a more informal way of sharing ideas and is usually best for introducing practical tips and examples of classroom practice; a conference allows for more in depth exploration of ideas, theory and research, including whole-school and department approaches to curriculum and assessment; a debate offers the opportunity to confront points of tension in curriculum and assessment design and to put one's ideas to the test.
- Approach speakers to be involved in the event – this will guarantee a good set of presentations and will also encourage other people to attend.
- For more guidance see the training plans and guides to running a TeachMeet and a conference (p 257–262).

Considering your audience

How you run your CPD will need to factor in the different needs of your audience:

- SLT
- Middle management
- Teachers
- NQTs

SLT

Recently, when running a session on coaching, I came across the video 'Three coaching examples in action, with the benefits outlined'. This video looked at coaching practice in three different schools. About five minutes into the clip, we see a coaching triad which includes an assistant head who admits to having had problems with a class, possibly as a consequence from taking on leadership responsibilities. She openly talks about her emotions surrounding the class and the feeling of shame about admitting it as she worries that it makes her sound 'incompetent' to be in leadership and having this issue.

This is a problem of the culture still remaining in many schools in the UK, where it is suggested that not being perfect, and certainly admitting to needing to improve, is a sign of weakness, particularly as you rise into the ranks of leadership. Of course you don't want a crumbling, insecure SLT who are constantly confessing their inadequacy, but it does suggest that we would benefit from more of what Carol Dweck calls 'a growth mindset' (p 95) in our approach to teachers and leaders. Otherwise you will encourage people to stall in their development and to mask problems; how many leaders avoid CPD sessions because of a fear that they'll look like they are incompetent or a false confidence that they no longer have anything to learn?

SLT attendance at training sessions and INSETs is often a point of contention. Members of leadership have a really bad reputation for deserting the rest of the staff and going off to do 'important, urgent things' when a training is taking place. It doesn't take a rocket scientist to work out that therefore the message to the rest of the staff is that THIS training is neither important nor urgent. Teachers with a full timetable find it hard to empathise with SLT needing more time to do their work.

It's also important that a leadership team puts on a united front and indeed is united on the main principles of the school – particularly when it comes to curriculum and assessment. For instance, if you're aiming to get staff on board with a new assessment system that focuses on using termly exams to assess pupils but you have members of leadership who believe that testing is damaging for pupils, you will struggle to persuade the rest of the school community.

Make it work

- Agree training plans in advance with SLT and ask for support in relevant areas, e.g. sharing a useful resource or worked example.
- Include leadership-focused workshops as part of a whole-day programme; these can be specifically targeted at aspects of leading a curriculum, but will also offer room for leaders to ask questions/share concerns from a leadership perspective.
- Advise leaders to admit to points of learning in front of other teachers but by phrasing these in a way that encourages confidence. Honesty commands respect only up to a point; we don't want leaders who are overly apologetic or in need of reassurance, e.g. instead of saying, 'I got this wrong' you could say, 'This could have been better if...' Likewise, instead of saying, 'I don't know what to do here', try asking others what they would do in the situation.

Middle management

These are the best people to give responsibility to as part of training and useful for gathering examples of best practice. At this stage it is also worth thinking about how to personalise the training so that middle managers can begin to carve out their career development. It's therefore important not to swamp them in bureaucracy in the guise of training. Middle managers often take the brunt of the admin side of teaching; whether it's tracking progress data, supporting and monitoring staff, creating behaviour and support plans for pupils or running meetings. Room for personal professional development is rare; yet it's this that will shape them to be a better leader. It's also essential for morale to have a leader who is motivated and enthusiastic about their work; the confidence and inspiration that can result from good CPD can create this.

Make it work

- Sit down with your middle leaders to assess their needs and carve out time in their timetable to focus on CPD.
- Avoid setting unnecessary demands in terms of paperwork and never set tasks in the name of Ofsted. Determine what is essential for the positive outcome of the pupils and do that – everything else goes.
- Make sure middle leaders are aware of the range of CPD options – visits to other schools are particularly helpful.

- Get middle leaders used to presenting and discussing training results within their departments, as well as gathering together evidence of good practice to share with SLT.
- Ask them to plot out their intended career trajectory and identify what CPD would be useful to complete this.
- Encourage them to think outside of the box of the usual CPD: a one day course on 'being a leader' is often much less effective and has less long-term impact than being involved in CPD such as a coaching a group, conducting a piece of academic/action research, education blogging or building a relationship with another department or school. I know if I'm looking at teacher's applications to work at the school, I'm more likely to be interested in a teacher who is invested in some meaningful continuous professional development than someone who holds a course certificate.

Teachers

With a range of experience and interests, this is a difficult target group and arguably your most important. For this group, especially those who have been teaching for around four years or more, it's about avoiding the 'OK plateau' (p xi) and making teachers feel comfortable with the idea of continually developing their practice. To do this, teachers need to be willing to take risks and also move away from the idea that there is such a thing as a 'perfect' or 'finished' teacher. At the same time you have to be careful; it's important to encourage teachers to find a path to development and to get them thinking about and trialling new approaches to curriculum and assessment, however you don't want to patronise or stamp out individuality. There are many horror stories about new teaching approaches being forced on teachers who were already doing a great job and then holding them to account for not following these approaches. This goes back to the idea of CPD being centred around the combined needs of your school, pupils and teachers.

Make it work
- Know your staff: take the time to have conversations about what they need, ideally in person but this can also be achieved through middle management.
- Encourage a range of different types of CPD – get middle managers and leaders to focus on this within meetings.
- Pick the brains of your most experienced teachers; if you can work out what would make them engage with CPD then you are likely to get a good picture of how to target the wider teacher body.

NQTs

Like Year 7s, NQTs are all wonder, enthusiasm and sheer blinding panic. Bounding out of their training and into the classroom with a mountain of ideas and strategies which come crashing down in the face of reality. Their first year is a time to support them to feel that they can do the job and to help them find their strengths. The determination of NQTs to succeed is something quite extraordinary. These are the future heroes of the school and their willingness needs careful guidance and mentoring.

Make it work

- Structure is key – experienced teachers can often be left to run with ideas, or to develop strategies and resources themselves based on the overall aims of the school, but unless you want tears and terror it helps to give NQTs a bit more guidance.
- Pair NQTs with teachers who lead on CPD – this will allow them to learn how the training can be applied in reality.
- Make observations a big part of the process – but make sure you have some which have a coaching focus rather than simply a performance management tool.

Top tips about running training – what not to do

'The Office' has some particularly sharp observations to make about the way we train staff. Watch Season 2, episode 4 'Motivation' where David Brent delivers a motivational speech as part of a corporate training day to see a cringe worthy example of the potential pitfalls of CPD (and school assemblies). It's a classic example of trying to focus on fairly vacuous ideas around positive motivation rather than imparting useful knowledge. So to avoid being a Brent: here are some tips about what **not** to do!

1. Do not confuse trainings with meetings/briefings
It's really easy to waste a good 30 minutes of a training by relating what has happened over the week, making announcements or setting deadlines. Whilst these are important for the smooth running of a school, they need to be kept away from the training space; instead have a morning briefing or send key information in an email/bulletin.

2. Do not talk non-stop for an hour

There's nothing wrong with a training taking the form of a lecture or talk but there are a few things you need to think about to make it worthwhile. For a start, it probably makes sense to keep talking to a maximum of 45 minutes to leave time for questions, or intersperse opportunities for questions throughout the talk. Consider including concrete examples of the material you are training teachers about and its impact such as a video of a lesson, or a lesson plan and the resulting pupil work.

3. Do not put your staff on the spot

I've definitely made this mistake – targeting staff as part of an example lesson to question them about something they've read or asking someone to give their viewpoint, without due preparation. In an ideal CPD culture, teachers will feel supported and confident enough to enjoy a challenge, but this takes a while to build especially when teachers have been used to working in schools where CPD is high stakes and to not have an answer means you are incompetent.

4. Do not shell out money for flash over substance

With limited resources, it makes sense to invest in staff rather than spend on external consultants or expensive courses. Especially because these are often generic and don't allow for the rich connections that in-school training provides. There's also a danger about buying in CPD that does not have much intellectual substance or is based on poor research; this will not lead to long-term positive impact on staff or pupils.

5. Do not make all CPD uniform and compulsory

Whilst there is some CPD that is absolutely essential for all, if you make every session compulsory then you take away the incentive. It just becomes another 'to do' added to the workload. This doesn't mean you can't provide regular CPD, but blanket approaches to training which don't take into account any of the criteria above will alienate and frustrate staff, as well as making it unlikely you'll move forward with staff development or have the desired push in outcome for pupils.

6. Do not let feedback/Q&A become a moaning session

Sometimes in a bid to get a democratic approach to training, you open up debate to the floor about some of the policies or ideas that the school wants to put into place. This is a valuable means of getting everyone on board with the ideas and also to ensure you have thought about it from every angle. Yet this has the danger of sometimes being let to slide into a bit of a moan about things that teachers don't think work and has the potential of limiting expectations for pupils. This should be avoided by making the aims of the feedback clear and asking for specific examples to support ideas; it's even worth talking through how the session can be used constructively if you disagree with something, then offer a positive alternative approach. Feedback of work completed after a day's training can also be a productive and constructive way to hear from staff.

Further reading

'Secret Teacher: don't waste my time on torturous training days' (www.theguardian.com)
Ross Morrison McGill: 'Training day pitfalls: what to avoid and how to put it right' (teachertoolkit.me)

Top Tips about running training – things that work well

1. Tailored approach to CPD
Encourage teachers to discover their own CPD paths. Shape your CPD around your teachers by assessing whole staff needs and making sure you also speak to individual teachers or their line managers to work out their individual strengths and passions. At some point this will allow teachers to begin their own CPD journey.

2. Encourage the three Rs: reading, research and reflection
One of the greatest elements of self-directed CPD is the importance of chances for reading, research and reflection. It's here that teachers can start to become the experts that we so desperately need if we are to take a school-led system seriously.

3. Create a clear vision for CPD and share this with staff
To invest in something, you need to know why it matters and how it will achieve successful outcomes. At the start of a year, there's a good opportunity to outline the school vision for CPD, the path through the academic year and the expected outcomes for teachers and pupils.

4. Keep it focused and respect the time
Especially important for after-school twilights: teachers should feel like their time is respected. Every minute that goes on further than the time allocated is an invasion of a teacher's time to plan, mark, read, research or indeed (shock horror) have a life beyond their work. This only creates stress and frustration, which takes away from any positivity of the training itself.

5. Support and challenge
This is a very hard balance – teachers need to be supported on their CPD journey and helped to navigate their workload, but also be challenged to think outside of their bias and to take risks with their work.

6. Make your staff feel valued
One of the easiest things to do is to make staff feel valued but it is often forgotten or put to one side in the face of pressures over pupil outcomes. Yet a valued and happy staff are the most likely to engage with CPD and therefore to give back to their pupils and lead to phenomenal outcomes. John Tomsett writes about this brilliantly on his blog (see below)

Oh, and don't forget the coffee. Seriously. Teachers need coffee.

Further reading

John Tomsett: 'This much I know about... why a happy staffroom is the best thing for our students' (johntomsett.com)
Coe, R., Aloisi, C., Higging, S. and Elliot Major, L. Developing teachers: Improving professional development for teachers. The Sutton Trust
Training and Development Agency: Continuing professional development guidance (CPD) (www.learntogether.org.uk/Resources/Documents/tda0530.pdf)

Chapter I takeaway

Teaching tip

Take CPD seriously

It is so important to spend time and thought on planning your CPD, especially when it comes to running sessions on curriculum and assessment design. Trying to introduce something as important as this without proper training is foolish. Luckily – as you can see from this chapter, there are so many great blogs and books to help you out. Make an action plan for CPD over the year and involve other leaders and teachers in helping you put it in place.

Pass it on

Work with the staff in your school

Ask for colleague's opinions on the training needs surrounding curriculum and assessment at your school. Working with other staff also means you can support them to pass on their knowledge at any trainings or events you run.

Share and tweet

Share tips and reflections on running successful CPD using the hashtag #BloomsCPD

CPD book club recommendation

Paul Bambrick-Santoyo, *Leverage Leadership*
(see Bibliography and further reading)

Bloggers' corner

Harry Fletcher-Wood has an excellent selection of blogs on teacher CPD as well as curriculum and assessment: improvingteaching.co.uk/

TO DO LIST:

- ☐ Ensure you have a clear vision about the CPD you want to run and how this will help realise your aims for new curriculum and assessment systems in the school.
- ☐ Create a CPD action plan which helps roll out the curriculum and assessment systems by training staff to gain expertise themselves.
- ☐ Model good CPD and lead by example.
- ☐ Be realistic about your aims and outcomes.
- ☐ Take time to find the experts within your school to share their knowledge.
- ☐ Check out Harry Fletcher-Wood's blog posts on CPD.
- ☐ Read *Leverage Leadership* by Paul Bambrick-Santoyo.

2 Training plans

In this chapter, you will find a range of different training plans to train others in your school in the art of designing curriculum and assessment, and to train your staff to engage with new whole-school systems in a meaningful way.

Breakdown of training plans

The first set of plans 'Training plans: Leadership' are tied directly with Chapters 1–6 of Part 1 and function as a way to introduce senior leaders to curriculum and assessment design, so that they can take responsibility for this within the school. These can be run as twilight sessions or even take the place of a senior leadership meeting.

The second set of plans 'Training plans: Whole school' are based around Chapter 7 and focus on training the whole school on curriculum and assessment design; specifically on how to put ideas into practice and therefore successfully launch new curriculum and assessment systems across the school. These are a combination of twilight and longer sessions including whole training days and events. They should follow on from the leadership training, as they will rely on the expertise of leaders and existing whole-school policies on new curriculum and assessment. (NB. When I refer to the 'current' school curriculum/assessment, it means the most recent, which should follow on from the leadership training where the curriculum and assessment should have already been designed/reformed to a certain extent. Although the whole-school trainings will help to develop this further.)

The final set of plans 'Training plans: Wider world' are aimed on embedding the curriculum and assessment through sharing practice in bigger events and with the wider education community.

Each training plan is structured in the same way – to tie in with the planning structure identified in Chapter 6:

- Aims
- Preparation for your audience – ensuring you have identified the training needs of your staff and that you have considered how to set up the session so that others will want to invest.
- Resources needed – PowerPoint slides for many of the training plans, recommended printouts and online resources. Staff are also recommended to compile notes from the training sessions and record what they learn as they go along, as this is a process which builds slowly.

- Planning documents – detailing how the training sessions will run, including timings, format and content. This is centred around the following stages, as detailed in Chapter 1 of Part 2:
  ○ Explain and model
  ○ Scaffold
  ○ Practice
  ○ Feedback, embed, evaluate.

Training plans: Leadership

Aims

These series of twilights are designed to help senior and middle leaders gain confidence in leading on curriculum and assessment design. It will also be a chance to introduce your learning from the first part of this book to the rest of your colleagues.

Preparation for your audience

These series of twilights will need to involve some self-assessment (for those taking part) prior to running the sessions otherwise you're in danger of either assuming knowledge or, alternatively, patronising your colleagues. You will also need to have strong knowledge yourself, so that you can deliver sessions confidently and guide your colleagues to feel expert enough to take on leadership of curriculum and assessment design in their own subjects or at whole-school level.

Resources needed

Create copies of the self-assessment quizzes from Part 1 for staff to complete prior to the sessions. Download the relevant PowerPoints from the online resources that accompany this book.

Training session 1: Gaining an overview

Twilight

Aims

This session aims to get leaders thinking about the history of curriculum and assessment and how this has impacted on decisions in these areas within the school. It's a chance to explore the context which has informed curriculum and assessment design. It should be an opportunity for a leadership team/group of leaders to reach a consensus about the school's approach to the big national questions about curriculum and assessment.

Preparation for your audience

Leaders will need to have completed the self-assessment quizzes. You will need to lead the session, or appoint someone who is also knowledgeable about the history of curriculum and assessment.

Resources needed

You will need to use the PowerPoint slides: 1. Gaining an overview to guide discussion. You might also want to create an action plan pro-forma for the final part of the session. (See template action plan, with example first line, Appendix 10).

Planning document: Gaining an overview

Routine	Timing	Format	Content
Explain and model	15 minutes	Presentation	❏ Present the key dates in curriculum and assessment design. Identify significant moments and their impact on curriculum and assessment. Explain the basic differences between the Traditional and Progressive approaches.
Scaffold	15 minutes	Guided questions	❏ Use the questions on the PowerPoint to guide this discussion. Discuss the impact of the significant moments and how this influences curriculum and assessment within the school.
Practice	20 minutes	Group discussion	❏ Discuss the school's stance on the big issues of curriculum and assessment design. In particular, how far the school's curriculum and assessment overlaps with National Curriculum and assessment. Is there a distinct school curriculum and assessment system?
			Is there agreement in the leadership team about the approach the school has to curriculum and assessment?
			What has this been informed by?

Routine	Timing	Format	Content
			❏ Explore the common mistakes from the past recent history of curriculum and assessment. Determine whether these are a problem in the school's current curriculum and assessment, and how these can be avoided moving forward. (Session leader to gather in and review the self-assessments during this time.)
Feedback, embed, evaluate	10 minutes	Presentation	❏ Session leader to sum up the discussions and self-assessment information to determine the training needs moving forward. ❏ Group to draw up an action plan of required actions, dates and responsibilities based on the outcomes of the session.

Training session 2: Theory and research

Twilight

Aims

This session aims to provide senior and/or middle leaders with an introduction to the thinking around curriculum and assessment design. This includes an overview of some of the key theories and research which have influenced design. A twilight session will simply allow for a quick glance at some of the ideas but is a useful launch pad for some more meaningful research and discussion. In this session, your role is to guide others to discover the different theory and research in this book and to allow them to begin their own journey. You are aiming to explore why looking at this material is an important part of curriculum and assessment design, and to encourage further reading and reflection.

Preparation for your audience

Get to know the reading and research habits of your leadership team. Use the self-assessment forms they have completed to draw out any prior knowledge of research and theory, which you can address in the session.

Resources needed

Ensure that you have downloaded the key extracts from Chapter 5 from the online resources. Use the PowerPoint slides: 2. Theory and research to display the different questions.

Planning document: Theory and research

Routine	Timing	Format	Content
Explain and model	5 minutes	Presentation	❑ Explain the reasoning behind looking at different research and theory. Describe your own experience with engaging with research and theory in respect to designing curriculum and assessment.
Scaffold	10 minutes	Guided questions/ discussion	❑ Guide the group to think about any research or theory they have engaged with as part of their practice. Use exemplars of their thinking to lead the discussion forward. Discuss what they discovered, and any concerns about how to use this to feed into the practical design. ❑ Display the biography boxes of the key experts from Chapter 5. Discuss these as a group and ascertain how much individuals know about these different people and their work on curriculum and assessment.

Routine	Timing	Format	Content
Practice	20-30 minutes	Paired discussion	❑ Sort the experts into the following groups: Curriculum content: Hirsch, Young, Freire; Assessment: Christodoulu, Wiliam; Ethic/ Mindset: Berger, Dweck.
			❑ In pairs, teachers should focus on one group and read through the 'key ideas' extracts from Chapter 5. They should aim to compare the different experts and consider the following questions: (This may need to be assigned differently in a larger group – some pairs may have to look at the same set of extracts.)
			What are the implications for curriculum and assessment design?
			How does the thinking match with the school's current curriculum and assessment?
			What are the pros and cons of the different theories/research?
Feedback, embed, evaluate	15 minutes	Feedback	❑ Pairs should feed back their findings to the rest of the group, particularly focusing on the implications for curriculum and assessment design.
			❑ The training session should end with determining further reading for the group/individuals and an expected outcome e.g. a report/ blog/presentation of the work and how it should be used to impact on the curriculum and assessment design. This outcome will be important for Training session 4: Main strategies

Training session 3: Purpose

Twilight

Aims

To explore the purpose of the school's curriculum and establish clarity about this purpose as a leadership group. You will also aim to review/revise the curriculum model based on your discussions around purpose.

Preparation for your audience

They should read Tom Sherrington's blog 'Curriculum models: A sharing initiative', so that they have a grasp of what this means and how a curriculum model can be shaped. You can find it here: headguruteacher.com

Resources needed

A copy of the school's current curriculum model. PowerPoint slides 3: Purpose

Planning document: Purpose

Routine	Timing	Format	Content
Explain and model	15 minutes	Presentation	❏ Explain the idea of school purpose and the question: what is the purpose of education? Draw this in more closely to look at the purpose of curriculum and assessment.
			❏ Explain why this is important and what the implications are for curriculum and assessment design.
			❏ Using your expertise and knowledge from reading Chapter 4, explain the four different approaches to purpose, including a quick summary of the pros and cons of each approach. (Leaders should be expected to make notes on these areas as you present.)
Scaffold	N/A	Checklist/spoken questions	❏ It's worth stopping the session at points to pose some guiding thoughts or questions in regards to what teachers should be considering e.g
			Is the purpose of the school clear?
			Is this indicated in the school curriculum and assessment?

Routine	Timing	Format	Content
			Does this include thinking about the extended curriculum and the curriculum model for the school day?
			How could the curriculum and assessment be shaped/designed to drive the school purpose?
Practice	30-40 minutes	Discussion	❏ Ask individuals/pairs/groups to rank the approaches to purpose in order of their importance (based on personal opinion). Feed back to the whole group, explaining their decisions. See if any of the four can be eliminated or if there is a clear front runner.
			❏ Brainstorm the implications for curriculum and assessment around the remaining purposes and tick off those which are already part of the school.
			❏ Look at the school curriculum model and compare this to other models: how does your understanding of the purpose alter the shape of this model? (See Tom Sherrington's blog: headguruteacher.com/2014/06/05/curriculum-models-a-sharing-initiative/
			❏ Do the same with the current assessment model.
Feedback, embed, evaluate	10 minutes	Discussion	❏ Identify to what extent the curriculum and assessment needs re-shaping to match the school purpose. Create an action plan to take this forward.

Training session 4: Main strategies

Twilight/Afternoon or full day session

This is a longer session, which could be run over two hours or staggered over a day or long afternoon, if you decide you want some breaks and some lengthier discussion and reflection time.

Aims

In this session, leaders will have a chance to explore how to begin the curriculum and assessment design process: moving from theoretical to practical.

Preparation for your audience

By this point, staff should have done a lot of thinking, reading, research and discussion about their curriculum and assessment. This means that there needs to be real action now, otherwise this will continue to live on only in the world of dreams. Remind those involved of this and direct them away from lengthy discussion, instead keeping to specific actions and dates to complete this action.

Resources needed

PowerPoint slides: 4. Main strategies need to be printed out for the group and you should ensure that the leaders involved have brought along their notes and ideas from the previous sessions. Choose some of the case studies from Chapter 6 to print out and share with the group.

Planning document: Main strategies

Routine	Timing	Format	Content
Explain and model	20 minutes	Presentation	❑ The leader of this session should begin by outlining the work that has been completed so far. The group should be clear on the following: purpose, key theories/research, curriculum model (shape of a school day/term).
			❑ Having re-capped this overview of curriculum, it is now helpful to break this down into the following areas: Expectations, Big ideas, Content, Sequencing.
			❑ Model how you can explore these areas, by looking at the key points made about 'Expectations' at whole-school and determining which aspects match with the current curriculum and assessment and which need to be incorporated into thinking about design going forward.

Routine	Timing	Format	Content
Scaffold	20 minutes	Guided exploration of case study	❏ Look at a case study together. Question the other leaders in the group about the case study and how it can inform thinking about curriculum and assessment design. ❏ Use Q&A to explore how you would use this knowledge about 'expectations' to set the expectations for curriculum and assessment at your school.
Practice	60 minutes (or longer if you prefer)	Independent work	❏ Provide the group with copies of key points and case studies to look at on: Big Ideas, Content and Sequencing. Leaders should read through the information, making notes and discussing - either in pairs or as a whole group - the implications for design going forward. ❏ First focus on curriculum, feedback ideas about this and then do the same again with assessment. You may need a break between these.
Feedback, embed, evaluate	10 minutes	Discussion	❏ End with a chance to feed back findings and also to come up with thoughts about the direction to take moving forwards. Consider how you will embed this – what training needs did it help you identify? Who is taking responsibility for the different elements of design? How will you communicate with subject leads to ensure the content is meaningful?

Training plans – Whole school

Aims

In this next set of plans, the strategies from Chapter 7 have been transformed into training plans. These can run as separate sessions or be held together as part of an inset day. They should cover the different strategies mentioned – see PowerPoint slide.

Preparation for your audience

It will be useful to glean from leaders and middle leaders the level of expertise amongst staff. It is advisable that subject leads have already spent time working with the SLT to think about curriculum and assessment, so that they can confidently lead their departments in the trainings.

Resources needed

PowerPoints are provided, and staff will also need to compile notes on their work. The expectation is that senior leaders will now be resources themselves as they have built up expertise from their own training, which they can transfer to their staff and can use to lead training sessions.

CURRICULUM TRAINING

Training session 1: Curriculum balloon debate

Twilight
Aims

This training comes first because it offers a way to engage teachers with their subject and to build confidence to talk about why their subject matters. This is an excellent light-hearted way to start discussions around mapping curriculum and to build a sense of academia and aspirational expectations in the school.

Preparation for your audience

There will be a range of confidence with your teachers, not only in terms of knowing their subject but also in regards to speaking in front of their colleagues, especially within a debate setting. Send out details of the event (which can run during a staff meeting) with clear guidance as to what you expect out of the session. Build a positive vibe around it so that teachers know that they can enjoy the session rather than feel like it's just another chore of a meeting.

Resources needed

Prepare the PowerPoint slides: 1. Curriculum balloon debate or print them to handout before the event to all attendees.

Premise: Civilisation has been destroyed! A few surviving humans are leaving a post-apocalyptic society in an air balloon.

Clincher: There is only room for one academic discipline on the air balloon to fly off to the new world.

Debate: Who deserves the last seat?

Winner: You decide!

Prize: Your subject is announced as the winner in the whole-school assembly tomorrow.

Rules

- Each subject area has up to two minutes to convince everyone that their subject should survive.

- Each subject area should aim to promote the greatest knowledge of their subject; what they might consider to be the 'powerful knowledge'.

- Only one person per subject can speak.

At the end of the debate, we will cast votes as to which subject should survive (you cannot choose your own subject!).

Planning document: Curriculum balloon debate

Routine	Timing	Format	Content
Explain and model	5 minutes	❏ Spoken explanation	❏ Introduce the event and remind teachers of the purpose and rules of the debate. ❏ Explain what will be expected from each subject department and suggest the types of things they might want to focus on, such as looking at either the practical or the aesthetic qualities of their subject. *Remember that at this point you are modelling the process of speaking in front of your colleagues, so do so with passion, enthusiasm and a light-hearted touch.*
Scaffold	10 minutes	❏ Targeted support	❏ Let teachers work in their departments to construct their arguments. *Some will have prepared for this in advance so can be left to add rhetorical flourish, whilst others might need some help and/or encouragement. As you're moving around the different departments, aim to encourage a wide range of teachers to take part in the debate – not just the usual vocal ones.*
Practice	30–35 minutes	❏ Debate	❏ Chair the debate, making sure that all subjects are represented and that each sticks to their two minute timing. ❏ After each has presented their case, you can open up the debate by getting the subject areas, including teachers who haven't spoken, to respond to the arguments made. *Your job is to ensure as many people as possible get involved and that it maintains a focus on the subjects not the people!*
Feedback, embed, evaluate	10 minutes	❏ Votes ❏ Blog/ written response ❏ Assembly	❏ Finally get each teacher to cast their vote and see which subject has won the debate. *To keep this purposeful, you can then write it up as a blog or other written response and use it to help teachers think about developing and demonstrating powerful subject knowledge. This should be the start of the 'Curriculum series'.* *It can also be fun to announce the results of the debate to pupils in assembly so that they know their teachers are spending time talking about curriculum.*

Training session 2: Curriculum INSET

Whole day INSET
Aims

I'm always a bit wary of whole-school INSET days, they often completely miss the point because they are aimed at such a disparate group of people with so many different needs, that they end up not matching anybody. But there are some things which demand the time that an INSET day provides, and one of these is getting a whole-school understanding of curriculum and what it means to design a curriculum. This day can either be the start of your curriculum journey or it can be a day to consolidate a number of twilight sessions on curriculum. I have created choices of different sessions targeted at specific groups of teachers – we have a small staff so these groupings make sense for us, but you might want to consider altering these or adding other options if you have a large staff body.

Preparation for your audience

Ensure that staff have been issued with the timetable for the day at least a week in advance so that they have an opportunity to consider some of the questions before the day. Prepare those teachers who will be leading sessions and have a shared discussion about the intended aims of the individual sessions and the day as a whole.

Resources needed

Download the relevant PowerPoint slides from the online resources. or prepare a handout to give to the attendees prior to the event.

- Handouts of readings about big ideas (see blog post suggestions on the PowerPoint).
- Example curriculum maps and curriculum design principles printed out to help guide discussion.

Planning document: Structure of the day (PowerPoint slide: 2 Curriculum INSET overview)

Session	Timing	Format	Choices
Opening session	30 minutes	❑ Keynote	All staff (led by headteacher/curriculum lead) ❑ Welcome ❑ Affirm school's values and purpose ❑ Set expectations for the day
Session 1	1 hour	❑ Workshops	Session 1a (NQTs/new teachers) **What is a curriculum?** Session 1b (subject leads/teachers) **What are the big ideas of your subject?** Session 1c (leadership) **What does it mean to design a curriculum?**
Break	30 minutes		
Session 2	1 hour	❑ Workshops	Session 2a (NQTs/new teachers) **What are the big ideas of your subject?** Session 2b (subject leads/teachers led by leadership) **What does it mean to design a curriculum?**
Session 3	1 hour	❑ Discussion	All staff (discussion between internal or external curriculum experts, followed by Q&A between staff and speakers). **What knowledge? How do we determine the content of our curriculum?** *Set up a debate between experts from the school or external speakers on the subject of choosing knowledge content for the curriculum. This will be an opportunity for analysing content choice and maintaining the academic rigour.*
Lunch	1 hour		
Afternoon session	2 hours	Department meetings	All staff (in departments) **Mapping your curriculum**
Plenary	15 minutes	Presentation	All staff **Presenting our curriculum**

Planning document
Session 1a (NQTs/new teachers) What is a curriculum?
(PowerPoint slides: 1a What is curriculum)

Routine	Timing	Format	Content
Explain and model	15 minutes	❏ Presentation	❏ Check prior knowledge: What do you think the curriculum is? ❏ Read extract from Part 1, Chapter 1 (What is curriculum?) ❏ Discuss differences between intended, implemented and enacted curriculum. ❏ Leader of the session should present the school's answers to the eight questions below *Some parts of curriculum design are mandated by leadership, however it is useful to explain the thinking and reasoning behind the decisions.* 1. When you are referring to curriculum, do you mean intended, implemented or enacted or a combination of these? *'You' – in this case means both presenter and school, it is good to maintain consistency.* 2. Do your staff know and understand the differences? *After reading the extract (see above) – check their understanding.* 3. Who should be involved in designing each type of curriculum? *Detail the roles that different staff take in this process and therefore what a new teacher should expect.* 4. To what extent does your intended curriculum need to match the National Curriculum? *If you are a school that is required to follow the National Curriculum explain to what extent this applies. If you are not required to follow it explain how far you deviate and why.* 5. How far does your curriculum extend – does it include activities/content that may have also been referred to as 'extra-curricular'. 6. What subjects should pupils study? *Whilst staff should have a knowledge of the subjects studied, it's worth explaining the hours assigned to which subjects and why.* 7. To what extent should your curriculum be based around knowledge and to what extent skills? 8. Will your curriculum encompass academic and vocational/technical?

Routine	Timing	Format	Content
Scaffold	10 minutes	❏ Guided questions	❏ Structured Q&A about the ideas presented so far. ❏ Lead trainer to give guidance about how to approach the curriculum.
Practice	20 minutes	❏ Paired discussion	❏ In pairs, examine the National Curriculum and how it compares to the school curriculum. What is the difference between the National Curriculum, GCSE specs and what your school currently offers? (NB. this will depend on the stage of curriculum design as to whether you are evaluating an old curriculum or looking at a 'current' curriculum bas on the design work from the leadership training.) • Teachers should discuss and evaluate the strengths and weaknesses of the different curricula. • How does the school curriculum set aspirational expectations based on the subject and avoid limitations of nationally prescribed curriculum?
Feedback, embed, evaluate	15 minutes	❏ Discussion	❏ Bring the discussion back to the whole group and reflect about the different thoughts and findings in response to the question 'What do you think the curriculum is?'

Planning document
Session 1b (subject leads/teachers): What are the big ideas of your subject? (PowerPoint slides: 1b What are the big ideas?)

Routine	Timing	Format	Content
Explain and model	15 minutes	❏ Presentation	❏ Explain the concept of threshold concepts/big ideas. Look at extracts from Chapter 6 in Part 1. Use a variety of blogs mentioned to explain the thinking behind these ideas. ❏ Introduce Harlen et al. 'Big Ideas of Science' as an example of big ideas (See Chapter 6). ❏ Present the school vision of what makes a 'big idea'.
Scaffold	10 minutes	❏ Guided exploration of big ideas	❏ Science teacher to lead discussion around big ideas and how they fit in with their ideas of the curriculum. What makes these work or not work? *Make sure teachers have a handout of readings and the big ideas so they can use these to determine their own ideas.*
Practice	30 minutes	❏ Subject teamwork	❏ In subject teams, work together to consider what the big ideas of the subject might be.
Feedback, embed, evaluate	5 minutes	❏ Discussion	❏ Create a neat list of the ideas to discuss in the next session. *Subject leader to photocopy these.*

Planning document
Session 1c (leadership): What does it mean to design a curriculum?
(PowerPoint slides: 1c What does it mean to design a curriculum?)

Routine	Timing	Format	Content
Explain and model	10 minutes	❏ Presentation	❏ Introduce the idea of designing a curriculum and what this means: ○ Being an expert in your subject: with a clear understanding of the subject construct ○ Understanding the big ideas and key content ○ Understanding how to effectively sequence the content ○ Knowing how to raise the bar of expectations when it comes to content ❏ Model an example curriculum map and the process of design.
Scaffold	N/A	❏ Written guidance	❏ Example maps and design principles printed out to help guide discussion. ❏ Use of guided questions for the lead trainer to structure the session.
Practice	40 minutes	❏ Subject teamwork	❏ Lay out the principles of the current school curriculum. Decide whether these fit with the school vision. ❏ Look in detail at the example curriculum map and where the strengths and weaknesses are. (NB. An example is provided, but it is better to use your own version to ensure you fit with your school vision.) ❏ If curriculum maps already exist, lay these out and discuss the general strengths and weaknesses. ❏ Focus specifically on how the curriculum matches with the principles. ❏ Refine the principles/design accordingly and make a list of the positive attributes of a well-designed curriculum.
Feedback, embed, evaluate	10 minutes	❏ Discussion	Create a checklist for designing a curriculum to be used with subject leaders in the following session, and use this to keep on track with the design process.

Planning document
Session 2a (NQTs/new teachers): What are the big ideas of your subject? (PowerPoint slides: 2a What are the big ideas?)

Routine	Timing	Format	Content
Explain and model	15 minutes	❏ Presentation	❏ Explain the concept of threshold concepts/big ideas. Look at extracts from Chapter 6 in Part 1. ❏ Introduce Harlen et al. 'Big Ideas of Science' as an example of big ideas (See Chapter 6). ❏ Present the school vision of what makes a 'big idea'. Present the list of big ideas from Session 1b – session lead (a leader who attended session 1b) to distribute photocopies of the ideas gathered.
Scaffold	10 minutes	❏ Guided questions	❏ Session lead to head up discussion around the big ideas of the curriculum. What makes these work or not work?
Practice	30 minutes	❏ Subject teamwork	❏ In subject teams, teachers will work to adapt/build upon the big ideas of their subject.
Feedback, embed, evaluate	5 minutes	❏ Create	❏ Create a completed list of the ideas to discuss as a whole department.

Planning document
Session 2b (Subject leads/teachers led by leadership): What does it mean to design a curriculum? (PowerPoint slides: 2b What does it mean to design a curriculum?)

Routine	Timing	Format	Content

Explain and model	15 minutes	❏ Presentation	❏ Introduce the idea of designing a curriculum and what this means:
			  ○ Being an expert in your subject: with a clear understanding of the subject construct
			  ○ Understanding the big ideas and key content
			  ○ Understanding how to effectively sequence the content.
			❏ Model an example curriculum map and the process of design. Present the principles which were determined in Session 1c.

Scaffold	N/A	❏ Written guidance	❏ Example maps and design principles printed out to help guide discussion.

Routine	Timing	Format	Content
Practice	30 minutes	❑ Subject teamwork	❑ Examine the big ideas alongside the principles and consider how these can be aligned. ❑ Begin to drill down to the more specific subject content which comes from the big ideas. ❑ In subject teams discuss the potential sequencing approaches that fit with your subject's construct.
Feedback, embed, evaluate	15 minutes	❑ Discussion	❑ Present the work you have completed in your teams and get feedback from other members of the group.

Session 3 (All staff): What knowledge? How do we determine the content of our curriculum?

This session doesn't have a planning document as it is very school dependent; determined by the issues that you want your staff to discuss and who you want to invite to speak.

This is an example of how we set up our discussion with Martin Robinson (@Trivium21c). We took the questions at heart and asked Martin to speak to us about his work on curriculum (Trivium 21c: Preparing young people for the future with lessons from the past) before asking him to debate the question: 'Are we in danger of atomising knowledge?'

Guest speaker
Our guest speaker for the morning is Martin Robinson, who was also a keynote speaker for the ELSS conference we ran last Easter. Martin is the author of Trivium 21c, a book that draws lessons from the ancient arts of the trivium: grammar, dialectic and rhetoric to examine both traditional and progressive approaches to teaching and learning to see if either are relevant to today's educational needs. Martin is an Education Associate for the RSA, advising on creativity, he writes regularly for the TES, is an in-demand speaker, and he provides consultancy to a wide range of schools and other establishments.
More information can be found about him and his education work here:
www.martinrobinson.net/
martinrobborobinson.wordpress.com/
twitter.com/SurrealAnarchy
www.facebook.com/Trivium21c

Discussion
The discussion topic: 'Are we in danger of atomising knowledge?' comes from the increased focus on knowledge in schools, including our own. Much of this knowledge focus has led schools to look into the importance of rote learning of

'facts' and testing of this through assessment such as multiple choice quizzes. Schools are also using cognitive science and ideas around memory as the basis for an understanding of why we should study knowledge. This has led some teachers and schools to argue that lessons should be scripted and curriculum content prescribed in minute detail. What does this mean for Socratic dialogue, the intrinsic value of knowledge, subject expertise, the history of ideas and the intellectual authority of the teacher? Where does our curriculum sit in this discussion? Discussing and debating these different elements will allow for a stronger understanding of what knowledge deserves to be found in our curriculum. We would like teachers to contribute to the discussion and to question the speakers. Please see below for some reading that might prompt questions.

Further reading
Pro-scripting and knowledge as facts
www.tes.com: 'Why teachers should become consumers of curricula and lessons planned and designed by others'

www.tes.com: 'Why new teachers should not have to plan lessons. They should just get on with the teaching'

thewingtoheaven.wordpress.com: 'Myth One – Facts prevent understanding'

Knowledge is more complex
www.theconfidentteacher.com: 'Should teachers follow the script?'

chronotopeblog.com: 'Standardised lessons is a Dystopian vision of education'

martinrobborobinson.wordpress.com: 'Engaging with a humane education'

martinrobborobinson.wordpress.com: 'Teaching the trivium'

Planning document
Session 4: Curriculum maps: working in subject areas to create curriculum maps (PowerPoint slides: 4 Curriculum maps)

Routine	Timing	Format	Content
Explain and model	15 minutes	❑ Presentation	❑ Feed back the ideas from the morning sessions – explain how this fits into what you need to consider now with the curriculum maps. ❑ Use the PowerPoint to explain the process of mapping the curriculum. (NB. Ideally the subject/department lead will be able to take charge of this through their work with the leadership team and the trainings from throughout the day.)
Scaffold	N/A	❑ Written structure	❑ List of principles, design checks and big ideas to guide the map making.

Routine	Timing	Format	Content
Practise	1 hour 45 minutes	❏ Subject teamwork	❏ Work in subject teams to create your curriculum maps. *See example in Appendix (p 269).*
Feedback, embed, evaluate	N/A	N/A	❏ Display and explain these in the final session of the day. *These will then need to be reviewed fairly consistently, with formal reviews taking place once in every academic year.*

Session 5: Plenary (All staff)

In this presentation of the curriculum work from the day, it is advisable to spread the curriculum maps out around a hall or other large space so that all staff can view the work. You might also want to get teachers to present their work within Faculties. (Department presentations at whole-school level will take too long and reduce the impact.)

Training session 3: Curriculum review

Twilight
Aims

This session should be run within six months of a new curriculum. It is an opportunity to push subject leaders to reflect on and critique their curriculum. It is also a chance to gain a firm understanding of the curriculum across the school and to hold teachers to account for the decisions they have made.

Preparation for your audience
For SLT

Before the review meeting, send out a list of key questions you want the subject lead to consider in advance (at least a week before). The meeting may want to focus on one part of the curriculum – such as one key stage – in order to get specific feedback. The aim is to have a quick turn around here to keep teachers constantly thinking about and critiquing their curriculum. You will want to guide subject leads to consider the specific qualities of their subject but also to think about how this fits within the whole-school curriculum and how it matches with the ethos and aspirations of the school.

For subject leads

This is a collaborative review – not a way of catching people out. Therefore it is important for you to be honest about your subject and look at it with a critical eye. However it is also useful to remember that you are the subject expert and if you believe something really needs to be in your curriculum then it is worth fighting to keep it there. You just need to be able to explain it, in connection with the school ethos and with pupil outcomes.

Resources

Download the PowerPoint slides from the online resources: 3 Curriculum review. Print out copies of the following documents (available online):

- Curriculum review sheet template (Appendix 2, p 272)
- Curriculum review questions (Appendix 3, p 273)
- Planning document

Planning document: Curriculum review. (PowerPoint slides: 3 Curriculum review overview)

Routine	Timing	Format	Content
Explain and model	5 minutes	❏ Spoken explanation	❏ Explain the purpose of the meeting: to get a grasp of the current curriculum and see where it needs strengthening and where celebrating. ❏ Model the 'Curriculum review sheet template' that you will be using (Appendix 2, p 272) and how you will be completing this.
Scaffold	N/A	❏ Guided questions	Use the 'Curriculum review questions' (Appendix 3, p 273) to scaffold the review discussion.
Practice	20–50 minutes	❏ Discussion *SLT to record important information on the 'Curriculum review sheets' (Appendix 2) during this time.*	❏ Ask the subject leads to present their reflections on their curriculum, including strengths and weaknesses. ❏ Once they have presented their thoughts, this leaves time for some structured dialogue about their/your findings. *The questions should guide the session but they are not a script. It helps to know what you want to get out of the session and be clear about that from the start. The whole session should run for around 30 minutes to an hour, depending on the time you have available.*
Feedback, embed, evaluate	5–10 minutes	❏ Discussion Written targets	❏ Discuss what resources are needed to ensure the curriculum is further strengthened. ❏ Create a set of action steps that need to take place and set a date to review these.

Routine	Timing	Format	Content
			There should be enough time for the subject lead to have embedded this practice e.g. to re-order the sequence of the Year 7 curriculum to fit with the 'big ideas' of the subject will take a few hours of department time, so it's pointless to ask for that to be completed over the next day.
			❑ Evaluation of the whole process can be implemented after the next review, though it's worth asking subject leads at the end of the session if the conversation was clear and if they felt there was anything missing – this will help structure following reviews.

ASSESSMENT TRAINING

These trainings all work individually but would work best as a series which will allow teachers to re-visit ideas. As we know assessment is at its best when it is driven by the curriculum, therefore it makes sense for these assessment sessions to follow from the curriculum training sessions. A number of these assessment trainings refer to documents produced in the curriculum CPD sessions.

As in the previous whole-school curriculum trainings, these sessions are intended to follow on from the leadership training. They represent how to put it into practice strategies 7–10 and rely on expertise at leadership level and the expectation that leadership will by now have introduced whole-school policy ideas about the reform of whole-school assessment.

Training session 1: Meaningful assessment – how do you know what your pupils know and how do you help them move forward?

Whole day INSET
Aims

The aim of this session is to encourage teachers to think about assessment design based around their subject expertise rather than being restricted by the thought of external examinations and the whims of an exam board.

Preparation for your audience

Provide teachers with a timetable of the day in advance so that they can consider the different questions to be debated. Remind them to bring curriculum documents with them to inform their thinking. Target teachers to lead on particular sessions, especially in the debate between the arts and sciences.

Resources needed

Teachers will need to bring their curriculum maps, big ideas and plans with key content in, so that they can determine the curriculum that they need to assess. See the training plans for the individual resources needed for each session, including the PowerPoint slides to download from the online resources.

Planning document: Structure of the day (PowerPoint slides: 1 Meaningful assessment overview)

Session	Timing	Format	Choices
Opening session	30 minutes	❏ Keynote	All staff (led by headteacher/curriculum lead) ❏ Welcome ❏ Affirm school's values and purpose ❏ Set expectations for the day
Session 1	1 hour	❏ Debate	**Making inferences: Can you assess the same way in the arts and the sciences?** All staff *Preferably to be led by experts from arts and sciences. Set this up as a debate to allow different ideas to be explored – you may need to ask a teacher to play devil's advocate.*
Break	30 minutes		
Session 2	1 hour	❏ Workshops	Session 2a (NQTs and new teachers) **Curriculum driven assessment** Session 2b (Option 1 – teachers/leaders) **Assessment for challenge** Session 2c (Option 2 – teachers/leaders) **Assessment for progress (struggling pupils)**
Session 3	1 hour	❏ Workshops	Choice of 2 workshops (All staff) Session 3a (Option 1) **Comparative assessment** Session 3b (Option 2) **Creating excellent questions**
Lunch	1 hour		
Session 4	2 hours	❏ Department meeting	All staff (in departments) **Mapping your assessment**
Plenary	15 minutes	❏ Presentation	All staff **Presenting your assessment maps**

Planning document
Session 2a (NQTs and new teachers): Curriculum driven assessment (PowerPoint slides: 2a Curriculum driven assessment)

Routine	Timing	Format	Content
Explain and model	5 minutes	❏ Keynote	❏ The lead trainer should present the main ideas of the session: thinking beyond qualifications and examinations to understand what it means to teach your subject at the highest level. They should pose the questions: ○ What would success in your subject look like in a life without examinations? ○ How do we match the assessment principles from Chapter 6?
Scaffold	20 minutes	❏ Discussion/ debate	❏ Hold a scaffolded discussion about the issues around preparing pupils for qualifications and how curriculum and assessment fit together. Some example question prompts might be: ○ How do you avoid the 'teach the specification' trap? ○ Does it matter if our pupils pass their exams? What is a pass? ○ Should we be preparing them to pass these exams or should we be teaching them our subject? ○ Can you do both? What does that look like? *The lead trainer can facilitate and scaffold the discussion to ensure a diverse range of voices and ideas.*
Practice	20 minutes	❏ Subject teamwork	❏ Subject groups should work together to create mission statements for both their curriculum and assessment, based on the ideas that have been discussed. ❏ They will use their curriculum maps – big ideas and key content, to determine what it means to succeed in their subject beyond qualifications. ❏ Teachers should then make a list of their current assessment, including summative and formative assessment in their subject. They should evaluate how far their assessment is driven by the curriculum and not the other way around.
Feedback, embed, evaluate	15 minutes	❏ Presentations	❏ Write up the mission statements by staff and share them. *These should be used within curriculum review meetings and subject trainings to evaluate whether these ideas are being seen in practice.*

Planning document
Session 2b (Option 1: Teachers/Leaders): Assessment for challenge
(PowerPoint slides: 2b Assessment for challenge

Routine	Timing	Format	Content
Scaffold *(This runs first in this instance as it is a way of assessing prior knowledge and therefore scaffolding learning throughout the training.)*	10 minutes	❏ Brainstorm/ discussion	❏ Get teachers to brainstorm the different forms of assessment that they already know. *Circulate, looking for good examples to share and to see if there are any that they are not aware of that need to be added.* ❏ Share these as a group. ❏ Then ask teachers to think about what is meant by 'challenge' and how this links to assessment. ❏ Collate ideas on a flipchart/board.
Explain and model	10 minutes	❏ Presentation/ film	❏ Get an expert teacher from your school to demonstrate either by film or through examples of work, how they have used assessment to challenge a pupil academically. *There are also excellent resources online to examine some of the possible techniques, such as: 'Check for understanding: Julia Goldenheim's 7th grade English class (video)' (teachlikeachampion.com)*
Practice	30 minutes	❏ Group work	❏ Divide into groups of three and give each group an example pupil from your school with a sample of their work. Choose work that is of high quality, the idea is to look at the next challenge rather than correcting basic errors. *Do not reveal who the pupil is, as this may lead them on to a discussion about personality/behaviour rather than work – ideally type up the examples.* ❏ Ask the groups to: 1. Identify the strengths 2. Identify the areas for improvement 3. Use the notes made on assessment and challenge them to think of three different forms of assessment they would use to help the pupil improve. 4. Determine how they would use these assessments within their subject areas.
Feedback, embed, evaluate	10 minutes	❏ Presentations	❏ Presentation of the different ideas and explanation of the reasoning by each group to the whole session. *The embedding will come through considering how these assessment elements can be included in the assessment map.*

Planning document
Session 2c (Option 2: Teachers/Leaders): Assessment for progress (struggling pupils) (PowerPoint slides: 2c Assessment for progress)

Routine	Timing	Format	Content
Scaffold *(This runs first in this instance as it is away of assessing prior knowledge and therefore scaffolding learning throughout the training.)*	10 minutes	❏ Guided discussion/ brainstorm	❏ Get teachers to brainstorm the different forms of assessment that they already know. *Circulate, looking for good examples to share and to see if there are any that they are not aware of that need to be added.* ❏ Share these as a group. ❏ Then ask teachers to think about what is meant by 'progress' and 'struggling pupils'. ❏ Consider how this links to assessment. Collate ideas on a flipchart/board.
Explain and model	10 minutes	❏ Presentation/ film	❏ Watch the Ron Berger clip of Austin's Butterfly (see Chapter 5) and discuss what this means for expectations and progress. ❏ Watch Dylan Wiliam on 'Hinge questions' https://www.youtube.com/watch?v= Mh5SZZt2o7k
Practice	30 minutes	❏ Group work	❏ Divide into groups of three and give each group an example pupil from your school with a sample of their work. Choose work that suffers from basic errors and misconceptions. *Do not reveal who the pupil is, as this may lead them onto a discussion about personality/behaviour rather than work – ideally type up the examples.* ❏ Ask the groups to: 1. Identify the strengths. 2. Identify the areas for improvement. 3. Use the notes made on assessment and progress to think of three different forms of assessment they would use to help the pupil improve. 4. Determine how they would use these assessments within their subject areas.
Feedback, embed, evaluate	10 minutes	❏ Presentations	❏ Presentation of the different ideas and explanation of the reasoning by each group to the whole session. *The embedding will come through considering how these assessment elements can be included in the assessment map.*

Planning document
Session 3a (Option 1): Comparative assessment (PowerPoint slides: 3a Comparative assessment)

Routine	Timing	Format	Content
Explain and model	20 minutes	Film/ discussion	❑ Watch Daisy Christodoulu talk about how to use comparative assessment for marking essays instead of using criteria. (23:00–31:38) https://www.youtube.com/watch?v=PGfIM_ b6loU ❑ Consider these questions as a group: 　○ Are we wrong to use criteria? 　○ What are the strengths and weaknesses of using comparative assessment?
Scaffold	N/A	N/A	❑ Use questions on the PowerPoint to support teachers as they work on their comparative assessment.
Practice	25 minutes	Group work	❑ In groups of three, teachers should look at a selection of pupil essays and try to comparatively assess them. ❑ One member of the group should write down their thoughts on strengths and weaknesses of this method, as they go along.
Feedback, embed, evaluate	15 minutes	Discussion	❑ Compare the feedback from the different groups and determine whether it is worth using this as an assessment tool. ❑ If not – is there anything to be learnt from it that is useful? ❑ If yes – then hold onto the ideas around these to use into your assessment map session later.

Planning document
Session 3b (Option 2): Creating excellent questions (PowerPoint slides: 3b Creating excellent questions)

Routine	Timing	Format	Content
Explain and model	20–30 minutes	Presentation	❑ Explain the motivation of the session, which is to: 　○ learn what common mistakes people make when designing test questions 　○ learn what makes a challenging high-quality question 　○ create your own test questions. ❑ Explain the three different types of questions: 　○ Rote learning 　○ Application of knowledge 　○ Challenging thinking about knowledge

Routine	Timing	Format	Content
			❑ Explain what can be inferred from these types of questions: what does it tell you about how much you have taught them and how does it help you and the pupils to know how to move forward. ❑ Look at some key examples of questions from examination papers and explain common errors such as badly phrased questions/weak allocation of marks. ❑ Then explore some key strong examples and why these are effective. Share criteria and ask teachers to create their own question(s).
Scaffold	N/A	Provide handout of assessment criteria	❑ Create a list of assessment criteria – either as a group or prescribed by the school. *See Appendix 4 for an example criteria.*
Practice	30-40 minutes	Subject teamwork	❑ Choose whether to have some of the practice time spent exploring examples and determining successful criteria or whether this can be all done through the explanation/model process. ❑ Teachers should then work in subject areas to create their own question(s) using the criteria to guide them.
Feedback, embed, evaluate	N/A	N/A	❑ Use these questions to form end of term tests and evaluate their impact after the results.

Planning document
Session 4 (All staff): Mapping your assessment (PowerPoint slides: 4 Mapping for your assessment)

Routine	Timing	Format	Content
Explain and model	20 minutes	❑ Presentation	❑ Use Dylan Wiliam's example of assessment mapping (*SSAT Principled Assessment Design*, see Chapter 7) as a guide for how to think about this, but subject departments should work as a team to consider how best to produce their own maps. *Wiliam suggests splitting the assessments into three categories: formative, summative and evaluative (accountability) and also considering the timescale for using these – in lessons, over a week, per half term, and annually.* ❑ Feed back on the ideas gathered throughout the day.
Scaffold	N/A	N/A	N/A

Routine	Timing	Format	Content
Practice	1 hour and 40 minutes	❑ Subject teamwork	❑ Create an assessment map, making sure that you do this in line with your curriculum – keep re-visiting what you want to teach and the best methods for assessing this. See exemplar on PowerPoint. ❑ Also consider the elements of a culture of excellence (see Berger, Chapter 5), challenge and progress for your range of pupils.
Feedback, embed, evaluate	15 minutes	❑ Presentation	❑ Present the assessment maps to the rest of the staff at the end of the day. These should be reviewed fairly consistently, with formal reviews taking place once in every academic year.

Training session 2: Multiple choice questions

Twilight
Aims

To introduce the idea of multiple choice questions (MCQs) and how to design effective questions which can be used in your subject to make reliable inferences about how much of the basic factual knowledge pupils have been able to learn.

This session lays out the basics of how to design a MCQ test and the reason behind using them.

Preparation for your audience

Teachers need to have thought out the key factual knowledge from their subject that they want pupils to learn and therefore be tested on in the quiz. MCQs can be used to test interpretation and analysis but factual knowledge is a good starting point. See Appendix 5.

Resources needed

Use the checklist (Appendix 6) and the PowerPoint slides: 2 Multiple choice questions that can be downloaded from the online resources to guide you on how to create these questions.

Planning document: Multiple choice questions

Routine	Timing	Format	Content
Explain and model	15 minutes	❏ Presentation	❏ Explain the reasoning and theory behind MCQs: ○ To assess key factual knowledge. ○ To measure what you value. ○ To help you make reliable inferences about what pupils know. *Researchers such as Dylan Wiliam have produced excellent work on how to use MCQs to assess higher order thinking (see Part 1: Chapter 5)* ❏ Model some key examples of questions looking at appropriate stems and alternatives. *Vanderbilt University has provided some excellent examples on their website: https://cft.vanderbilt.edu/guides-sub-pages/writing-good-multiple-choice-test-questions/ Additionally, you might like to show an example of a complete MCQ test on one of your subjects, as an exemplar.*
Scaffold	N/A	❏ Written checklist	❏ Use a checklist for teachers to check off against whilst they are designing their questions (see Appendix 6, <XREF>). This is a useful way to help teachers shape their own questions without losing sight of the ideas you have explored around effectiveness. *The lead on this should also be around to help teachers as they generate questions.*
Practice	35 minutes	❏ Subject teamwork	❏ In subject teams, teachers should now work on creating their own MCQs with the scaffolded checklist to help them. *It makes sense, if you have a large enough venue, for everyone to stay in the same space so that the trainer can help people as they go along.*
Feedback, embed, evaluate	5 minutes	❏ Q&A	❏ Most of the feedback, embedding and evaluating will come as a consequence of having used the tests with pupils. This is when you can determine how it impacts on their outcomes, both in the taking of the test and how it helps them understand improving their learning going forward. ❏ At the end of the training session, a quick Q&A about the process of developing MCQs isn't a bad idea though and it flags up any needs teachers might still have from the training. *See Appendix 7 for an example survey on this for teachers.*

Training session 3: Marking party

This is an idea that one of our vice principals introduced to our school, he had found the idea during some online research, as a way to share examples of good marking and excellent pupil work. It was also an opportunity to further the discussion we were already having about how our marking was/was not enabling pupils to access the curriculum and reach our high expectations.

Twilight

Aims

This is very much a chance to celebrate the work that has been done and for everyone to have a look at each others' work. This means you need to mostly just let people get on with it.

Preparation for your audience

Teachers need to know about this in advance so that they can prepare to have a set of books to bring to the marking party. They also need to be clear on what is expected of them – are they going to be judged on their marking or is it really an opportunity to share?

Resources needed

Teachers will need to bring a selection of exercise books with them to demonstrate a range of pupil work. Use the PowerPoint slides: 3 Marking party that can be downloaded from the online resources as a resource for the checklist/spoken questions.

Planning document: Marking party

Routine	Timing	Format	Content
Explain and model	10 minutes	❑ Presentation	❑ Explain the reasoning behind having the marking party, including what type of things you are looking for. *This might mean you want people just to have a general look at books or focus on something specific such as quality of pupil work/evidence of re-drafting/key examples of marking helping to move a pupil forward. You can give an example of this yourself – describing what you've inferred from a piece of marking you have looked at.*

Routine	Timing	Format	Content
Scaffold	5 minutes	❑ Checklist/ spoken questions	❑ It's worth stopping the session at points in order to put out some guiding thoughts or questions about what teachers should be looking for, e.g. ○ Has anyone found a piece of marking that demonstrates a demand for excellence? How have the pupils responded? ○ Is there evidence of positive outcomes from any of our trainings, such as the use of multiple choice questions? How do you know these are positive outcomes? Are there any particularly strong examples of assessment which you would like to use? ○ Where can you see pupils making progress in their thinking and learning? ○ Where can you see examples of pupils being supported to access the curriculum or challenged to push themselves further?
Practice	20–30 minutes	❑ Discussion	❑ Lay all the books out around the room in different subjects or by year group depending on what exactly you are looking for. ❑ Teachers should then take time to walk around the room and discuss the different examples they look at, as well as asking questions of each other in regards to the marking/work set.
Feedback, embed, evaluate	10 minutes	❑ Feedback	❑ End with a chance to feed back findings and also to come up with thoughts about the direction to take moving forwards. ❑ Consider how you will embed this: what training needs did it help you identify? What examples of good practice did you find to share?

Training plans - wider world

Training session 1: TeachMeet

One of the best things that ever happened to me as a teacher was being introduced to the concept of TeachMeets. I've been to a number now both as guest and speaker, in all kinds of destinations – even on the top deck of a London bus! I've also been involved in running TeachMeets in my school. These can either be run as internal (to the school) or external (open to wider education community) events – it is a really fantastic way to get all staff involved in their CPD and allow a range of people to present their ideas without it being an official training. This means you don't have quite the same pressure about ensuring every presentation is perfect or that it needs some kind of immediate outcome. It is more about encouraging a culture of shared ideas and risk-taking.

Evening event

Aims

Choose a theme for the TeachMeet which embraces some of the ideas that you are trying to explore. This could be something like the use of assessment within the classroom or tackling challenging knowledge. I recently ran a TeachMeet where colleagues presented on excellent practice that they had observed in someone else's classroom – this is a good way of encouraging shared engagement and offers a chance for the more shy or humble to present ideas.

- Be really clear on the format of the presentations: will people be using technology or just talking? How strict are the time limits?
- Approach people directly (either in person or via personal message) to encourage them to sign up to present. As soon as you get a couple of volunteers to present, you are likely to encourage others. I try to ensure that at least one of the first sign-ups is someone who has not presented before, this helps to build confidence amongst other staff and ensures you don't simply listen to the same voices over and over again.
- Treat the event seriously – set it up in advance and publicise it, as if it was an external event. Eventbrite is a great resource for setting up an event and distributing tickets (they can still be free of charge but having tickets gives the event have more gravity and takes it away from a regular staff training).
- Consider when to run the TeachMeet. I think it works well to run it at the end of term as a celebration event, but some terms are better for this than others. You want enthusiastic energy so if you know that staff in your school tend to be burned out by the end of the school term then consider holding it earlier.
- Make it a proper event by including refreshments and a special layout – perhaps with a later start than a regular meeting. This detail sounds a bit vacuous but I think it's important to establish this kind of event as distinct from a meeting, it's more about a culture of shared thinking.
- I would recommend making it a voluntary event – there's nothing worse than forcing teachers who don't want to be there to come along and engage positively. It's better to establish this kind of event, build a buzz around it and then wait for others to come on board.

Preparation for your audience

Ensure you are there at the start or have nominated another teacher to be the host. You'll need someone to keep the momentum going and to bridge the gap between presentations. You'll also need someone to keep up a relentlessly positive approach in the face of any cynicism.

- Decide early on whether you want the audience to engage critically with the presentations and apply this rule to all. There is a danger of letting people get up to present a 'great idea' only to be torn down by colleagues. If you feel as a

school that you're ready for some constructive criticism then great, but make sure that's true for everyone.
- Use Twitter to tweet out ideas from the different presentations. If you have any prolific Twitter users amongst the staff you can even set up your own hashtag and ask them to make the most of this.
- After the TeachMeet has ended I think this is a great opportunity for a social amongst staff – you'll often find that the ideas being discussed are developed and thought through in conversations in the pub later.
- Once the event is all over, try to release some kind of summary/blog/recap of the Tweets from the event. This will help to keep the momentum going. It's also worth asking teachers to feedback about when they use any of the ideas that were presented – this might even be worth a follow-up TeachMeet.

Resources needed

You will need a computer and a big screen to display presentations, you might also want to consider another screen to show Twitter interactions. You'll also need internet wifi access for your visitors, a timer and name shuffle tool. It's also a good idea to provide a selection of refreshments for your guests.

Planning document: Stucture of the TeachMeet

Session	Timing	Format	Content
Opening	5–20 minutes *(depending on whether it's an internal/ external event)*	❏ Keynote	❏ Have some music on whilst people arrive and some refreshments so that people feel like they are at an event rather than a meeting. ❏ Introduce the event. ❏ Give out wifi and # details so that people can Tweet about what is going on. *If you have access to two screens, you can use one for the presentations and another to show the live stream of Tweets.* ❏ Be clear about the format such as how strict you are with timings and when people can/cannot ask questions. ❏ Briefly explain the inspiration behind the event and then kick off!
Session 1	45–60 minutes	❏ Presentations	❏ Invite a set number of presenters to give their presentations. *Use either a random shuffle approach – by putting names into an online system – or ask for presenter's material in advance and structure a timetable which balances different types of presenters and content. In this way you can avoid repeated information or the perils of an experienced presenter speaking directly before a newbie.*

Session	Timing	Format	Content
Break	15 minutes (refreshments and music)		
Session 2	30–45 minutes	❑ Presentations	❑ Same as Session 1. *You may want to remind people to Tweet.*
Plenary/ networking	5 minute thank you Flexible timing for networking	❑ Keynote and informal conversation	❑ A quick thank you and links to relevant blogs/presentations will suffice here, though you may also choose to add a Q&A. ❑ Informal conversation and networking (wine usually helps) – to further interesting discussions about the presentations.

Training session 2: Education conference

One of the best ways to set a whole-school vision is to put yourself on the stage. If you can put your ideas out to test in the wider education world and still stand firm, you know you're doing well. It's not about being a publicity stunt for the school, although of course hosting an education event isn't bad PR, it's more about engaging with the education world outside of your school. Much of this book has been dedicated to the idea of looking outside of yourselves in order to make it work within; not dissimilar to the idea of a curriculum that takes pupils beyond their own experiences. Hosting an event for some of your online collaborators and for other educators perhaps not in the Twitter and blogosphere (yes there are some), allows you to take this to the ultimate level.

Day event

Aims

Decide on what you want the theme of the event to be; what do you want it to be about, is this something that other people are interested in/talking about? Don't be afraid of being controversial – education types love something that will create a bit of a ruckus.

Determine the format for the event: keynotes, debates, workshops? I tend to favour the top and tail keynote, with a selection of debates/panel discussions in between. I'm not a massive fan of practical workshops at these kind of events – I like going to hear experts present and discuss, but that's a personal preference.

Preparation for your audience

- Consider your audience: what type of events do they usually attend and respond well to?

- Make a list of presenters that you want to speak. You'll want some well-known names in order to get the event off the ground and to encourage others to speak. However, I think it's also good to get some new speakers involved to avoid the conference broken record. It's also good to think about the diversity of your speakers – if you want to fully represent the profession, you need that represented in your line up.
- Harass them. OK, not literally but it's good to make as much contact as possible. If you know them, then speak to them directly and get their name signed up as quickly as possible; then when you are contacting other speakers you can start mentioning names of others who are involved. Send individual, personalised messages which explain why you have chosen to ask them for the event – don't eulogise, keep it brief – but it's important that people feel they have been chosen for a reason. It's better if you can approach them with a specific purpose in mind: e.g. we'd like you to be in a debate about whether we should be testing pupils more.
- Use Eventbrite to set up an online event for free; you can organise the sale of tickets from here as well as using it to publicise.
- Aim to start publicising the event a few months in advance – the education calendar gets pretty busy. Make sure you don't clash with any of the big events such as ResearchEd, WomanEd, Pedagoo or the Education Festival.
- Make sure you get the programme out there as quickly as possible – people are more likely to sign up when they know who is speaking.
- Use Twitter and other social networks to spread the word – this is the best publicity and encourages others to join in.

Running the event

Unlike the other trainings, there is no clear or specific structure for running the event, though you need to think about these key aspects.

- Practicalities – this is the basics from providing refreshments, to having someone help open the venue (usually your school) at the beginning of the day. You will not have time to set up the whole place, so you will need a team of teachers/pupils/volunteers to get everything in place. You also need to think about how you plan to register people, signs and logistical information, as well as ensuring a good open wifi connection for the day. Speakers will also need to be looked after, you may want to consider having a specific room where they can base themselves and you'll need someone on hand to deal with technical requests and issues.
- Chairing – it's important to think not only about who you have speaking, but who will chair debates, discussion and introduce speakers. A good chair needs to know when to hold back and when to insist that you switch to another

speaker or take a question. They also need to be able to field questions from the floor – preferably taking three or so at a time, and ensuring that they write them down in case the speaker loses their way. They also need to deal with the inevitable question from the audience, which instead of being a question is actually a long speech about their opinion – knowing when to cut in and demand a question or an end to the statement is a real skill.

- Participation – it's useful to think about how much participation you want from your audience, both in person and online. Carve out opportunities for questions and discussion, as well as encouraging the use of Twitter and other social networks to share thoughts through the day. You can use specific hashtags, as well as competitions to keep people Tweeting, as well as Tweeting a lot yourself!
- Outcomes – after an event, it is a good idea to write up some of your thoughts in the form of a blog or a paper. You should also encourage other speakers to share their ideas, as well as audience members. You can use the hashtag to carry on collating the ideas from the day or even film speakers so that these can be shared online.

3 Evaluation and next steps

At last. You have put in all the work to develop a curriculum and linked assessment system, you've established a CPD programme to ensure this is embedded across the school and you've started to transform your school culture. Time for a sit down? Who are you kidding. Well maybe, a glass of something congratulatory, but now you have the difficult process of determining whether what you are doing is working and how to continually refine and review it. As it's been said already: in teaching you never stop learning to be better.

We have already determined that for CPD to be effective it needs to result in positive outcomes for teachers, pupils and the whole school. Great CPD will impact on all these groups and will become truly continuous, embedded in the everyday life of staff and school.

How do you evaluate the success of your CPD and whether or not it is achieving these outcomes?

There are a number of different evaluation tools that you can use to help this process, but you need to ensure that when combined, they allow you to ascertain the following:

- What have teachers learnt?
- What has been the impact on pupils?
- How can the school maximise the impact of CPD?

There should be a timeline for evaluation and somebody in charge of keeping on track of the different CPD in the school, particularly off-site CPD for individual teachers. We use a simple form which asks teachers to explain the nature of the CPD, who it is designed to impact upon (personal/department/ school level) and how learning from the training will be disseminated.

Use of surveys

Surveys are a good way to get an understanding of both pupil and teacher ideas about the effectiveness of CPD.

Pupil surveys

At his school, Nick Rose has used pupil surveys to evaluate the impact of their coaching programme. These surveys were used pre-coaching to identify areas of focus, in this case 'classroom control' and after the coaching process to see if there had been any improvement. Whilst the surveys do seem to show some improvement, he is quick to say that this is not completely reliable evidence but that it can help us to inform planning.

Nick Rose on pupil surveys

Name: Nick Rose
Twitter handle: @Nick_J_Rose
Website: evidenceintopractice.wordpress.com
What to read: 'Using student surveys to measure the impact of coaching'

Teacher surveys

You can survey teachers to find out both what they think needs to be the focus of CPD and as an evaluation after training. You can anonymise surveys to get the most genuine responses or use named surveys to help target specific teachers. Ensure you tailor your questions – much like designing test questions, you could do well with some multiple choice questions and also some specified critiques. If it is too open-ended people will either moan or just give a general 'it is good'. (See Example multiple choice questions survey, Appendix 7 p 277.)

Looking at work

By work here, I mean both that produced by pupils, but also the work that has come out of the trainings from teachers.

Pupils' work

Here you are looking firstly at the work that you can find in books, which will be whether it demonstrates the demand for excellence in both quality and quantity. This needs to clearly link to the aims of the training – does the work demonstrate an application of the ideas that have been discussed during training sessions? Is there evidence of any marked improvement in pupils' work in these areas? The same applies for data, which often gets a bad name but is an important part of school life. We're in danger, by ignoring data, of trying to say that it doesn't matter; that pupils achieving in tests is not an important part of school life, and this has the potential of lowering expectations.

Teachers' work

Here you want to look for evidence of the different curriculum and assessment documents demonstrating the thinking and discussions that have happened as a part of the training session. You need to be able to determine from this what it is that teachers have learnt and how they have applied this. Really great training will also lead to teachers writing up, either in blog or paper form, and presenting their work. This will demonstrate the start of an engagement with their own CPD journey; the more they begin to take ownership of this, the more evident it is that the training is having a positive impact.

Observations

In tandem with looking at work, looking at lessons and also training is a good way to observe how training impacts on outcomes for teachers and pupils in a more practical fashion.

Observing pupils

Is it clear in the observations of lessons that pupils are being assessed in a way that helps support the curriculum and are being challenged to reach the high expectations of the school? Seeing pupils responding in lessons is a good way to evaluate this and it also is key to working out the next steps; what is still not happening that should be or vice versa? What are the current needs that need to be addressed in training?

Observing teachers

Here you can evaluate whether teachers are using any of the different varieties of ideas that have come about in relation to enacting the curriculum within the classroom. You can also determine how effective the coaching model has been – especially if this information has all been recorded centrally. Additionally, it works as a way of determining which training is having an impact on which teachers and their classes. Each teacher will have taken something different from their training and it is useful to look at how they have applied it in different ways. This could be done by comparing departments, or comparing groups of teachers, such as NQTs, against more experienced teachers. Again, alike to observing impact on pupils, you can gain a clearer idea of teacher needs from CPD. This can also be effectively observed in training sessions where other teachers take on the role of trainer.

Dialogue

One of the central aspects of any school is the conversations that happen: between pupils, between pupils and teachers, between teachers, between teachers and line manager and SLT. All of them carry a different component that can help evaluate CPD provision.

Dialogue with pupils

By talking with pupils you can easily work out whether the trainings are filtering down; if a pupil can easily articulate what they are studying and why, then you know that the understanding of subject curriculum must be strong. If a pupil, rather than just telling you a data point in terms of their progress, can identify specific things that they need to do to achieve more highly in their subject, then again you know that you are onto the right track.

Dialogue with teachers

Talking with teachers – both formally (in review meetings/conversations between line managers and teachers), and informally (in the staffroom or at the end of training sessions or socially) can help to glean what has been successful in terms of CPD and where there needs to be more investment. It also shows you how clearly teachers are able to articulate the vision of the school. (See Appendix 8 (p 278) for example guided questions to use with teachers.)

CPD reviews

You, or the person responsible for training at your school, should be clear about setting a timeline for reviewing curriculum and the key strategies you will use.

- Be clear on how and when the feedback will be implemented – it can be worthwhile to start the next training session with feedback about how you have shifted the training based on previous evaluations.
- Demand outcomes from the training sessions and then re-visit these at subsequent training sessions – make sure there is enough space between these but ensure there are expectations of how and when this will happen.
- Determine to what extent CPD is an embedded part of the school culture and how you can make progress towards achieving this.
- Include specific dates to review CPD with key teachers.

See Appendix 9 (p 279) for an example of a review to complete as a CPD lead.

School culture

As a whole school, CPD should have an impact on the entire culture. This is especially true of curriculum and assessment; this has all been trying to lead others to shift an entire way of thinking within a school and establish new curriculum and assessment systems. This is a huge upheaval, but when implemented carefully through training, it should have a positive impact on the school culture. This means that:

- you will hear conversations around the school about curriculum
- you will have passionate subject teachers and the beginnings of a culture of expertise
- pupils will be living up to the high expectations of the curriculum and want to celebrate their work
- you will have a staff who are fully invested in their CPD journey.

Next steps

After evaluating the training that has gone, you now have the immense task of working out where you travel to next. This whole process of design and implementation, as well as training, is likely to be the work of at least one, if not two, academic years. It will seem like a lifetime but it is only the beginning.

- There should be a thorough review process implemented within the school, which means an action plan of dates, times and potential outcomes (see Appendix 10 (p 281) for an example).
- The evaluations may have also thrown up particular concerns about certain aspects of curriculum and assessment design which need to be immediately investigated.
- If a teacher is unable to effectively help their pupils to move forward from the way in which your reporting data is presented, for instance, then you have an emergent problem to address.
- More likely is that there will be a continued ebb and flow of discussion over curriculum content, as well as refining the different techniques and formats of assessment.

You will also be in the early stages of having persuaded teachers to come on board with your ideas – if you're at a new school then this can be an easier task, but if you are trying to shift long-established methods you will need to work harder at bringing everyone on side. Equally, committing to a whole-school culture of CPD, including personal investment in developing through research and reading is not something that can be achieved overnight. It will take significant outcomes to prove to those around you that what you are doing does indeed work. Unfortunately these outcomes will mostly be long-term outcomes such as pupils results – we can't get away from that being the biggest current judgement of success in education. Therefore there is a lot of holding your steel, of being determined, in the face of others' insecurity or fear and sometimes in the face of those who argue that you should turn back the clock and return to the policies of before, because 'this works for us'.

Whilst this can be both exhausting and frustrating, you can't do this alone. It's not enough to be a pioneer, a trailblazer all on your own – you need to grow a community of trailblazers. If great change is going to happen, it will be by all teachers owning their profession and holding themselves up as experts. You can be the one who enables other to do this, who frees teachers at your school to think and challenge and fight for what they know is right for the children in their care. Let teachers become the experts once again.

Appendix 1

Example curriculum maps

English curriculum maps 2016 – Summer Turner
(East London Science School)

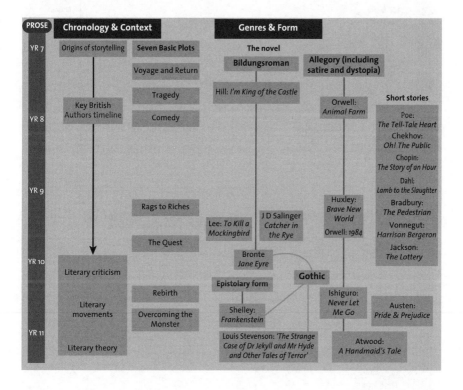

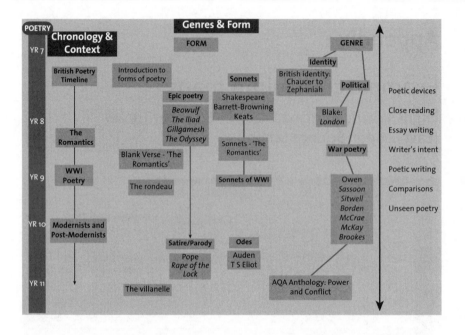

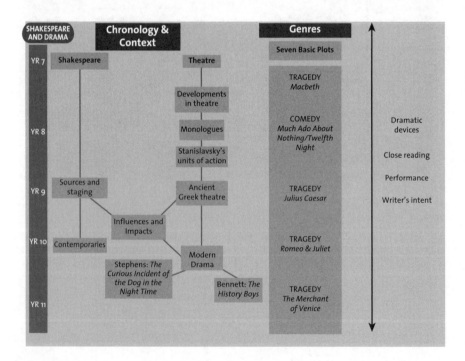

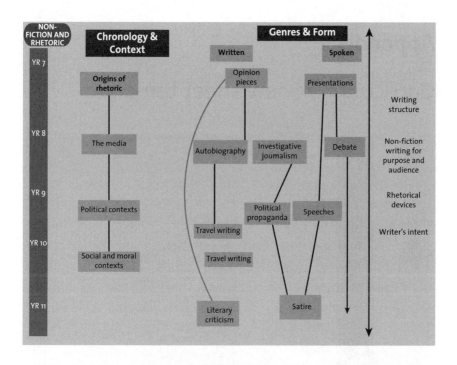

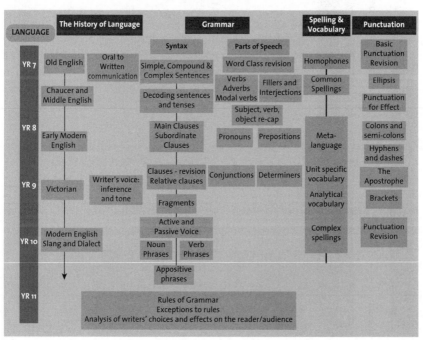

Appendix 2

Curriculum review sheet template

KS3 Curriculum Review February 2015			
Subject:		Subject Lead:	

Curriculum Feature	Strengths	Areas to improve	Actions
High Aspirations -AT LEAST NC			
Knowledge led			
Preparation for GCSEs			

Appendix 3

Curriculum review questions

Example questions for a Key Stage 3 review:

- What are the strengths of your KS3 curriculum?
- Where do you see the weaknesses in your KS3 curriculum?
- What adaptions have you made to your KS3 curriculum?
- How confident are you that the pupils have retained the key knowledge from your subject and will be able to demonstrate this in an exam?
- How confident are you in your department's ability to deliver your curriculum?
- How confident are you that your curriculum and assessment match the school ethos?
- How have you validated your curriculum and assessment; can you demonstrate the strength of your curriculum and assessment in comparison with other schools?
- Do you/your department need training/advice/visits to help develop your ability to deliver the curriculum? If so please give specific details.

Example questions for a Key Stage 4 review:

- What are the strengths of your KS4 curriculum?
- Where do you see the weaknesses in your KS4 curriculum?
- What adaptions have you made to your KS4 curriculum since the new changes in the GCSE programmes?
- How do you see the curriculum developing over the next few years?
- Where, in KS3, do you need to focus your attention in order for the pupils to be ready for KS4?
- How confident are you in your department's ability to deliver a KS4 curriculum?
- Are you aware of the current DfE guidelines/draft specifications/recently published specifications for your subject?
- Have you taken part in the DfE consultations on your subject for the new GCSEs?
- Are you aware of specific changes to the qualifications arrangements being developed by Ofqual for your subject? If so does this raise any questions and specific needs for training/CPD?

Appendix 4

Example assessment criteria

Answer these questions as a way to check that you are setting appropriate tests.

1. Could you answer the question?
2. Does it confuse you?
3. Do your fellow subject teacher come to the same answers as you in response to the questions?
4. Have you taught all the vocabulary that is included in the questions – including question words?
5. Do the questions test what you want the pupils to learn?
6. Do the questions avoid giving clues?
7. Are the marks awarded precise?
8. Have you avoided having to give 'benefit of the doubt' marks?
9. Have you included a range of question types?
10. Have you ensured that pupils have to use correct terminology and definitions?
11. Is there a range of challenge in the questions?
12. Have you included opportunities to subtract marks where pupils make mistakes in the basics?

Appendix 5

Example questionnaire on using multiple choice questions

Prior knowledge

1. Do you know what a multiple choice quiz is?
   (a) Yes   (b) No

2. Have you used multiple choice quizzes before when teaching?
   (a) Yes   (b) No

(If your answer is (a) then go to Question 3 then skip to Question 5. If your answer is (b) then skip to Question 4.)

3. How often have you used multiple choice quizzes in your teaching?
   (a) Never   (d) Frequently (every half term)
   (b) Once or twice   (e) I use them every week
   (c) Several times

4. Why have you not used them before?
   (a) Hadn't thought about it   (d) I don't think they are relevant
   (b) I don't think they are useful   to my subject
   (c) I don't know how to make them   (e) Other (Please specify)

   _____

   _____

5. Do you know how to design an effective multiple choice quiz?
   (a) Yes, I have read a lot about this/studied this and know how to create an
       effective MCQ.
   (b) I think I know how to do it, from my own experience.
   (c) I have some idea about this.
   (d) I'm not really sure.
   (e) I have no clue.

Any other comments, such as what you would like to achieve from a training on this topic.

_____

_____

Appendix 6

Checklist for designing multiple choice questions

Designing your mid-term test

Content
- Do the questions link to your areas of knowledge?
- What inferences do you want to be able to make from the answers?
- Does it include the key factual knowledge of the term?

Stems
- Does the stem present a clear and definite problem?
- Does it include only relevant material?
- Have you avoided negative phrasing?
- Is it a question or a partial sentence?
- Have you used more questions than partial sentences?

Alternatives
- Are all the alternatives plausible?
- Are all the alternatives homogenous?
- Are they all free from clues (same grammar, length etc)?
- Have you avoided 'all of the above' and 'none of the above' phrases?
- Are the alternatives presented in a logical order?
- Have you included any probing questions?

Further Reading
https://pragmaticreform.wordpress.com/2014/03/08/whymcqs/
https://cft.vanderbilt.edu/guides-sub-pages/writing-good-multiple-choice-test-
    questions/
https://thewingtoheaven.wordpress.com/2013/10/06/closed-questions-and-
    higher-order-thinking/
https://joeybagstock.wordpress.com/2013/11/29/there-is-a-place-for-multiple-
    choice-in-english-part-ii-2/

Appendix 7

Example survey: multiple choice question training review

Name: _____

1. Do you feel that the training helped you with your MCQ test design?
    (Please circle)

    Yes
    No
    A bit

2. Have you now designed a mid-term test? (Please circle)

    Yes
    No

    Have you started and know how to complete it?
    Yes
    No

3. Was the training pitched at the right level?
    (Please circle)

    Yes – perfect
    It was too easy – I already knew all this.
    There were some bits that were obvious.
    It was too difficult – I'm confused/overwhelmed.

4. How did you feel about the quantity of material covered?
    (Please circle)

    The right amount was covered
    There wasn't enough for me
    There was too much information
    We needed more time

5. What structure of training do you find most useful? (Please circle)

    Lecture/presentation   Working on own
    Workshop (practical)   Working in self-selected groups
    Whole-school meeting   Working in assigned groups
    Working in faculties   Other (please specify)
    Working in departments

Appendix 8

Example guided evaluation questions to use with teachers

1. What was the nature of your CPD?
   - (a) In-school training
   - (b) Education event
   - (c) External course
   - (d) Personal research/reading
   - (e) Coaching
   - (f) Other, please specify

2. What was the intended aim of your CPD?
   Pupil aim:
   Teacher aim:

3. What were the outcome measures that you planned to use to judge whether this aim had been met?
   Pupil outcome
   Personal outcome
   Department/whole-school outcome

4. To what extent did you meet the aim and what evidence have you got from the outcome to determine this?

5. To what extent did you not meet the aim, why was this?

6. How reliable do you think your outcomes are?

7. Were there any other unexpected outcomes from the CPD?

8. Will you now be altering/reviewing your aim?

9. How did you disseminate what you learnt?

10. How have you used what you have learnt to alter your practice?

11. What are the next steps you think you need to take to fulfil your aim or to meet your new aim?

12. Would you recommend this CPD to other members of staff/to be introduced as part of the whole-school training programme? Please explain your answer.

Appendix 9

Example guided evaluation questions: CPD lead

1. How many in-school trainings have been run this year?

2. What different formats and focuses have these trainings taken? (Create separate spreadsheet with this information – see example table below)

3. What were the aims for the year's CPD?
   (a) Pupil aims
   (b) Teacher aims
   (c) Whole-school aims

4. What were the measurable outcomes for this year's CPD?
   (a) Pupil outcomes
   (b) Teacher outcomes
   (c) Whole-school outcomes

5. Complete the spreadsheet, including ratings of how successful each training was according to the evidence that you have gathered.

6. If you use a spreadsheet format to log this information, you can quickly look across the sheet to see the relative merits and flaws of the different training offered. From this determine: what are the next steps for CPD? When will you review this again?

CPD name	Format	Intended aim: pupil/ teacher/ school	Intended outcome: pupil/teacher/ school	Success rating (1–5)	Evidence of outcomes being achieved	Next step and date for review

Fig. 25 Training spreadsheet

7. Using this information, consider who needs to be involved to help ensure the CPD programme develops in the right direction. This may become clear from seeing which teachers ran the successful training sessions.

8. Collate the information about the CPD that teachers have been completing outside of whole-school training sessions. Consider what the different strengths and weaknesses of this have been and how consistent this is across the staff body.

9. Identify teachers who have embraced the CPD culture and ask them about what has inspired them to take the reins of their professional development. Do the same for those who have not reacted so positively.

10. Use this to structure the next year's set of CPD provision, including targeted individual provision through department leads. If possible, appoint CPD leads from amongst the teachers who have made the most of the programme. They can help to build the CPD culture and disseminate their learning.

Appendix 10

Curriculum/Assesment Action Plan

AIMS & OBJECTIVES	ACTIONS	SUCCESS CRITERIA	DATE TO BE COMPLETED	LEADS
Develop understanding of common errors in curriculum and assessment design within departments.	• ST [Example staff leader] to make a list of the common errors, with examples from our previous curriculum/assessment model and suggested revisions. • List to be reviewed by SLT and distributed to all staff.	• SLT will have agreed revisions to the curriculum/assessment and have begun to action these. • Departments will demonstrate a clear understanding of the errors and how they can be avoided. [Will present in Faculty meeting].	3/5 9/5	ST SLT

APRIL 2016

Bibliography and further reading

'Assessment without levels: Using SIMS to create a new assessment system' (assessmentwithoutlevels.com)

'Secret Teacher: don't waste my time on torturous training days' (theguardian.com)
(www.theguardian.com/teacher-network/2015/sep/12/secret-teacher-waste-time-torturous-training-inset-days)

'Teachers: The Real Masters of Multitasking' (busyteacher.org)

'Richard Branson rejects "one size fits all" education' (edtechnology.co.uk)

'Da Do Ron Ron' (rug62.edublogs.org/2013/01/07/da-do-ron-ron)

'The growth mindset: telling penguins to flap harder?' (disidealist.wordpress.com/2014/12/05/242)

'Dangerous conjectures' (horatiospeaks.wordpress.com/2016/01/01/dangerous-conjectures)

Allison, S. and Tharby, A. (2015), Making Every Lesson Count: Six Principles to Support Great Teaching and Learning. Crown House Publishing Limited

Arnold, M. (2009) *Culture and Anarchy*. OUP.

Ashman, G. (2015), 'I refute it thus; can a false choice be an object of research?' (gregashman.wordpress.com)

Ashman, G. (2015), 'Why educational theory is flawed (gregashman.wordpress.com)

ATL 'Common ground on assessment and accountability in primary schools' www.atl.org.uk/policy-and-campaigns/policy-library/common-ground-assessment-accountability.asp)

Bagstock, J. (2015), 'Miltonic vision part 1: Trivium 21C, threshold concepts and the power of "powerful knowledge"' (joeybagstock.wordpress.com)

Bartle, K. (2014), 'Heads up 1: Live it. Learn it.' (dailygenius.wordpress.com)

Bartle, K. (2013), 'Ten commandments for school leaders' (dailygenius.wordpress.com)

Bartle, K. (2013), 'The pedagogy leaders project: how our staff drive teaching and learning' (the guardian.com)

Berger, R. (2003), *An Ethic of Excellence: Building a Culture of Craftsmanship with Students*. Heinemann

Bishop, P. (2015), 'The new CPD: film lessons and train teachers to be coaches' (schoolsweek.co.uk)

Blake, D. (2015), '"Beware the Ids that march" – to the barricades fir Ofsted at Michaela' (johndavidblake.org)

Boakye, J. (2015), 'And then, "Killamanshank": stumbling my way towards curriculum diversity'. (unseenflirtspoetry.wordpress.com)

Boyle, D. (2016), 'School tells A-level students to wear target grades around their necks' (http://www.telegraph.co.uk/news/2016/04/17/school-tells-a-level-students-to-wear-target-grades-around-their/)

Bullock, A. (1975), *A Language for Life: Report of the Committee of Enquiry*. Crown copyright

Centre for the Use of Research and Evidence in Education (CUREE) Evaluation of CPD providers in England 2010-2011. Report for School Leaders. Commissioned by the Teachers Development Agency for Schools (TDA)

Children, Schools and Families Committee (2009), National Curriculum: Fourth Report of Session 2008-09. House of Commons

Christodoulu, D. (2015), 'Guide to my posts about assessment' (thewingtoheaven. wordpress.com)

Christodoulu, D. (2013), 'Research on multiple choice questions' (thewingtoheaven. wordpress.com)

Christodoulu, D. (2015), 'Tests are inhuman – and that is what is so good about them' (thewingtoheaven.wordpress.com)

Coates, S (2015), *Headstrong*. John Catt Educational Ltd.

Coe, R., Aloisi, C., Higging, S. and Elliot Major, L. (2014), What makes great teaching? Review of the underpinning research. The Sutton Trust

Coe, R., Aloisi, C., Higging, S. and Elliot Major, L. (2015), Developing teachers: Improving professional development for teachers. The Sutton Trust

Coles, T. (2014), 'Critical pedagogy: schools must equip students to challenge the status quo' (www.theguardian.com)

Coles, T. (2014), 'No input, no output' (taitcoles.wordpress.com)

Department for Education (2014) 'Assessment Principles.' Crown Copyright

Department for Education (2014), 'England to become a global leader of teaching character.' Crown copyright

Department for Education (2014), 'The National Curriculum in England: Framework Document.' Crown Copyright

Department for Education (2014), 'Schools win funds to develop and share new ways of assessing pupils.' Crown Copyright

Department for Education (2016) 'Purpose and quality of education in England inquiry.' www.parliament.uk/business/committees/committees-a-z/commons-select/education-committee/inquiries/parliament-2015/purpose-quality-education-england-15-16/

Didau, D. (2013), 'Improving peer feedback with Public Critique' (learningspy.co.uk)

Didau, D. (2014), 'Grit and growth: who's to blame for low achievement?' (learningspy.co.uk)

Didau, D. (2015), 'Using threshold concepts to think about curriculum design' (learningpsy.co.uk)

Dweck, C. (2012), *Mindset: How You Can Fulfil Your Potential*. Ballantine Books

Facer, J. (2015): 'Just one book: curriculum' (readingallthebooks.com)

Facer, J. (2015), 'At what cost?' (readingallthebooks.com)

Fawcett, D. (2013), 'Creating a culture of Critique' (reflectionsofmyteaching.blogspot.co.uk)

Fleetham, M. '7 tips to making coaching feedback formative' (blog.irisconnect.co.uk)

Fletcher-Wood, H. (2014), 'Hinge questions hub' (improvingteaching.co.uk)

Fletcher-Wood, H. (2013), 'A "superior rival" to the draft history curriculum' (improvingteaching.co.uk)

Fletcher-Wood, H. (2015), 'Practice files: everything is practice' (improvingteaching.co.uk)

Fletcher-Wood, H. (2014), 'Being the 1% – what does it take to make CPD effective?' (improvingteaching.co.uk)

Fletcher-Wood, H. (2014), 'Archimedean leadership (2): what are leverage observations? Or, how would Yo-Yo Ma feed back?' (improving teaching.co.uk)

Fordham, M. (2015), The merits of the academic disciplines. (clioetcetera.com)

Fordham, M. (2015) 'What are schools not responsible for?' (clioetcetera.com)

Fordham, M. (2014), 'A radically traditional secondary curriculum model' (clioetcetera.com)

Fordham, M. (2015), '10 signs that you teach in an academic school' (clioetcetera.com)

Fordham, M. (2014), '90% of teacher training should be subject-specific' (clioetcetera.com)

Freire, P. (1996), *Pedagogy of the Oppressed*. Penguin

Fromm, E. (2001) *The Fear of Freedom*. Routledge Classics

Gibb, N.(2015), 'The purpose of education' (www.gov.uk/government/speeches/the-purpose-of-education)

Gibson, S., Oliver, L. and Dennison, M. (2015), Workload Challenge: Analysis of Teacher Consultation Responses. CooperGibson Research report, Department for Education

www.gov.uk/government/uploads/system/uploads/attachment_data/file/401406/RR445_-_Workload_Challenge_-_Analysis_of_teacher_consultation_responses_FINAL.pdf

Golby, M., Greenwood, J., & West, R., eds. (1975) *Curriculum Design*. London: Open University Press

Harlen, W (2010), Principles and Big Ideas of Science Education. Association for Science Education.

Hirsch, E.D. Jr. (1987), *Cultural Literacy: What Every American Needs to Know*. First Vintage Books

Hirsch, E.D. Jr. (1999), *The Schools We Needs and Why We Don't Have Them*. Anchor Books

Hirsch, E.D. Jr. (2006), *The Knowledge Deficit: Closing The Shocking Education Gap For American Children*. Houghton Mifflin Company

Hildrew, C. (2014), 'Becoming a growth mindset school' (chrishildrew.wordpress.com)

Hildrew, C. (2016) 'Refining assessment without levels' (chrishildrew.wordpress.com)

Isaksen, B. (2015), 'How should I revisit past content?' (blog.bodil.co.uk)

Isaksen, B. (2015), 'Just say no to junk data: assessment at Michaela' (blog.bodil.co.uk)

Isaksen, B. (2015), 'Seven principles of maths at Michaela' (blog.bodil.co.uk)

Jones, K. (2003), *Education in Britain: 1944 to the Present*. Polity Press

Kidd, D. (2013), '7 myths about education – an alternative view' (debrakidd.wordpress.com)

Kirby, J. (2013), 'What can science tell us about how pupils learn best?' (www.researched2013.co.uk/310)

Kirby, J. (2013), 'What can we learn from Core Knowledge and E.D. Hirsch?' (pragmaticreform.wordpress.com)

Kirby, J. (2013), 'Why we shouldn't close down the skills–knowledge debate' (pragmaticreform.wordpress.com)

Kirby, J. (2013), 'What makes a great school curriculum?' (pragmaticreform.wordpress.com)

Kirby, J. (2015), 'Knowledge organisers: specify subject knowledge in meticulous detail' (pragmaticreform.wordpress.com)

Kirby, J. (2013), 'What can we learn from Dylan Wiliam and AfL?' (pragmaticreform. wordpress.com)

Lemov, D. (2015), 'Harry Fletcher-Wood's checklist for practice sessions' (teachlikeachampion.com)

Lemov, D. (2015), 'Giving feedback as a coach – Isabel Beck and the secret life of guided discovery' (teachlikeachampion.com)

Lofthouse, R. Leat, D. and Towler, C. (2010), 'Coaching for teaching and learning: a paractical guide for schools'. CfBT and National College for Leadership of Schools and Children's Services (www.gov.uk/government/uploads/system/ uploads/attachment_data/file/327944/coaching-for-teaching-and-learning.pdf)

Lofthouse, R. (2015), 'Opening up a discussion: do coaches and mentors make successful educational leaders?' (blogs.ncl.ac.uk)

Luther King, M. (1947), 'The purpose of education' published in campus magazine Maroon Tiger (January – February 1947)

Manzione, J. (2015), 'Whose knowledge is it anyway?' (schoolsweek.co.uk)

McInerny, L. (2012), 'Things to know about E.D. Hirsch and the "common cultural literacy" idea (lkmco.org)

McLaughlin, K. and Mercieca, M. (2015), What's wrong with education for education's sake? *The Telegraph*

Meyer, J. and Land, R. (2003), 'Threshold concepts and troublesome knowledge: linkages to ways of thinking and practicing within the disciplines'. ETL project (www.etl.tla.ed.ac.uk//docs/ETLreport4.pdf)

Morrison McGill, R. (2015), '8 teaching ideas to bin in 2016' (teachertoolkit.me)

Morrison McGill, R. (2012), 'Training day pitfalls: what to avoid and how to put it right' (teachertoolkit.me)

Oates, T. et al (2011), The Framework for the National Curriculum: A Report by the Expert Panel for the National Curriculum Review. Department for Education (https://www.gov.uk/government/uploads/system/uploads/attachment_data/ file/175439/NCR-Expert_Panel_Report.pdf)

Oates, T. 'Opening the door to deeper understanding' (cambridgeassessment.org.uk)

Obama, B. (2015) 'Running Wild with Bear Grylls' Channel 4.

O'Shaughnessy, J. (2013), Why Character is the key to a perfect education. *The Telegraph*

Perks, D. 'Primary Curriculum Review. Primary Science Review' Campaign for Real Education

Playfair, E. (2015), 'What is powerful knowledge?' (eddieplayfair.com)

Peterson, C. and Seligman, M. (2004), *Character Strengths and Virtues: A Handbook and Classification*. Oxford University Press

Pollard, A. (2012), 'Proposed primary curriculum: what about the pupils?' (ioelondonblog.wordpress.com)

Plowden (1967), Children and their Primary Schools: A Report of the Central Advisory Council for Education (England). Crown copyright

Quigley, A. (2014), 'Multiple choice questions: a) use regularly b) don't use' (huntingenglish.com)

Quigley, A. (2012), 'A taste of Berger: reading "An Ethic of Excellence"' (huntingenglish.com)

Quigley, A. (2014), 'The problem with growth mindset' (huntingenglish.com)

Quigley, A. (2016), 'Thinking hard and why we should avoid it' (huntingenglish.com)

Quigley, A. (2013), 'A new English curriculum' (huntingenglish.com)

Quigley, A. (2013), 'Overcoming the ok plateau: how to become an expert teacher'. *The Guardian* (www.theguardian.com/teacher-network/teacher-blog/2013/apr/11/expert-teachers-ok-plateau-professional-development)

Quigley, A. (2013), 'Teacher coaching and improving "continuous professional development"' (huntingenglish.com)

Radice, A. (2015), 'National testing should be broader, simpler and more frequent' (thetraditionalteacher.wordpress.com)

Reddy, B. (2014), 'Design your own mastery curriculum in maths' (mrreddy.com)

Robinson, M. (2015), 'Memory' (martinrobborobinson.wordpress.com/2015/05/05/memory)

Robinson, M. (2015) 'Educate for freedom'

(martinrobborobinson.wordpress.com/2015/11/08/educate-for-freedom/).

Robinson, M (2013) Trivium 21c: Preparing young people for the future with lessons from the past. Independent Thinking Press.

Rose, N. (2014), 'Using student surveys to measure the impact of coaching' (evidenceintopractice.wordpress.com)

Rosen, M. (2012), 'Tim Oates lengthy reply to my request for evidence' (michaelrosenblog.blogspot.co.uk)

Sherrington, T. (2014), 'The progressive-traditional pedagogy tree' (headguruteacher.com)

Sherrington, T. (2013), 'Lessons from Berger: Austin's Butterfly and not accepting mediocrity' (headguruteacher.com)

Sherrington, T. (2015), 'The Trivium and the Baccalaureate: the flesh and bones of a great education' (headguruteacher.com)

Sherrington, T. (2015), 'Proposals for our new curriculum' (headguruteacher.com)

Sherrington, T. (2015), 'Our comprehensive curriculum for all' (headguruteacher.com)

Sherrington, T. (2013), 'The anatomy of high expectations' (headguruteacher.com)

Sherrington, T. (2013), 'Great lessons 1: Probing' (headguruteacher.com)

Smith, M. (1997, 2002), 'Paulo Freire: dialogue, praxis and education' (infed.org)

Stock, P. (2016), 'The unexamined life' (joeybagstock.wordpress.com)

Stock, P. (2015), 'Miltonic Vision Part 1: Trivium 21C, Threshold concepts and the power of "powerful knowledge"' (joeybagstock.wordpress.com)

Tharby, A. (2014), 'Adventures with gallery critique' (reflectingenglish.wordpress.com)

Theobald, J. (2016), 'I was a teenage progressive: a defence of the debate' (othmarstrombone.wordpress.com)

Theobald, J. (2016), 'The reconciliation of the debate (Is it possible? Is it desirable?)' (othmarstrombone.wordpress.com)

Tidd, M. (2015), 'My message for Lucy Powell' (michaelt1979.wordpress.com/2015/10/07/ my-message-for-lucy-powell)

Tidd, M. (2014), '7 questions you should ask about any new "post-levels" assessment scheme' (michaelt1979.wordpress.com)

Tomsett, J. (2013), 'This much I know about...developing a Dweck-inspired Growth Mindset culture' (johntomsett.com)

Tomsett, J. (2015), 'This much I know about...why we are developing Growth Mindset Learning tools' (johntomsett.com)

Tomsett, J. (2014), 'This much I know about...why a happy staffroom is the best thing for our students' (johntomsett.com)

Tomsett, J. (2013), 'Examples of GROW coaching questions: Goal Reality Options Wrap up' (johntomsett.files.wordpress.com/2013/12/grow-coaching-questions. pdf)

Training and Development Agency (2008), Continuing professional development guidance (CPD). TDA

Tyler, R. (1949), *Basic Principles of Curriculum and Instruction*. University of Chicago Press

White, J. (2012), 'Powerful knowledge: too weak a prop for the traditional curriculum?' (www.newvisionsforeducation.org.uk)

Wiliam, D. (2013), Redesigning Schooling –3: Principled Curriculum Design. SSAT (The Schools Network)

Wiliam, D. (2014), Redesigning Schooling –8: Principled Assessment Design. SSAT (The Schools Network)

Wiliam, D. 'Planning assessment without levels – article by Dylan Wiliam' (thehub. walthamforest.gov.uk)

Wiliam, D. (1998) 'Inside the black box'. GL Assessment.

Willingham, D. (2009), *Why Don't Students Like School?: A Cognitive Scientist Answers Questions About How the Mind Works and What it Means for the Classroom.* Jossey Bass

Willingham, D. (2002) Allocating Student Study Time: "Massed" versus "Distributed" Practice http://www.aft.org/periodical/american-educator/summer-2002/ask-cognitive-scientist

Young, M. (1971), *Knowledge and Control: New Directions for the Sociology of Education.* MacMillan

Young, M. (2007), *Bringing Knowledge Back In: From Social Constructivism to Social Realism in the Sociology of Education.* Routledge

Young, M., Lambert, D., Roberts, C. and Roberts, M. (2014), *Knowledge and the Future School: Curriculum and Social Justice.* Bloomsbury

Zizek, S. (2008), 'Rumsfeld and the bees' (https://www.theguardian.com/commentisfree/2008/jun/28/wildlife.conservation)

Videos

'The attack on knowledge: Interview with Michael Young' (www.cambridgeassessment.org.uk)

'National Curriculum: Tim Oates on assessment' (www.youtube.com/watch?v=-q5vrBXFpmo)

'Austin's Butterfly' (https://vimeo.com/38247060)

'Shonda Rhimes: "Ditch the dream and be a doer, not a dreamer"' (2014) (jezebel.com/shonda-rhimes-ditch-the-dream-and-be-a-doer-not-a-dre-1588352106)

'Three coaching examples in action, with the benefits outlined' (2014) (http://www.creativeeducation.co.uk/video/245)

Lemov, D. (2014), 'Check for understanding: Julia Goldenheim's 7th grade English class (video)' (teachlikeachampion.com)

Christodoulu, D. 'Life beyond levels' (https://www.youtube.com/watch?v=PGfIM_b6loU)

Index